LESSONS FROM
HISTORY

Essential Understandings and Historical Perspectives
Students Should Acquire

LESSONS FROM

HISTORY

Essential Understandings and Historical Perspectives
Students Should Acquire

Edited By

Charlotte Crabtree

Gary B. Nash

Paul Gagnon

Scott Waugh

A Project of

THE NATIONAL CENTER FOR HISTORY IN THE SCHOOLS

A COOPERATIVE UCLA/NEH RESEARCH PROGRAM

Printed in the U.S.A.

ISBN: 0-9633218-0-3

Published by the National Center for History in the Schools
University of California, Los Angeles
405 Hilgard Avenue
Los Angeles, California 90024-1521

Available at special discounts for bulk orders for educational use.

Cover design by Robin Weisz
Book layout and design by Brenda Thomas

Center Information

Directors

Charlotte Crabtree, Center Director
Graduate School of Education
University of California,
Los Angeles

Gary B. Nash, Center Associate Director
History Department
University of California,
Los Angeles

Linda Symcox,
Center Assistant Director
University of California,
Los Angeles

NEH Project Officer

Jeffrey Thomas
National Endowment for
the Humanities
Washington, D.C.

Advisory Panel

Francie Alexander
Associate Superintendent
California State Department
of Education

Gordon Craig
Department of History
Stanford University

Wayne Ginty
Lockport High School
Lockport, New York

David Millstone
Marian W. Cross School
Norwich, Vermont

Marguerite Navarrete
Carmenita Junior High School
Cerritos, California

Gordon Wood
Department of History
Brown University

Participation and titles of Advisory Panelists and Center Scholars are given as current at the time this volume was under development.

Center Scholars

Kathleen Conzen, Professor
University of Chicago

Don Fehrenbacher, Professor
Stanford University

Paul Gagnon, Professor
University of Massachusetts,
Boston

Nikki Keddie, Professor
University of California,
Los Angeles

Bill Rowe, Professor
Johns Hopkins University

Richard Saller, Professor
University of Chicago

Thaddeus Tate, Professor
The College of William and Mary

Scott Waugh, Professor
University of California,
Los Angeles

Michael Winston, Professor
and Vice President for
Academic Affairs
Howard University

Staff

Brenda R. Thomas
Senior Publications Coordinator

Pamela Hamilton
Administrative Coordinator

Leticia Zermeno
Copyright Procurement

Alexey Root
Copy Editor

Teacher Associates

Outstanding classroom teachers appointed to work collaboratively with the Center's Scholars, institute leaders, and consultants in the activities of the Center.

Table of Contents

Chapter Four: Essential Understandings in World History

Preface

This volume, with its 1992 publication date, could not have appeared at a more timely moment. Nearly four years in development, it has reached completion just as the nation has turned with special urgency to the central questions this volume seeks to address: What history should the schools teach? From the vast storehouse of historical knowledge, what is of most significance for students to learn if they are to be prepared for those central challenges of life to which the study of history contributes in unique and important ways? What historical understandings, habits of historical thinking, insights, and perspectives are of most importance if students are to be prepared for the challenges of active citizenship in the years ahead, for a satisfying career of work, and, most important, for personal fulfillment, for a healthy sense of self and of one's place in the great stream of human history? These are the central questions this volume has addressed, arguing first the rationale on which this search was undertaken; confronting next some very real constraints of classroom time and feasibility with which teachers presently must cope; and turning, finally, to the task of working toward consensus on what of United States and world history is of central importance for students to understand by the time they graduate from high school.

What historical understandings and perspectives are of most importance if students are to be prepared for the challenges of active citizenship and if they are to develop a healthy sense of self and of one's place in the great stream of human history?

When this task was first undertaken in June 1988, the evidence was clear that history in the nation's schools was in serious decline. Reports of students' distressingly low achievement levels in history on respected national assessments were matched by evidence that the time devoted to history in the schools had steadily declined to a state of genuine risk. Responding in March, 1988 to what was clearly a national problem, the National Endowment for the Humanities established, in cooperation with the University of California, Los Angeles, a National Center for History in the Schools. Its purpose would be to engage in a broad program of research and dissemination activities to improve history teaching and learning in the nation's elementary and secondary schools. The cornerstone of this program was to be a volume setting forth the essential understandings and historical perspectives students should acquire. Its primary audience was to be teachers, curriculum leaders, parents, school boards, and legislators—all who share a concern for improving history in their schools. This present volume is the product of that mission.

This is a consensus report. Collaborating in its development have been the distinguished historians serving as Center Scholars and Advisory Panelists, the Center's curriculum leaders and teachers serving on the Advisory Panel, the many historians enlisted for their special expertise as Consultants to this project, and Teacher Associates of the Center who served as reviewers and provided important perspectives on the development of this project.

This is also a practical volume, intended to provide the goals toward which good programs in history should be directed, the justifications for those goals, and sufficient background for teachers to plan their own teaching, formulate their own interpretation of events, and engage students in lively discussions and worthy investigations.

Finally, this is a volume that provides teachers an interpretation of United States and world history that is contemporary in its scholarship, broadly integrative of political and social history, and rich in its inclusion of the many peoples and constituent groups of each society under study. Working toward these ends required hard choices from among the great riches that have been mined by historians over the last 30 years in this liveliest of research fields in the university today. Building the new syntheses in United States and world history is one of the great challenges confronting historians today. Doing so for the precollegiate curriculum is especially demanding, for constraints of learners' sophistication and the purposes of general education must be taken into account. That the eminent historians working with the Center were willing to devote so much time and dedicated attention to this task over the past three years is testimony itself to the importance they attached to this aim, and to the respect in which they hold the work of teachers in the schools.

The Center offers this volume, then, in the hope that teachers and school leaders will find within its pages good

This is a volume that provides teachers an interpretation of United States and world history that is contemporary in its scholarship, broadly integrative of political and social history, and rich in its inclusion of the many peoples and constituent groups of each society under study.

guidance, encouragement, and essential support for this most important task confronting us all—engaging our students in productive and deeply rewarding studies of the human journey, and of their own connections within it. For discovering who we are, for understanding how we came to our present state of affairs, and for moving with confidence and wisdom to meet the challenges ahead, no field of the curriculum is of greater or more enduring worth.

—Charlotte Crabtree & Gary B. Nash

Los Angeles, California
January 1992

Acknowledgments

A volume as comprehensive as this one, developed through nearly four years of work by the dedicated historians, teachers, and curriculum experts associated with the National Center for History in the Schools, owes special recognition to all who gave so generously of their time and expertise to bring it to completion. As a consensus document, it has been repeatedly reviewed and revised on the basis of scholarly and professional judgments. In the end, it bears the imprint of all who contributed to its development.

Special acknowledgment is due the historians, classroom teachers, and curriculum leaders serving as Advisory Panelists and Center Scholars of the National Center for History in the Schools. Their support has been continuous throughout the development of this volume, contributing to its organization and definition of major themes and understandings; serving as contributing authors of chapters of this work; and providing continuing and incisive reviews and recommendations for revisions throughout its many stages of editing.

Deep appreciation is due each of them: Center historians **Gordon Craig** (Stanford University), **Kathleen Conzen** (University of Chicago), **Don Fehrenbacher** (Stanford University), **Paul Gagnon** (University of Massachusetts, Boston), **Nikki Keddie** (University of California, Los Angeles), **Bill Rowe** (Johns Hopkins University), **Richard Saller** (University of Chicago), **Thaddeus Tate** (College of William and Mary), **Scott Waugh** (University of California, Los Angeles), **Michael Winston** (Howard University), and **Gordon Wood** (Brown University); and teachers and curriculum leaders **Francie Alexander** (who at the time was Associate Superintendent for Curriculum, California Department of Education), **Wayne Ginty** (Lockport High School, Lockport, New York), **David Millstone** (Marian W. Cross Elementary School, Norwich, Vermont), and **Marguerite Navarrete** (Carmenita Junior High School, Cerritos, California).

Special recognition is due the contributions of Center Scholar **Paul Gagnon** (University of Massachusetts, Boston) who authored Chapter I, drawing upon preliminary drafts by Center Scholars and the considerable contributions of Gary B. Nash, and bringing his own vision and broad experience to this important chapter as well. In addition, Professor Gagnon contributed importantly to the units in modern United States and world history, provided major assistance in developing the sections titled "Habits of the Mind," and provided considerable assistance in the editing of the volume as a whole.

Major contributions were also made to Chapter III, "Essential Understandings in United States History," by Center Scholars **Thaddeus Tate** (College of William and Mary and at the time Director of the Institute of Early American History and Culture) who collaborated with Gary Nash in the development of Unit 2, The Colonial Era; **Gordon Wood** (Brown University) who contributed importantly to Unit 4, Nation Building; **Don Fehrenbacher** (Stanford University) who largely authored Unit 7, The Civil War and Reconstruction; and Center Consultant **Robert H. Ferrell** (Indiana University) who contributed importantly to Units 9-14, devoted to 20th-century United States history.

Important contributions to Chapter III were also made by the many scholars of United States history who were invited, as Center Consultants, to prepare papers setting forth the content and perspectives they considered most important in their era or area of scholarly study. Presented in Institute meetings before the Center's 65 Teacher Associates, these papers also served as major resources in the development of Chapter III. All of the following assisted importantly in providing their perspectives on United States history and several played a role, as well, in reviewing various drafts of the chapter: **Joyce Appleby** (University of California, Los Angeles); **Harold Barron** (Harvey Mudd College); **Richard Beeman** (University of Pennsylvania); **Joseph Boskin** (Boston University); **Robert Dallek** (University of California, Los Angeles); **Ellen DuBois** (University of California, Los Angeles); **Steven Hahn** (University of California, San Diego); **Julie Jeffrey** (Goucher College); **Michael Johnson** (University of California, Irvine); **Leon Litwack** (University of California, Berkeley); **Eric Monkonnen** (University of California, Los Angeles).

In the development of Chapter IV, "Essential Understandings in World History," Center Scholar **Scott Waugh** (University of California, Los Angeles) provided major contributions in chairing the committee of world historians and classroom teachers who worked for consensus on the major content and essential understandings that should be included in this chapter. Professor Waugh provided also a preliminary draft of European history, developed the five "Spheres of Human Activity" from which the major narrative themes of world history were derived, and formulated the basic approach to synthesizing world history—chronological and comparative—that was adopted in this volume. Professor Waugh also contributed important assistance in editing this volume and turned his own pen to refining sections as the need arose.

Among the Center Scholars contributing importantly to the development and review of Chapter IV were **Nikki Keddie** (the history of the Islamic world); **Bill Rowe** (the history of East Asia); and **Richard Saller** (classical civilizations of the Mediterranean world). A number of historians recognized for their scholarship in particular regions or eras of world history served as Consultants to the Center and contributed also to the development of this chapter. Among these were **Stanley Burstein** (California State University, Los Angeles), who largely authored the unit on ancient Egypt**; Ross Dunn** (San Diego State University), who provided an important draft on African history; **Arnold Kaminsky** (California State University, Long Beach) who contributed drafts on the history of both South and Southeast Asia; **James Lockhart** (University of California, Los Angeles) who assisted with the history of the Americas; and **Geoffrey Symcox** (University of California, Los Angeles) who provided critical reviews and assisted with revisions in the history of the European and Islamic worlds between 600 and 1450 A.D.

Important contributions to Chapter IV were also made by the many scholars of world history who were invited, as Consultants, to prepare papers setting forth what they considered to be the most important content and perspectives in their areas or eras of study. Again, these papers were presented in Institute sessions before the Center's 65 Teacher Associates, and provided important resources for the development of

Chapter IV. Among these scholars were **Dorothy Abrahamse** (California State Polytechnic University, Pomona); **Ned Alpers** (University of California, Los Angeles); **Joseph Block** (California State Polytechnic University, Pomona); **Chris Ehret** (University of California, Los Angeles); **Benjamin Elman** (University of California, Los Angeles); **Tom Martin** (Pomona College); **Ronald Mellor** (University of California, Los Angeles); **Kate Norberg** (University of California, Los Angeles); **Herman Ooms** (University of California, Los Angeles); **Amanda Podany** (California State Polytechnic University, Pomona); **Richard Rouse** (University of California, Los Angeles); **Ann Walthall** (University of Utah); and **Norton Wise** (Princeton University).

We note, too, with special appreciation the incisive and very helpful reviews at various stages of the manuscript provided by historians **Ned Alpers** (University of California, Los Angeles), **Bernard Lewis** (Princeton University); and **William McNeill** (University of Chicago).

Acknowledgment is also due the 65 Teacher Associates of the Center who attended the three years of Institute sessions when these many presentations of United States and world history were made and who offered, in turn, their important reactions and professional insights into the historical content and approaches appropriate for history instruction in the precollegiate years.

Linda Symcox, Assistant Director of the Center, oversaw the selection of the photographs and documents included in these pages and provided important historical research and editing service, assisted by copy-editors **Alexey Root**, **Margaret McMillen**, and **Gwynn Lewis**, Research Assistants in the Center. **Leticia Zermeno** procured copyright releases for the photographs and documents, and **Pamela Hamilton** assisted with typing the manuscript. Special recognition is due **Brenda Thomas**, Senior Publications Coordinator, who designed and desktop-published the volume.

Overseeing all these operations were the Center's Director and Associate Director who coordinated all these activities, contributed to the editing of the manuscript, and turned their hands to the materials on many occasions as well. Our sense is one of deep satisfaction in seeing this volume brought to completion, and of pride in the superb contributions of the more than one hundred historians, teachers, and staff who together made possible this major contribution to worthy programs of history in the nation's schools.

We are deeply grateful as well to the National Endowment for the Humanities whose generous funding over the past four years has supported the completion of this important endeavor.

—Charlotte Crabtree & Gary B. Nash

CHAPTER ONE:
The Case for History in Our Schools

Americans have long said that universal education is essential to securing the people's rights to life, liberty, and the pursuit of happiness. But those who run our schools have rarely agreed on what is most worth teaching to every learner in a modern democratic society. So difficult has this question appeared that we have repeatedly turned away from it, to busy ourselves instead with methods and logistics, as though these were more important and could be applied without regard to the subject matter we choose to teach, or our purposes in choosing it. The consequences are evident. All subjects and disciplines have suffered, at all levels of schooling from kindergarten through the graduate years.

By its nature, history has suffered more than most subjects from permissive or simply ill-founded curriculum making. History's enormous scope and detail require more choices than many people, educators and historians included, are able or willing to make. It is, and ought to be, complex and often controversial. In its style and methods, it is both an art and a science. As a school subject, it embraces both the humanities and the social studies, neither of which can prosper without history's context and perspectives. It is the most synthesizing of all the disciplines, not just another bundle of subject-matter, but a way of ordering and apprehending reality. To be well taught it calls for more than ordinary knowledge and pedagogical skill on the part of those who teach it. As historians and teachers of history, we must admit its difficulties and labor to overcome them, for if the proper place of history in our schools is not accepted by the public and those who shape the schools, the larger campaign to improve the quality, and equality, of American education will surely fail.

As a school subject, history embraces both the humanities and the social studies, neither of which can prosper without history's context and perspectives.

Above: Teacher Associate David Vigilante working with his class in San Diego, California.

We need to begin by answering fundamental questions. What history, and how much of it, needs to be taught?

We need to begin by answering fundamental questions. Why does history deserve to occupy a broad and central place throughout the school curriculum? What are its uses, its purposes? Which history, and how much of it, needs to be taught? What is the essential knowledge we should expect all graduates of high schools in the United States to possess about the history of their own country and of the world? And much beyond knowledge, what kinds of historical understandings, perspectives, and ways of thinking are necessary to the private person and to the public citizen in a democratic society?

Such questions defy easy answers. Historical knowledge is far more than lists of facts, dates, epic events, and famous or infamous people. How are details related to significant questions that stimulate understanding rather than only memorization? How can students achieve historical perspective and learn historical ways of thought? Our answers proceed from two assumptions. First, that we cannot specify what people ought to know about history until we settle upon the larger educational purposes to be served by historical study. Second, that the methods used to teach and study history are nearly as important as the subject matter of our courses, and that, in turn, they must be consonant with the larger educational purposes we have set for ourselves. Purposes, method, and subject-matter are inextricably intertwined and must be dealt with all at once. That this proposition, so obvious and so often ignored (sometimes by the historical profession itself), is resurfacing in current debates over school reform in this nation is an encouraging sign that improvement is possible in how we educate ourselves.

WHY STUDY HISTORY?

The purposes of historical study must reflect the three ultimate purposes of education in a free society: to prepare the individual for a career of work, to sustain life; for active citizenship, to safeguard liberty and justice; and for the private pursuit of happiness. The last of these purposes—personal fulfillment, whether it be defined in secular or spiritual terms— is of first importance, providing the reason we struggle to maintain life and liberty, its necessary conditions. Each of the three aims of education, of course, calls for traits of mind and character that are useful to the other two. Historical study contributes to all three, but in preparing the individual for citizenship and for personal fulfillment its offerings are unique, and together with those of literature and philosophy, are indispensable.

The argument for more history in the schools and for its centrality to the social studies has usually stressed its role in preparing informed, sophisticated citizens. Thomas Jefferson long ago prescribed history for all who would take part in self-government because it would "enable every man to judge for himself what will secure or endanger his freedom." History's main use, he believed, was to prepare people for things yet to come. By reflecting on the past, on other times, other people, other nations, they would be able "to judge of the future" and to make up their own minds on the "actions and designs of men."

In 1892, the Committee of Ten's subcommittee on History, Civil Government, and Political Economy (which included Woodrow Wilson) urged that four years of history be required for all secondary school students, whether or not they were destined for college, because history, more than any other subject, readied the student to exercise "a salutary influence upon the affairs of his country." It was, they said, vital to "the invaluable mental power which we call judgment." A succession of committees, from the American Historical Association's "Seven" in 1899 through its study panels in the 1930s, pressed similar arguments for history as the basis for civic education.

Nearing the end of the 20th century, in a populous and ethnically and racially diverse society caught up in an interdependent global society, we reaffirm the central importance of history in preparing students to exercise their rights and responsibilities in the democratic political process. As historians of human behavior, we know better than to claim too much. "Neither history nor any social studies course intended to teach citizenship can *make* good citizens," said the Council for Basic Education's Commission on the Teaching of History in 1982; but without knowing the past, citizens cannot know the choices before them. And historian William McNeill, in a report for the American Historical Association in 1985, similarly argued that "democratic citizenship and effective participation in the determination of public policy require

Thomas Jefferson long ago prescribed history for all who would take part in self-government because it would prepare people for things yet to come.

citizens to share a collective memory, organized into historical knowledge and belief."

Lacking a collective memory of important things, people lapse into political amnesia, unable to see what newspapers are saying, to hear what is in (or left out of) a speech, or to talk to each other about public questions. A historical education should prepare us for times of trouble, when we are tempted to put aside inefficient democracy and to lash out, to exclude, or to oppress others. Why have past societies fallen or survived, turned ugly or retained their humanity? Citizens need to know and to be able to tell each other, before it grows too late, what struggles and sacrifices have had to be accepted, what comforts given up, to keep freedom and justice alive. Historical knowledge and historical perspective ward off panic, cynicism, self-pity, and resignation.

Citizens need to know what struggles and sacrifices have had to be accepted, what comforts given up, to keep freedom and justice alive.

Students of history come to see, as James Howard and Thomas Mendenhall said in Making History Come Alive, that not every difficulty is a problem and not every problem is a crisis. To take but one example, democracy must cherish both liberty and equality. The two impulses repeatedly clash, yet each is necessary to the other. This "concept" may serve as a starting point, but only history can teach us why it is so, by presenting the tough human experience that has convinced us of it. Students then grasp why conflict is to be expected—even welcomed—and is not some failure of a system that should run itself and leave them alone. They also understand how hard it has been to improve human life but how often it has nonetheless been done in the past. Historical study has a way (annoying to some) of rejecting both optimism and pessimism, of refusing us the comforts of either. In sum, it offers citizens the sense of reality and proportion that is the first mark of political wisdom.

It is hard to see how better to prepare students for life in the 21st century, about which there is so much talk these days in the social studies field. Unhappily, enthusiasts for "futures studies" are quick to reject history and the humanities in general as "past-oriented" and thereby useless in preparing citizens for what is to come. Apart from flying in the face of centuries of human experience, such notions ignore—as they would have our young people do—everything that can be learned from the lives of countless men and women whose historical and humanistic education prepared them for great work in the "futures" of their own eras. If they knew how to meet the unexpected, it was not out of formulas and "skills" but out of first knowing themselves and the human condition. History, philosophy, biography, literature, and the arts had liberated their imaginations, informed their judgments, and imbued them with a sense of human dignity. The social sciences standing alone help to describe today's and tomorrow's problems, but they alone cannot explain them; nor should they be expected to nourish those values and qualities of mind required to deal with them wisely. For these purposes the long-term explanatory perspectives that history provides and the habits of thought it uniquely develops are essential.

Along with educating citizens for public affairs—a role it shares with the social sciences—history has a deeper, even more fundamental responsibility: the cultivation of the individual private person, in whom self-knowledge and self-respect support a life of dignity and fulfillment. The public and private purposes of education and historical study are, of course, inescapably interrelated. Only the self-respecting, fully-rounded person is likely to make a good citizen for a self-governing society, as ready to serve as to resist, depending upon the circumstances of the hour. Only a free society can provide a setting for personal dignity and fulfillment, what Jefferson called the pursuit of happiness.

The liberal education of the private person is preeminently the role of history and the humanities. The study of history reveals the long, hard path of human striving for dignity. It can be, as Jerry Martin puts it, "a source of *pietas*, the reverent acknowledgment of the sources of one's being." Historical memory is the key to self-identity, to seeing one's place in the stream of time, in the story of humankind. We are part of an ancient chain and the hand of the past is upon us— for good and ill—as our hands will rest on our descendants in the future. Such perspective is essential to one's morale, perhaps even to sanity, in a complex, troubled present. "It is true that history cannot satisfy our appetite when we are hungry, nor keep us warm when the cold wind blows," says the New York Chinatown History Project. "But it is also true that

Historical memory is the key to self-identity, to seeing one's place in the stream of time, in the story of humankind.

5

if younger generations do not understand the hardships and triumphs of their elders, then we will be a people without a past. As such, we will be like water without a source, a tree without roots."

The human mind seems to require a usable past. Unfurnished with historical knowledge that approximates reality, we are likely to conjure up a past that is false or nostalgic, misleading in one form or other. Or we may subscribe to versions of the past peddled by partisan or special interests. Either way we are deluded, lose our way, perhaps even become dangerous to ourselves and our contemporaries, not to speak of posterity. We remain prisoners of our milieu, ignorant, in bliss or despair, of the possibilities for personal liberation that history opens to us by revealing the immense range of approaches people have taken to political, economic, and social life, to personal integrity and salvation, to cultural creativity.

Unfurnished with historical knowledge, we remain prisoners of our milieu, ignorant of the possibilities for personal liberation that history opens to us.

The dignity of free choice can proceed only out of knowing the alternatives possible in private and public life, the knowledge that only history, and the humanities taught in conjunction with history, can provide. Is such education "past-oriented" and obsolete? Exactly the contrary. The study of history opens to students the great case book of centuries of human experience. The quicker the pace of change, the higher the flood of "information," the more troubled and confused we become, the more relevant and essential history becomes in preparing people for private life and public action.

As to the third purpose of education—preparation for work—historical studies are central for such careers as journalism, law, diplomacy, international business, government service, politics, the military, teaching, and management of many public and private enterprises. Knowledge of history informs many other academic disciplines and creative professions. Insofar as personal morale, integrity, and dignity are conducive to all kinds of good work, history's contributions are obvious, as is its development of analytical skills and modes of critical judgment. As more and more employers assert the importance of a liberal education to their workers' inventiveness, their aptitude for continued learning and changes of career, the uses of historical studies should be more commonly appreciated.

Given the importance of history for all three purposes of education, and its centrality to citizenship and personal life, it is clear that both the amount and the quality of history taught in American schools must be sufficient to the task. That they are clearly not sufficient has alarmed many observers in recent years. In 1975, a report by the executive secretary of the Organization of American Historians, Richard S. Kirkendall, found history enrollments shrinking and history being displaced by other social studies subjects. In 1982 the Council for Basic Education's Commission on the Teaching of History deplored both the quantity and the quality of history being taught in the schools. History, said the Commission's report, was "overshadowed and undervalued in the curriculum, often neglected by professional historians, and found boring by many students."

Data reported by the National Center for Education Statistics indicated that in 1981-82 only 69 percent of the nation's high schools were offering a comprehensive course in United States history, though courses in state history, special eras, or special topics were being offered in some of the schools not providing the basic United States history course. By 1989-90 this picture had improved, probably as a result of the curriculum reforms launched in 1983. A national survey conducted in 1989-90 by the National Center for History in the Schools found that 89.9 percent of the high schools were offering one or more General Enrollment classes in United States history, and an additional 5 percent not offering the General Enrollment course were offering one or more special enrollment classes such as Advanced Placement or Remedial. Fully 5 percent of the high schools, however, were offering no United States history courses, and of the courses that were offered, only 81 percent provided a full year of instruction; the rest were offered for one semester or less. Only 70.2 percent of the high schools were offering a General Enrollment course in world history, with only 66 percent of these schools requiring the course for graduation. Only 3.7 percent were offering a course in Western Civilization, a significant decline

Given the importance of history and its centrality to citizenship and personal life, both the amount and the quality of history taught in American schools must be sufficient to the task.

from a decade earlier when 14 percent were offering such a course. Serious problems were observed in the middle school/junior high school offerings. Close to 40 percent were offering no courses in United States history and 87 percent reported offering no courses in world history. For a significant number of students, then, the only history they currently study is what is offered in a year or less of high school instruction.

The gap between what a modern democratic school system needs and what the curriculum in this country now provides is very great. Putting aside for a moment the paucity of history in the elementary and middle school curriculum of most schools, there is simply no way that the one and one-half years, or less, of history now taken by the average American high school student can possibly fulfill the purposes we have set forth above, or develop the essential knowledge and understandings we shall presently discuss. This view is shared by every major reform proposal of recent years. Theodore Sizer, in Horace's Compromise (1984), makes the joint study of history and ideas one of his four required areas of learning throughout the secondary years.[1] The Paideia Program (1984) places narrative history and geography at the core of the social studies from the upper elementary years through high school.[2] In the Carnegie report, High School (1983), Ernest Boyer recommended a year of United States history, a year of Western Civilization, and at least a term's study of a non-Western society.[3] The Council for Basic Education's report of 1984 set an "irreducible minimum" of two years of American history, one of European and the historical study of at least one non-European society in depth.[4] In 1987, the American Federation of Teachers published Education for Democracy: A Statement of Principles, signed by 150 national leaders across the political spectrum, and calling for the reordering of the entire social studies curricu-

The gap between what a modern democratic school system needs and what the curriculum in this country now provides is very great.

[1] Theodore R. Sizer, Horace's Compromise, Boston, Houghton-Mifflin, 1984.

[2] Mortimer J. Adler, et al., The Paideia Program, New York, Macmillan, 1984.

[3] Ernest L. Boyer, High School, New York, Harper and Row, 1983.

[4] Thomas C. Mendenhall and James Howard, Making History Come Alive, Washington, D.C., Council for Basic Education, 1984.

lum around a continuing core of history and geography.[5] Also in 1987 the National Endowment for the Humanities issued American Memory, Lynne V. Cheney's report on humanities in the schools, which urged that "both history and enduring works of literature" be a part of every school year for every student.[6] Most recently, the Bradley Commission recommended that the social studies curriculum from kindergarten through grade six be history-centered and that no fewer than four years of history be required of all students sometime during the six-year span from 7th through 12th grade.[7]

All of these reports set reasonable goals, and they also agree that a reformed social studies curriculum should be required of all students in common, regardless of their "track" or further vocational and educational plans. Only such a common core is democratic, because wherever the curriculum in history and ideas is truncated or optional, the students' right to know is violated and democracy is wanting. Something is wrong when the learning often considered necessary and appropriate for university-bound students is treated as unnecessary or irrelevant for the others. This first principle of democratic education, enunciated by the Committee of Ten a century ago, is an idea whose time has come again. In order that it not again be abandoned, diverse and imaginative teaching methods must be applied in developing the common core of what is most worth learning with all of our diverse learners. A common core and varied methods are the twin imperatives for democratic schooling. A curriculum that is trivial, optional, or differentiated according to track produces a class system of education, no matter how innovative the methods or how many students receive a diploma. But the most wondrous subject matter just as surely produces a class system of education if inflexible teaching methods and school structures impede its being conveyed to the great majority of

Diverse and imaginative teaching methods must be applied to develop the common core of what is most worth learning with all our students.

[5] Education for Democracy: A Statement of Principles, Washington, D.C., American Federation of Teachers, 1987.

[6] Lynne V. Cheney, American Memory, National Endowment for the Humanities, Washington, D.C., 1987.

[7] The Bradley Commission on History in Schools, Building a History Curriculum: Guidelines for Teaching History in Schools, Washington, D.C., 1988.

young people.

WHAT HISTORY SHOULD WE TEACH?

Concerning what history to teach, we must hope that the American educational debate has moved to a higher stage, that we have left behind the futile dialogue between "content" people and "methods" people. It is just as critical to transcend the false dichotomy between facts and conceptual analysis. Historical understanding requires both knowledge of facts and ways of thinking about facts. Less obvious is how to go about choosing the facts, skills, and concepts that are most worth our time and effort. In the following chapters, we address the questions of the essential content, both factual and conceptual, and the major historical themes that all of our students should explore, those larger developments without which they will not understand themselves or their society, or the larger world outside.

Among these essential understandings is the story of the long human struggle for liberty, equality, justice, and dignity. Americans need to understand the ideas, conditions, and people all over the earth that have carried the struggle forward and those that have hobbled, betrayed, or defeated it wherever, whenever, the struggle has been waged. The collective memory of that story is particularly important for us as a young and ever-changing nation. Kenneth Jackson, Chairman of the Bradley Commission on History in Schools, reminds us that unlike many other peoples, "Americans are not bound together by a common religion or a common ethnicity. Instead, our binding heritage is a democratic vision of liberty, equality, and justice. If Americans are to preserve that vision and bring it to daily practice, it is imperative that all citizens understand how it was shaped in the past, what events and forces either helped or obstructed it, and how it has evolved down to the circumstances and political discourse of our time."[8]

Americans are not bound together by a common religion or a common ethnicity; our binding heritage is a democratic vision of liberty, equality, and justice.

If we are to secure and extend freedom, justice, and respect for each other in an increasingly diverse society, we must arrive together at a common realization of what it has

[8] Ibid., p. 2.

taken to keep democracy alive through crises of the past and what it will likely demand of us in the future. A democratic people's power to make critical judgments on the choices thrust upon them requires a common grasp of a particular body of knowledge. To engage productively in public debate on issues of national importance, citizens need to know the forces that have shaped us, our country, and our world, and brought us to this moment of human history. What does the past tell us of the alternatives we shall confront and of the possible consequences of our choices among them? At bottom, democracy is a gamble that great numbers of people of all kinds and conditions will be wise in public affairs and devoted to the greater good of all. Otherwise, elected leaders have little choice but public obfuscation, bending to the most powerful current interest groups, and hoping for the best.

What people need to know in order to raise the level of public discourse, and the integrity of public institutions, is no small order. First, as Kenneth Jackson says, they must understand the fundamental ideas making up the political vision of the 18th-century founders expressed in the Declaration of Independence, the Constitution, the Federalist Papers (together with the anti-Federalist arguments), and the Bill of Rights. Understanding requires that we know not only what the words say, but where such ideas arose, how they evolved from earlier ideas, back to the ancient world. What historical conditions encouraged people to hold such views? What conditions were hostile? What did people assume about human nature? About their relation to God? About the meaning and direction of human history?

Students must understand the fundamental ideas expressed in the Declaration of Independence, the Constitution, the Federalist Papers, and the Bill of Rights.

In particular, students should understand the close connection between the foundations of representative self-government in the United States and its English antecedents: (1) the English jurisprudential tradition that established the rule of law as a constitutional restraint upon the authority of the Crown and, through the development of common law, protected such rights as trial by jury, *habeas corpus*, and Parliamentary representation; (2) the influences of the Glorious Revolution and the English Bill of Rights; and (3) the ideas of John Locke on natural rights and the social contract and of Montesquieu on the separation of powers. Without this background, the principles of democratic government are not fully comprehensible; they are words alone, floating free of source, drama, and meaning.

Second, to understand the democratic system, its strengths and its weaknesses, requires that students also understand the alternative systems of governance, benevolent and otherwise, that have predominated throughout most of European and world history. Without this comparative background, students will neither appreciate the democratic alternative nor understand the sources, comparative strengths, durability, and costs of the various centrally controlled and imperial regimes under which most Europeans lived until the 19th century and most other societies have been governed well into the 20th. Essential to this story is the rise of 20th-century totalitarian regimes and the unprecedented scale of their human rights violations.

Students should consider how democratic ideas have been turned into practice, and how they have been strengthened, violated, or defeated altogether. Who has defended such societies and how? Who has sought their defeat and why?

Third, in observing the origins, struggles, and achievements of free societies, past and present, students should consider how democratic ideas have been turned into practice, and how they have been strengthened, violated, or defeated altogether. Who has defended such societies and how? Who has sought their defeat and why? What forces—economic, social, cultural, religious, military, technological—have supported democratic practices? What forces have obstructed or destroyed them? Such knowledge empowers people to draw distinctions between democratic ideals and their violations in practice, and to understand the passion for reform in American history, and in the history of many other societies, as continuing struggles they themselves may join to bring reality closer to aspiration.

To be effective in so doing, students will need to confront the realities of modern history. All of the major ideologies and mass movements of the 19th and 20th centuries were shaped, directly or indirectly, by the forces and human expectations flowing from the American, French, and Industrial revolutions: nationalism, liberalism, conservatism, republicanism, social democracy, trade unionism, Marxism, socialism, Communism, Fascism, Nazism. Indeed, the history of the world since the early 1800s can be told as the ebb and flow of a great three-sided revolution, driven by people's desire to achieve three things for themselves: national unity, dignity, and independence; political democracy and civil equality; and a full measure of economic and social justice. Students must see how these three kinds of revolutionary pressure have acted upon the established order and upon each other in very different ways, in nearly every society on every continent, depending upon which of the three aims has seemed most urgent to rival interests within each society, or which have earlier been frustrated, or achieved.

Fourth, democratic citizens need a comprehensive understanding of their late 20th-century world. The triple revolution has dominated global changes since the advent of the new imperialism, with its tremendous consequences for both the colonized and the colonizers. The 20th century opened, for most Western nations at least, in a flush of optimism and high promise of progress in all spheres of human life. But it brought with it total wars, depression, the collapse of liberal regimes, the rise of totalitarianism, racism, oppression, and the mass extermination of human beings. How has it all happened? How have the highest human aspirations for national dignity, self-government, and social decency been so often turned to violence and tragedy? What lessons can we draw out of recent history as we confront our present choices? How, for example, may knowing the consequences of earlier societies' reactions, or inaction, in the face of unprecedented danger help us to meet the emerging threats to the global environment?

If we are to see ahead more clearly than did our predecessors of 1900, we must grasp more surely than they did the history, the cultures, and the daily workings of all the world's societies.

Today's world confronts its own array of changes and upheavals, some hopeful and others ominous. If we are to see ahead more clearly than did our predecessors of 1900, we must grasp more surely than they did the history, the cultures, and the daily workings of all the world's societies. Hence the declaration of the Bradley Commission on History that democratic citizens must grasp three sorts of historical reality: the American past, to tell us who we are, what we have done, and who we are becoming; the Western, or European past, to understand our moral and political heritage and the causes of its advances and its failures; and the history of non-European civilizations, to know the nations and peoples with whom we shall live out a common destiny. Each of the three tells us things we must know that the other two cannot. None is sufficient by itself.

Students should also build their capacities for judgment and analysis, those ways of thinking that are powerfully developed by historical study. Such habits of mind are not limited to the formal skills called "critical thinking," but range from the rational to the affective to traits we may call moral and temperamental. Among the analytical skills worth having is the ability to distinguish between fact and conjecture, between the trivial and the consequential, and between the general and the particular. Particularity must be respected in order to avoid careless generalizations and false analogies. The study of history should promote the ability to grasp the complexity of causation—how change occurs in society, how human intentions matter, but also how consequences are shaped by the means of carrying them out, in what William McNeill has called the tangle of purpose and process. History inculcates an understanding of paradox and a readiness to distinguish between that which is beyond and that which is within human control—the inevitable and the contingent. It trains students to detect bias, to weigh evidence, and to evaluate arguments, thus preparing them to make sensible, independent judgments, to sniff out spurious appeals to history by partisan pleaders, to distinguish between anecdote and analysis.

Knowledge of history is the pre-condition of political intelligence. Without it, one cannot undertake any sensible inquiry into political, economic, social, or moral issues in society.

Knowledge of history is the precondition of political intelligence. Without it, one cannot undertake any sensible inquiry into political, economic, social, or moral issues in society. And without inquiry, one cannot move to the active, discriminating citizenship essential to the survival of democratic processes and the fulfillment of the democratic ideals expressed in the central texts of American history. History illuminates the roots of contemporary issues and problems; it reveals the ambiguity of choice, the unresolved questions every society has faced; it promotes wariness about quick, facile solutions, which have so often brought human suffering in their wake.

To care about the human consequences of human choice is to enter the affective realm. History, like literature, biography, and the arts, helps students to confront "otherness." By studying other societies, students can develop understanding of people of other cultures and other eras, who have lived under different ideas and conditions from their own. They may gain at one and the same time an appreciation of different cultures and of a shared humanity with common problems. They may acquire the habit of seeing matters through others' eyes and come to realize that they can better understand themselves as they study others, and the other way around. To understand does not require approval or forgiveness, either of others or ourselves. But it is conducive to the kind of mutual patience and civic courage required to bring to life those values that are so much needed in our pluralistic, multicultural society. Such are a few of the habits of mind and temper that history, properly presented, can help to develop.

HOW SHOULD HISTORY BE PRESENTED?

The kind of history teaching and learning needed to fulfill the purposes of historical study outlined so far will necessarily differ from much of the history taught in American schools in this century. This is not to deny that history is already well taught by good teachers in those schools that help them to work at their best. Our object is to open chances for many more of our teachers and students to reap the benefits of more history, more effectively presented. We have already argued the need for more curricular time for history in the education of all Americans. But the problem is not only to teach *more* history as it has been conventionally conceived. The problem is also *how* history is taught, upon what principles of presentation teachers build their courses, select their readings, set up discussions and student activities, assign paper topics, and construct examinations. Among the most vital principles of presentation are the following.

■ **Chronological, Analytical Narrative**. History's unique power to educate flows from its narrative character, its respect for verifiable fact, its passion for accuracy but, at the same time, its allowance for interpretation. It reveals connections, consequences, drama, and change. Well-wrought narrative is also analytical, pursuing critical themes and questions, making clear as it goes along the importance of all the other principles of presentation offered below. To place it at the continuing, organizing core of the social studies is to recognize that history is not the enemy of the social sciences but is instead their indispensable source of nourishment, order, and perspective. It is manifestly impossible for stu-

History's unique power to educate flows from its narrative character, its respect for fact, its revelation of connections, consequences, drama, and change.

dents to comprehend economic, political, social, and cultural questions without examining them in their historical context, and their interrelatedness in that context. To organize curricula around concepts or current issues abstracted from the historical narrative not only confuses students but is bound to obscure the human condition. Taught in historical context, the formulations and insights of the social sciences take on life, drama, and human significance. And, in turn, their organizing concepts and questions can help rescue history from the unrelated recital of dates and facts that so many students have complained of and which has contributed to its unpopularity in many instances.

Just as history and the social sciences are interdependent allies, so are history and the humanities. Literature, religion, philosophy, and the arts are best understood by students in the context of societal evolution over time. History offers both organization and illumination. And, in turn, the humanities greatly enliven and reinforce students' comprehension of historical place and moment. Narrative history is by its nature an interdisciplinary subject. It should be much richer than a thin recital of successive facts. It should emerge as what has been called "thick narrative," which combines lively storytelling and biography with conceptual analysis drawn from all relevant disciplines. Apart from its greater interest for students, "thick narrative" makes plain that ideas and institutions do not spring up in a vacuum but are developed over time and shaped by changing historical contexts, forces, and people.

> *Narrative history is by its nature an interdisciplinary subject. It should merge as what has been called "thick narrative," which combines lively storytelling and biography with conceptual analysis drawn from all relevant disciplines.*

■ **Interpretation of Narrative.** One of the most common questions students ask as they embark on history papers is "Am I on the right track?" or "Is this what you want?" They feel compelled to find the one right answer, and the teacher's urging that they think about the difference between an answer and an argument is met with confusion. Their problem is deeply rooted in the conventional ways in which textbooks have presented history as a succession of facts marching straight to a single, settled outcome or resolution, whose significance one can neatly evaluate. But once students have learned the fundamental importance of keeping their facts straight, they need to realize that historians may disagree widely on how those facts are to be interpreted. Thus, "history" is usually taken to mean what happened in the past;

but *written* history is a dialogue among historians not only about what happened, but about why and how it happened, whether it was good or bad, how it affected other happenings, and how much importance it ought to be assigned. The study of history is not only remembering answers. It requires following and evaluating arguments, and arriving at usable, even if tentative, conclusions based on the available evidence.

■ **Inclusiveness**. Students can genuinely comprehend the processes of history only if they understand the roles played by the many different people and constituent groups of the society under study. Without knowing them all, and how they interacted, students will understand none very well and will misconstrue both social and political history. What is needed is the effective integration into the historical narrative of men and women from all classes and conditions, ethnic and racial origins, national and religious backgrounds. Such integration is important, for we Americans have our origins in every region on earth—Africa, Asia, Europe, the Middle East, the Pacific, and all of the Americas—as well as in the many different cultures within each region.

The study of history requires following and evaluating arguments, and arriving at usable, even if tentative, conclusions based on the available evidence.

Such integration is not yet an easy task for teachers to carry out. There is the ever-present problem of time. Social history, no less than political history, requires careful selection from among the numberless topics available. The sheer scope of the historical record requires the imaginative synthesis of political and social, cultural, economic, and religious history around central, significant themes and questions. But many teachers' own university training in history has been weak in such syntheses. Moreover, their historical studies of diverse people have rarely been so comprehensive as we would wish. Until very recently, even college-level textbooks have not been inclusive enough of the nation's ethnic and cultural diversity, and the experiences of these many groups are often still not well-integrated into the main narrative. Many texts, both at school and college level, tack them on in brief sketches, side-bars, and tail-ends of paragraphs that are awkward and condescending. The realities of history are obscured, and its interest for students dimmed, when the role of diverse groups is slighted or presented in a disjointed way. American history has been especially disfigured by the minimal or demeaning treatment of African Americans, despite guage, and infrastructure of a dynastic system that was to endure for two thousand years.

The military revolution in Europe between 1500-1700 A.D. contributed to profound changes in Europe and eventually throughout much of the rest of the world. It triggered a European arms race, strengthened rivalries between European nation states, and was a major factor in the gradual conquest of the Americas, Indonesia, and large parts of Africa and India by rival European states before the end of the 18th century. In our own century the consequences of World War I prepared the way for the rise of the totalitarian regimes of the Left and Right: the Soviet Union under Stalin, Germany under Hitler, Franco's Spain and Mussolini's Italy. None of these developments can be fully explained without understanding the influences of military revolution and war in the affairs of nations.

Students should search out the wider interactions between major technological and economic developments and their effects upon social and political institutions.

Students should similarly be encouraged to search out the wider interactions between major economic developments and their effects upon social and political institutions, at home and abroad. Thus, questions of the degree to which economic motives were responsible for imperialism in the ancient as well as the modern world should be examined alongside the broader questions of what was happening to the (imperialist) society at home, what prior events were influential, how other societies were affected, and what role was played by tradition or ideology. This broader historical approach will bring to life, far better than economic analyses alone, most economic questions, whether the means of capital accumulation or the causes of depression.

Following this theme of economic development across the centuries, students should also come to understand that regional and global economic dominance has constantly shifted from one people to another. In turn, India, Islam, Italy, Holland, England, the United States, and Japan have led the world in trade and reaped great benefits for their peoples. This insight should dispel notions that any given people is somehow naturally endowed with qualities that perpetuate economic success or stagnation. And it should also dispel the notion that economic dominance over others, or even their exploitation, requires the military and political control commonly associated with imperialism. Whatever form economic dominance takes, students should examine its effects on both the dominated and the dominating societies, not only in general but in regard to particular classes and interests in each society. The question of who profits and who pays, and how much, always interests students and leads them to perceive complications they may not have expected, whether in their home economy or in the international economy of the late 20th-century world.

In following this theme, teachers will want students to consider the effects of humankind's increasing control of the environment, the destructive as well as benign effects of such control upon the planet and upon human life itself, and the different effects of "modernization" upon peoples and cultures throughout the world. In this regard, students might consider how much developments such as the internal combustion engine and the art of flying have shaped human life and death in the 20th century. Students may ask, as Churchill did, whether such inventions arrived too soon upon a civilization still too primitive to prevent them from generating unprecedented horror and destruction. The question of harnessing the powers of science and technology has never been more urgent and should inspire students to look all the more deeply into those economic, social, political, and ethical spheres of human life that have encouraged or inhibited the work of science and technology, and out of which have come the decisions that have made the difference betweer their benign or destructive application.

Finally, through this theme students will confront another of the most significant questions of our day: the nature of alternative economic systems, and their respective consequences in the social, economic, and political fortunes of their societies. As with the issue of directing science and technology to benign ends, no question has had more significance for nations in the 20th century. Its meaning for students will depend upon their ability to examine basic alternatives in economic systems within the larger context of social, political, and philosophical beliefs to which those systems are closely linked.

Students should consider the effects of humankind's increasing control of the environment, its destructive as well as benign effects upon the planet and human life itself.

■ ***Major Theme III: People's Development and Representation of Their Understandings of Them-***

been both winners and losers over the course of time. They may not see what was lost from the way things turned out, or what was nonetheless passed on by those who lost, to influence the victors and the future. Only a step away is the trap of inevitability. Unless students can conceive that things could have turned out differently—that history is contingent (which accounts for its unpopularity in some quarters)—they may unconsciously accept the notion that the future is also inevitable or predetermined, that human agency and individual action will count for nothing. No attitude is more likely to feed civic apathy, cynicism, and resignation—precisely what we hope the study of history will fend off. Whether in dealing with the main narrative or with a topic in depth, we must always, in Gordon Craig's words, "restore to the past the options it once had."

■ **Exploring Causality.** Depth and narrative cannot do without each other. The one cannot be effectively taught without a nearby treatment of the other. Nowhere is their combination more necessary than in bringing students to grapple with the historical question of causality. Why and how do things happen as they do? How has change occurred? How does one event relate to the next? How have people managed reform or revolution or restoration, or fallen into war, and won or lost? Few things can be more fascinating to students than unpeeling the often dramatic complications of cause. And nothing is more poisonous to whole societies than a simple, monocausal explanation of their past experiences and present problems. It can stir unwarranted pride or shame or fury, raise up scapegoats and single enemies, and hopelessly tangle public debate on the most critical issues at hand. Historical sophistication is the best, probably the only, inoculation against this kind of poison.

Whereas some social scientists search for universal, predictable laws explaining change, historians generally look for all possible factors and contingencies of the moment, while drawing upon the hypotheses of other disciplines. They attempt to weigh the importance of ideas and human values, as well as the force of special interests and material conditions. They seek to measure the importance of the individual in history, the influence of individual will, intellect, and character. And they look for chance, for the accidental and the irrational, and the extent to which human choice may be inhibited, or stimulated,

Unless students can conceive that things could have turned out differently—that history is contingent—they may unconsciously accept the notion that the future is also inevitable or predetermined, that human agency and individual action will count for nothing.

by memories of the past. Very often, historians cannot help but conclude that things could well have happened another way.

■ **Active learning and critical inquiry**. If things could have happened otherwise, it follows that historians and their students often cannot rest content with received myth or settled certainty recorded in textbooks. As school history courses proceed, teachers should pause at a number of turning-points to remind students again that certain judgments about the past are tentative and arguable, that historians regard their work as critical inquiry. They pursue ongoing explorations and debates with other historians that are sometimes impolite and often unresolved. On certain topics, where there is relevant evidence, students can themselves actively engage in critical inquiry by exploring primary sources and documents. In 1892, the Committee of Ten strongly recommended active learning, in saying that students should always read more than one account of important events, should employ original documents, frame questions for discussion and debate, write and speak their own minds frequently on significant topics. We repeat the Committee's concern with even greater urgency today, for by active engagement in questions honestly posed, students can learn for themselves why historians are continually reinterpreting the past and why new interpretations emerge not only from uncovering new evidence but from rethinking old evidence in the light of new ideas springing up in our own times. Students can see why the good historian, the good teacher, is interested not in manipulation or indoctrination but in acting as the honest messenger from the past—not interested in possessing students' minds but in presenting them with the power to possess their own.

On certain topics, where there is relevant evidence, students can themselves actively engage in critical inquiry by exploring primary sources and documents.

HISTORY AND THE POWER TO CHOOSE

To confer such power upon all citizens equally is the first aspiration of education in a democracy, for it is essential to self-governing people. The broad and deep historical knowledge we ask for is vital not only for the individual's role as citizen but also for the self-knowledge and the sense of place in the human story that lie at the heart of personal wholeness. To this end, the study of history should be accompanied by biography and literature, philosophy, religion, and the arts.

changing character of culture. Technology of radio, film, and television, for example, changes the look and frequency of our amusements, if not their worth. Printing and Protestantism transformed the curricula of schools and universities and gave rise to autonomy and a greater sense of individualism. Economic and social changes have altered the character of spectator sports in our time, just as they helped to shape the arts and literature of the Renaissance and of every century since.

Students should also understand, however, that the realm of culture cannot be explained simply by the action of outside forces, or as the direct expression of what people valued. Each of the arts and every genre of literature has its own inner history, its own developments of craft and imagination. Not only did printing, Protestantism, economic and social change reshape the look of churches, but the historical evolution of architecture, painting, music, and sculpture did so as well. Every sort of literature has been influenced by imitation, rivalries, dialogue, and debate among its practitioners and between generations. And students should not assume that only "high" culture has been marked by such adventures. Almost every form of sport and amusement has a long history of its own, replete with innovation, tradition, and quarrels between the two. The circus, vaudeville, popular song and dance, the banquet, races on foot and wheel, to mention only a few, are almost as old as history and are changing still. Understanding the developments in culture, as in every other sphere of life, requires that students follow the chronological story, in main outline if not in detail.

Culture cannot be explained simply by the action of outside forces, or as the direct expression of what people valued. Each of the arts has its own inner history, its own developments of craft and imagination.

■ *MAJOR THEME IV: The Development of Political Theories and Organization, variously expressed in people's quest for effective order, power, and for just and humane relationships.*

World history reveals the variety of arrangements people have developed in their efforts to live successfully and peaceably together, in communal and tribal relationships and in the increasingly differentiated and complex social and political structures accompanying the historical emergence of city- and nation-states, of great bureaucratic empires, and of modern nations increasingly linked through systems of international economic and political cooperation and control.

Measured by its difficulty and by its limitless human consequences, politics is the highest of the arts to practice well. Struggles to achieve and to preserve law, justice, and security for any society, in the face of innumerable forces bearing upon it from within and without, make captivating stories. Democracy's great vision of doing so under conditions of human liberty and equality adds a whole new level of challenge.

As argued in Chapter I, the major eras of political change and development provide the chronological framework students need for historical perspective, for understanding cause and effect, change, and continuity. The central human drama is played out in the political arena where, always within the limits imposed by other forces (from geography to public passion to the power of other nations), citizens and leaders must make their choices. The sense or folly of these choices determines again and again whether the lives of most people and their children are to be relatively long or short, bearable or unbearable. It is, then, imperative that students concerned with democratic politics and human well-being follow the development of political history: the origin and growth of law and states; the variety of governmental systems; the forces and decisions that have brought war and peace, reform, and revolution; the urge toward empire; the rise of modern mass politics; decolonization and the evolution of regional and world mechanisms to promote international law and policy-making.

The major eras of political change and development provide the chronological framework students need for historical perspective, for understanding cause and effect, change, and continuity.

One important sub-theme to follow in the unfolding of all these events in world history, and one particularly important in the study of United States history, is the evolution of democracy—the story of the long human struggle for liberty, equality, justice, and dignity; the ideas, conditions, and people who have carried the struggle forward; and those that have hobbled, betrayed, or defeated it. In world history, students need to think about the meaning of terms like democracy, freedom, and liberty in modern mass society and how these terms have been differently used and misused to justify practices that in fact violate the central premises of democracy.

In world history students need also to follow the evolu-

3. The years of history recommended above should include **no less than three full years of United States history for all students,** with two of those years offered between grades 7 and 12.

4. The years of history recommended above should also include for all students **no less than two full years of world history** with at least one of those years offered at the senior high school level, when students will have attained the intellectual maturity to grasp major issues, debate their causes, and develop the historical perspectives needed for interpreting unfolding events in the modern world.

Richer, more inclusive programs of history have been recommended by every major curriculum reform proposal of recent years.

The recommendations in Chapters III and IV of the important historical understandings and habits of thought that all students should acquire were developed on the assumption that schools will be moving toward the richer, more inclusive programs of history recommended by the Center and by every major curriculum reform proposal of recent years. Such changes, moreover, are essential if students are to achieve the "world class" standards in history espoused in the national goals established by the nation's governors,[1] endorsed in the national agenda, America 2000,[2] and enthusiastically supported by 81 percent of the American public.[3]

How to go about selecting what history is essential in producing the level of understanding envisioned in these goals is the question we turn to next. This chapter will then conclude with an examination of the problems confronting teachers in districts not yet providing the time required to accomplish these purposes with their students, and the criteria for selection they might use in planning their programs under the duress of clearly insufficient teaching time.

---

[1] National Goals in Education. Washington, D.C., U.S. Department of Education, July 1990.

[2] America 2000, An Education Strategy. Washington, D.C., U.S. Department of Education, 1991.

[3] Stanley M. Elam, Lowell C. Rose, and Alec M. Gallup. "The 23rd Annual Gallup Poll of the Public's Attitudes Toward the Public Schools." Phi Delta Kappan, (Sept. 1991), 41-56.

MAJOR SPHERES OF HUMAN ACTIVITY

To bring students into the process of historical interpretation and to answer the dynamic questions of *why* and *how*, it will be most helpful for both teachers and students to develop the habit of looking at life and history—at least part of the time—as the playing-out of five kinds of human endeavor: social; scientific/technological; economic; religious/philosophical/cultural; and political. History is the story of human strivings and aspirations in each of these spheres of activity. It follows that the major themes and questions closest to human concerns—including the concerns of students—arise from each and all of these spheres of life.

History is the story of human strivings and aspirations in five spheres of activity: social, scientific/technological, economic, religious/philosophical, and political.

■ SOCIAL SPHERE OF ACTIVITY

Indispensable to an understanding of human history, this sphere confronts students with the enduring question, what is human society? It includes the different and changing views of men's and women's roles across time and place and the different forms and roles that family life has taken, including African and American Indian matrilineal and matriarchal family structures as well as western patrilineal and patriarchal families. This sphere includes, also, the different conceptions of childhood, adolescence, and old age; status and characteristics of the various groups and classes in society; their relationships to each other and to society at large. It considers how economic, religious, cultural, and political changes have affected social life, and it incorporates developments shaping the destiny of millions: the history of slavery; of class conflict; of mass migration and immigration; the human consequences of plague, war, and famine; and the longer life expectancy and rising living standards following upon medical, technological, and economic advances.

■ SCIENTIFIC/TECHNOLOGICAL SPHERE OF ACTIVITY

What we call science, the quest for understanding nature and humanity itself, is as old as recorded history. So, too, is humanity's effort to do better, or more efficiently, everything from hunting food to intercepting missiles to caring for the ill. Science and technology have propelled each other. Technical advances have eased the way for scientific research; scientific knowledge of how they would turn out than are our decisions today. The historical context selected to develop these essential habits of the mind will necessarily be rich in controversy—controversies of the time among those caught up in these events but controversies, also, among historians as they seek to interpret the significance of events and their lasting influences upon the fortunes of people of various groups, classes, and national allegience.

SELECTION AND THE PROBLEM OF TIME

The two following chapters demonstrate the advantage of a curriculum that begins historical studies in the early grades and continues them throughout the middle and high school years.

In studying both the history of the United States and the world, students will find it extremely helpful to focus their exploration and discussion of the past upon major continuing themes and habits of the mind. But as we began by saying, such a thought-provoking study of history depends upon sufficient time in the school curriculum. The two following chapters will further demonstrate the immense advantage of a curriculum that begins historical studies in the early grades, continues them throughout the middle and high school years, and provides exposure to world history as well as to the history of the United States. Such curricular reform is proceeding in several areas of the country to provide a history/geography core for the social studies throughout the school years. For teachers fortunate enough to work in these settings, the essential understandings and perspectives recommended in Chapters III and IV will be wholly practicable, provided there is careful planning by school districts of how best to sequence historical studies across the elementary, middle, and senior high school grades.

In schools that have not yet adopted the necessary curricular reforms, the chances are strong that the whole of United States history will be collapsed into a single year-long "survey course" or less at the secondary level, preceded for some but not all students by a year of United States history in the middle or junior high school, and preceded for even fewer students by an elementary school offering in United States history. For teachers of world history or Western civilization in such schools, the senior high school course, when offered at all, will likely be the first introduction most students will have had to any history of regions beyond their borders.

Given all that should be learned for a historically literate society, and given the absence of an adequate historical background on the part of so many students today, what are teachers in these districts to do? For them, the essential understandings set forth in Chapters III and IV will almost certainly appear to be more than can be thoughtfully developed within the short time they have for instruction. We have already argued that "coverage" is not enough by itself; it is a recipe for boredom, superficiality, and, worst of all, for serious misunderstanding of the nature of history. Racing over the 800 or so pages of a textbook simply does not allow for the active and thoughtful study of the past that results in understanding. How can teachers, then, go about the drastic kind of selection that is imposed and yet leave intact a vital narrative story line that follows significant, engaging themes and questions throughout each course?

Quite obviously, not all of the major topics and essential understandings set forth in Chapters III and IV can possibly be given equal weight or even "covered" in any single course that is built around the principles of presentation set forth in Chapter I. Teachers will therefore be compelled to select from these topics and essential understandings those that they wish to develop in depth; those that they will present in moderate detail or in a lean narrative which serves as a bridge to the next topic; and those they may leave to homework in the text, which very often amounts to leaving them out, altogether.

Racing through the 800 or so pages of a textbook simply does not allow for the active and thoughtful study of the past that results in understanding.

In practice, no such selection should be made without first answering three questions. First, is the choice made in the light of the arguments in Chapters III and IV for its significance? Second, is the choice consistent with the aims of historical study and the principles of presentation offered in Chapter I? Third, is the choice better suited than other possible choices to serve the teacher's own course design and objectives? Otherwise said, trimming and cutting may be necessary, but they should never be easy! One good test of whether decisions, to keep or to cut, have been carefully arrived at is whether they can be explained to students in ways that promote their understanding of what history is all about.

Two finals points deserve emphasis. First, it is important that study of times past be linked to the present day. Students need, and very much want, to perceive how everything they have learned possesses meaning for them and their society in

Major themes move across the great sweep of human history, illustrating the interplay of major forces for continuity and change in the unfolding of the human story.

framework (a "cognitive map") in which major events and turning points in the history of the nation and the world are causally linked to their antecedents and their consequences, contextually linked to other forces at work at the time, and clarified as to their continuing significance in the present.

In the paragraphs which follow, we present four major narrative themes, capable of bringing together for students the story of human history. Each has been derived from one of the major spheres of human activity described above, in interaction with one or more of the others. Figure 1 illustrates this relationship between the five spheres of human activity and these four major narrative themes in world and United States history. The narrative which follows explains each in greater detail.

■ *MAJOR THEME I: The Development and Changing Character of Human Societies*

An understanding of society is indispensable to an understanding of human history. Basic to United States history, for example, is the story of the gathering of the many and diverse peoples and cultures that have created and are still transforming American society. Basic to an understanding of world history is comprehension of the many and diverse societies that constitute humankind, the long road they have traveled from their earliest beginnings, the rich diversity of social forms developed along the way, and the continuing significance of their interactions throughout history and into the modern era.

To examine how these various social forms and developments have evolved over time, through what patterns of continuity and change, this theme reaches back for its beginnings to the earliest prehistoric societies in their immediate family and kinship groupings; and it continues through time to the development of late 20th-century mass societies in which today's students now live and which shape, in important ways, their outlook, opportunities, and their futures.

To understand the dynamic force behind the historical evolution of social groups, students must first understand the human commitment to social life, evident throughout all of

Figure 1. Relationships Between Major Spheres of Human
Activity and Major Narrative Themes in U.S. and World History

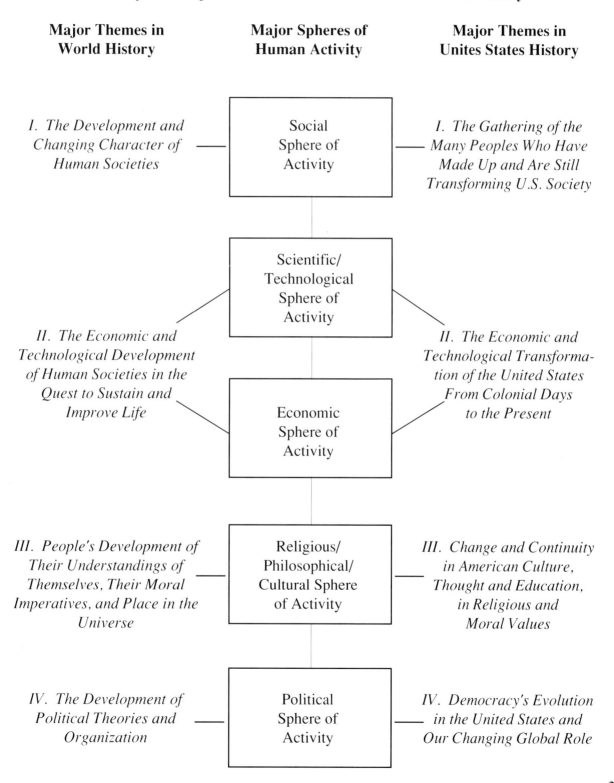

Major Themes in World History	Major Spheres of Human Activity	Major Themes in Unites States History
I. The Development and Changing Character of Human Societies	Social Sphere of Activity	*I. The Gathering of the Many Peoples Who Have Made Up and Are Still Transforming U.S. Society*
II. The Economic and Technological Development of Human Societies in the Quest to Sustain and Improve Life	Scientific/ Technological Sphere of Activity Economic Sphere of Activity	*II. The Economic and Technological Transformation of the United States From Colonial Days to the Present*
III. People's Development of Their Understandings of Themselves, Their Moral Imperatives, and Place in the Universe	Religious/ Philosophical/ Cultural Sphere of Activity	*III. Change and Continuity in American Culture, Thought and Education, in Religious and Moral Values*
IV. The Development of Political Theories and Organization	Political Sphere of Activity	*IV. Democracy's Evolution in the United States and Our Changing Global Role*

Textbooks are often not helpful in setting forth and carrying through such themes and questions. But teachers should do so, choosing from among those that are obvious and finding new combinations of their own. One unending story is the **gathering of the many diverse peoples and cultures that have made up, and are still transforming American society.** Who have we been; who are we becoming? The story runs from the earliest American Indians occupying this continent, through the 15th- through 17th-century arrivals of Europeans and Africans in the "Great Convergence" of these three worlds, through the successive waves of 18th-, 19th-, and 20th-century arrivals from every part of the world, to the new immigrants of the day after tomorrow.

Another inescapable theme is the **economic transformation of the United States from pre-industrial colonial days to our highly technological, post-industrial society.** How has such change, more rapid and complex with each passing decade, affected social and family life, work, political balances, and human aspirations? A third related theme is the story of **change and continuity in American culture, in thought and education, and in religion and moral values.**

Without question, the story of **democracy's evolution in North America** should form a fourth continuing, central theme, unifying the study of the nation's history from its beginning until now. What have we aspired to and how far have we succeeded? Nowhere more than in a diverse society plunged in rapid change is understanding political ideals and acknowledging political realities essential to amity and shared purpose. On the one hand, students must grasp the American vision of liberty, equality, justice, and human dignity, and how these ideals were first defined and then redefined as time has passed. Students should follow the development of the reform impulse, which has repeatedly surfaced in our history. Just as surely, they need to follow the true story of the slow, unsteady journey of turning ideals into practices, how and where they have been applied and have been violated, the people and forces that have opened or obstructed the way.

Finally, related to the nation's political history is **our changing role in the world** from a few tiny, quarrelsome colonies in rebellion to a great power of the 20th century,

Students must grasp the American vision of liberty, equality, justice, and human dignity; just as surely, they need to follow the slow, unsteady journey of turning ideals into practices.

entangled in an interdependent world marked by breathtaking economic and political changes.

Students should see that each of these continuing stories—the gathering of our people, the transformation of our economic, social, and cultural life, the adventures of democracy in the United States, and the changes in our global role—is affected by all the others. It should also become clear to students that most questions worth asking about the history and life of the United States have no final answers and that no themes worth following have endings, happy or otherwise. The students themselves will be actors in the unfinished drama and it should burst upon them, long before the end of their studies, that they will not escape responsibility for some of its turns, any more than earlier generations have. They too will be blamed or praised, held up as bad or good examples, by historians, teachers, and students in the future.

The study of United States history should also quickly reveal to students that their own experiences of pain and conflict are not unique. They will learn that Americans in every generation have struggled to defend or extend their own and others' rights and well-being, very often at high personal cost, in peacetime as well as at war. They will learn that people here and around the world have cherished liberty and justice not because they bring affluence, efficiency, or repose—these are not, in any case, the promises of liberty and justice—but for their own surpassing value. Only historical perspective and the sympathetic understanding of men and women in the past can teach such lessons, and the many others that ought to emerge from well-conceived studies of our own history.

It should become clear to students that most questions worth asking about the history of the United States have no final answers, that students themselves will be actors in the unfinished drama.

ORGANIZATION OF CHAPTER III

To aid teachers in the work of planning their programs, each major historical era or teaching unit in Chapter III is presented under three major headings: **Significance and Teaching Goals; Major Topics;** and **Major Topics and Their Development: Essential Understandings and Related Background for Teachers**. The first, **Significance and Teaching Goals,** argues the importance of the subject at hand and some of the most worthwhile goals to be sought in teaching it. What major historical themes should be pursued?

complishment, and the emphasis, by contrast, that other cultures have placed on the class, group, or community.

■ *Major Theme II: The Economic and Technological Development of Human Societies, resulting from humankind's increasing control of the environment, in the quest to sustain and improve the quality of life.*

This major theme has been central throughout human history, appearing first in earliest prehistoric societies in their harnessing of fire and tool-making capabilities; and continuing over time with developments in hunting/gathering, agriculture, trade, mining, banking, industrial manufacturing, and the modern technological innovations that have transformed the post-industrial world and its increasingly global economic systems. In world history this major theme follows the development of entire economic systems down to the present, including their effects on people's lives and on the social and political structures under which they have lived. In United States history, this major theme is circumscribed by the time frame of the nation's history and focuses therefore on the economic transformation of the United States, from pre-industrial colonial days to our highly technological post-industrial society.

This basic theme draws upon events in two major spheres of human activity—the scientific/technological and the economic. In world history, the emergence of agriculture, navigation, printing, and industrialization are among the most obvious of the world-shaking technological changes that challenge students' imaginations. In United States history, the technological development of the iron-tipped plow, the steam engine, and electrical power are but three examples of innovations on which major transformations of the nation's economy have turned.

Students must understand the basic struggle for human survival itself, the ongoing interaction between man and environment in that struggle, and the related quest to improve the quality of life, once life itself is sustained.

To understand the dynamic force behind all these developments, students must understand **the basic struggle for human survival itself, the ongoing interaction between man and environment in that struggle, and the related quest to improve the quality of life, once life itself is sustained.** Students will observe the unfolding of this struggle from the earliest records of human history: the nomadic hunting/gathering activities of the Paleolithic Age, and the dramatic changes begun with the Neolithic Revolution, a major turning point in human history.

With agriculture came the development of simple farming villages; of cities such as Ur, once irrigation was developed to support agriculture on the dry plain of the Tigris and Euphrates; and of new technologies stimulated by the changing needs of an agricultural economy. Among these developments of the Neolithic age were the plow to till the hard clay soils; metal smelting for tools, utensils, and weapons unavailable through stone-tool technology; the wheel to shape pottery and to transport surplus grain for storage and trade; and systems of numeration and writing for purposes of record-keeping and administration.

Economic specialization, developed to conduct these various activities for a growing population, led in turn to the development of hierarchically differentiated social classes, of central government, and of law to administer the increasingly complex economic and political affairs of these early city states. Examining these developments, dynamically unfolding over centuries in the basic quest for survival, students will see that **major technological and economic developments have been the source of profound changes in people's lives and in the social and political structures under which they have lived.**

Studying succeeding historical eras, students should similarly be encouraged to search out the wider interactions between major technological and economic developments and their effects upon social and political institutions, at home and abroad. Among these have been the major consequences of military revolutions in the weaponry, tactics, and organization of war for the social, economic, and political affairs of societies. The military revolution of third century B.C. China, for example, not only allowed the Ch'in Dynasty forcibly to end more than a half-century of warfare in China by defeating all other states and by creating a unified empire; its new military tactics of utilizing massed conscripts exceeding one million men, its new mass-produced iron weaponry of war, and its formidable centralization of authority also influenced the development of the administrative structure, penal codes, lan-

Economic specialization led to the development of hierarchically differentiated social classes, central government, and law to administer the increasingly complex affairs of early city states.

guage, and infrastructure of a dynastic system that was to endure for two thousand years.

The military revolution in Europe between 1500-1700 A.D. contributed to profound changes in Europe and eventually throughout much of the rest of the world. It triggered a European arms race, strengthened rivalries between European nation states, and was a major factor in the gradual conquest of the Americas, Indonesia, and large parts of Africa and India by rival European states before the end of the 18th century. In our own century the consequences of World War I prepared the way for the rise of the totalitarian regimes of the Left and Right: the Soviet Union under Stalin, Germany under Hitler, Franco's Spain and Mussolini's Italy. None of these developments can be fully explained without understanding the influences of military revolution and war in the affairs of nations.

Students should search out the wider interactions between major technological and economic developments and their effects upon social and political institutions.

Students should similarly be encouraged to search out the wider interactions between major economic developments and their effects upon social and political institutions, at home and abroad. Thus, questions of the degree to which economic motives were responsible for imperialism in the ancient as well as the modern world should be examined alongside the broader questions of what was happening to the (imperialist) society at home, what prior events were influential, how other societies were affected, and what role was played by tradition or ideology. This broader historical approach will bring to life, far better than economic analyses alone, most economic questions, whether the means of capital accumulation or the causes of depression.

Following this theme of economic development across the centuries, students should also come to understand that regional and global economic dominance has constantly shifted from one people to another. In turn, India, Islam, Italy, Holland, England, the United States, and Japan have led the world in trade and reaped great benefits for their peoples. This insight should dispel notions that any given people is somehow naturally endowed with qualities that perpetuate economic success or stagnation. And it should also dispel the notion that economic dominance over others, or even their exploitation, requires the military and political control commonly associated with imperialism. Whatever form economic dominance takes, students should examine its effects on both the dominated and the dominating societies, not only in general but in regard to particular classes and interests in each society. The question of who profits and who pays, and how much, always interests students and leads them to perceive complications they may not have expected, whether in their home economy or in the international economy of the late 20th-century world.

In following this theme, teachers will want students to consider the effects of humankind's increasing control of the environment, the destructive as well as benign effects of such control upon the planet and upon human life itself, and the different effects of "modernization" upon peoples and cultures throughout the world. In this regard, students might consider how much developments such as the internal combustion engine and the art of flying have shaped human life and death in the 20th century. Students may ask, as Churchill did, whether such inventions arrived too soon upon a civilization still too primitive to prevent them from generating unprecedented horror and destruction. The question of harnessing the powers of science and technology has never been more urgent and should inspire students to look all the more deeply into those economic, social, political, and ethical spheres of human life that have encouraged or inhibited the work of science and technology, and out of which have come the decisions that have made the difference between their benign or destructive application.

Finally, through this theme students will confront another of the most significant questions of our day: the nature of alternative economic systems, and their respective consequences in the social, economic, and political fortunes of their societies. As with the issue of directing science and technology to benign ends, no question has had more significance for nations in the 20th century. Its meaning for students will depend upon their ability to examine basic alternatives in economic systems within the larger context of social, political, and philosophical beliefs to which those systems are closely linked.

■ *Major Theme III: People's Development and Representation of Their Understandings of Them-*

Students should consider the effects of humankind's increasing control of the environment, its destructive as well as benign effects upon the planet and human life itself.

selves, Their Moral Imperatives, and Their Place in the Universe, a theme concerned with people's quest for meaning as they confront the great questions of human existence and give such meanings cultural expression.

Such questions as humankind's place in the universe, worthy relationships with others, and the nature of justice and injustice, equality and inequality, the worth of the individual—and thereby the degree of individual liberty that is called for—take us to the realm of religious and philosophical beliefs and values. This realm, like the others, embraces an enormous range of human thought and faith, but fundamental questions cut across it all, and most religions, ethical systems, moral philosophies, and political ideologies have their own answers to offer. What is worthy human behavior and what is not? What brings out the best in people? What constitutes human salvation or human fulfillment on earth? To achieve either or both, what should the individual do, and how is the society best governed to help people individually and collectively attain the good, true, beautiful, and the honorable or holy life?

From the great questions of human existence, answers have emerged with astonishing power to move entire peoples to action.

These are the great questions of human existence; answers have emerged with astonishing power to move entire peoples to action, and often to conflict. In the case of religious faith, events such as the Crusades, the Reformation, Hindu/Moslem strife in India, and the Iranian revolution all illustrate the power of religious conviction in determining historical change. And such conviction has also inspired massive acts of charity and self-abnegation, of healing and consolation, movements for social reform from ancient to modern days, and great works of art and learning.

Students should be able to compare the moral imperatives of the world's major religions and ethical systems, not merely as lists of right and wrong, but as they are related to the basic concepts of human nature that underlie all organized thought about the person, society, and the purpose of human life on earth. To understand the varieties of spiritual experiences among humankind, students need to understand the origins, development, and historical and ethical significance of the great religious and ethical systems which arose in the ancient world and which have been major forces throughout world history, influencing the beliefs and behaviors of millions—Judaism, Christianity, Hinduism, Buddhism, Confucianism—and, from its origins in the Middle Ages, Islam. Students should be introduced to the basic precepts and moral teachings of these faiths and they should understand, as well, the ideas of spirituality of African and American Indian societies, to be developed in the context of their historical study of these cultures.

In the realm of morality, students should address basic questions: Are people born with altruistic or aggressive natures? With potential for both? If the last, do they have the free will to choose for themselves? What part do environment, upbringing, and schooling play? Is human nature itself really changeable, or only outward behavior? Are human beings equal? Are they alike? What can one expect of them, and how should they be treated? It matters little how profoundly students can discuss these questions at first. What matters is that they see how people like themselves have always had to wrestle with such questions to form their own ideas about the important things in life—morals, values, politics, bringing up children—and to develop the power to judge the ideas of others, especially the major prescriptions of competing political ideologies, economic and social theories, and educational philosophies.

Students should understand the moral teachings and imperatives of the world's major religious and ethical systems.

With such a definition, students may explore, for example, the culture of the European Middle Ages at several levels: the influence of the Church on intellectual and cultural life, the cathedral of Chartres, the mystery plays acted at its portals, feasts and festivals, wrestling, sword-swallowing and bear-baiting, the curriculum of the universities, the songs of troubadours, the dash and violence of knightly tournaments, the pleasures of lordly tables. Similarly, students can compare the several levels of cultural life in medieval Japan: the high culture of the Japanese court in Kyoto with its refined manners, courtly poetry, and literary achievements of Lady Murasaki; the ceremonial arts of dance-drama and tea ceremonies; and such new forms of popular culture, developing with the rise of the merchant class, as the Kabuki theater, public baths, and wrestling.

Most obviously, all other aspects of life influence the

changing character of culture. Technology of radio, film, and television, for example, changes the look and frequency of our amusements, if not their worth. Printing and Protestantism transformed the curricula of schools and universities and gave rise to autonomy and a greater sense of individualism. Economic and social changes have altered the character of spectator sports in our time, just as they helped to shape the arts and literature of the Renaissance and of every century since.

Culture cannot be explained simply by the action of outside forces, or as the direct expression of what people valued. Each of the arts has its own inner history, its own developments of craft and imagination.

Students should also understand, however, that the realm of culture cannot be explained simply by the action of outside forces, or as the direct expression of what people valued. Each of the arts and every genre of literature has its own inner history, its own developments of craft and imagination. Not only did printing, Protestantism, economic and social change reshape the look of churches, but the historical evolution of architecture, painting, music, and sculpture did so as well. Every sort of literature has been influenced by imitation, rivalries, dialogue, and debate among its practitioners and between generations. And students should not assume that only "high" culture has been marked by such adventures. Almost every form of sport and amusement has a long history of its own, replete with innovation, tradition, and quarrels between the two. The circus, vaudeville, popular song and dance, the banquet, races on foot and wheel, to mention only a few, are almost as old as history and are changing still. Understanding the developments in culture, as in every other sphere of life, requires that students follow the chronological story, in main outline if not in detail.

■ *MAJOR THEME IV: The Development of Political Theories and Organization, variously expressed in people's quest for effective order, power, and for just and humane relationships.*

World history reveals the variety of arrangements people have developed in their efforts to live successfully and peaceably together, in communal and tribal relationships and in the increasingly differentiated and complex social and political structures accompanying the historical emergence of city- and nation-states, of great bureaucratic empires, and of modern nations increasingly linked through systems of international economic and political cooperation and control.

Measured by its difficulty and by its limitless human consequences, politics is the highest of the arts to practice well. Struggles to achieve and to preserve law, justice, and security for any society, in the face of innumerable forces bearing upon it from within and without, make captivating stories. Democracy's great vision of doing so under conditions of human liberty and equality adds a whole new level of challenge.

As argued in Chapter I, the major eras of political change and development provide the chronological framework students need for historical perspective, for understanding cause and effect, change, and continuity. The central human drama is played out in the political arena where, always within the limits imposed by other forces (from geography to public passion to the power of other nations), citizens and leaders must make their choices. The sense or folly of these choices determines again and again whether the lives of most people and their children are to be relatively long or short, bearable or unbearable. It is, then, imperative that students concerned with democratic politics and human well-being follow the development of political history: the origin and growth of law and states; the variety of governmental systems; the forces and decisions that have brought war and peace, reform, and revolution; the urge toward empire; the rise of modern mass politics; decolonization and the evolution of regional and world mechanisms to promote international law and policy-making.

The major eras of political change and development provide the chronological framework students need for historical perspective, for understanding cause and effect, change, and continuity.

One important sub-theme to follow in the unfolding of all these events in world history, and one particularly important in the study of United States history, is the evolution of democracy—the story of the long human struggle for liberty, equality, justice, and dignity; the ideas, conditions, and people who have carried the struggle forward; and those that have hobbled, betrayed, or defeated it. In world history, students need to think about the meaning of terms like democracy, freedom, and liberty in modern mass society and how these terms have been differently used and misused to justify practices that in fact violate the central premises of democracy.

In world history students need also to follow the evolution of alternative governmental forms, of the astonishing variety of governmental systems that have been created including, in the medieval and early modern eras alone, the feudal kingdoms of northern Europe, feudal Japan, the republican city-states of Italy, the Moslim caliphates, the leaderless society of Iceland, the African kingdoms, the pre-Columbian empires in the Americas, and the Chinese empire. How did they emerge and flourish and why were they so different?

A third political sub-theme students might follow is the history of wars, conquests, slavery, colonization, and empires as well as the violent side of modern political movements mobilized to seize and maintain power. Illustrative are the Terror in Revolutionary France, the Holocaust, Stalin's forced collectivization of the Soviet Union, and such recent events as those in Cambodia, Argentina, the Chinese Cultural Revolution, and the Baltic Republics demonstrating the use of state apparatus, technology, and mass mobilization to destroy opposition and control peoples.

Accompanying the chronological study of events should be the study of political theory and the ideologies that have moved people to action.

Finally, accompanying the chronological study of events should be the study of political theory and the ideologies that have moved people to action. Influential writings and documents should be examined in their historical context: Confucius and Aristotle on right kinds of government; Magna Carta; Bossuet on kingship; Hobbes and Locke on human nature; the Declaration of Independence; The Federalist Papers; the Declaration of the Rights of Man and Citizen; the Communist Manifesto; Mein Kampf; Mao on revolution. All demonstrate—and some of them frightfully—the power of ideas to shape human life.

Clearly Major Theme IV, tracing the development of political organization and its many corollaries, confronts teachers with important choices. Where classroom time sets absolute limits on what can be included, teachers must remember that what is essential is not that students encounter every event, episode, and development in the political histories of the world but that those they do explore be carefully selected to illuminate the deeper understandings identified in these themes, and that sufficient time be given to developing those basic understandings in depth.

ESSENTIAL UNDERSTANDINGS AND HABITS OF THE MIND

Judging what historical understandings are of most worth is best done in terms of the major historical themes just examined. In each of the units on United States history (Chapter III) and world history (Chapter IV), therefore, these major themes have provided the criteria for selecting essential understandings, specific to the unit, which students should have opportunity to acquire. In addition, examples of historical reasoning and analysis which are particularly well developed in the context of these specific units are set forth under the heading, Habits of the Mind.

As suggested in Chapter I, the long perspectives and ways of judgment that arise from the study of history carry students beyond the formal skills of logical, critical thinking to certain traits of mind that amount to real wisdom about life and history. Developing these habits of the mind, students become aware of the past's shaping influences on their own lives and their society. They see the past as it was lived by people at the time, with historical empathy rather than present-mindedness. They recognize how people and their cultures differ, while sharing a common humanity. They grasp the interplay of change and continuity, as history demonstrates to them that neither is necessarily more to be expected, or more desirable, than the other. They understand that not all problems have solutions, that people have always had to live with uncertainty and unfinished business. They see the complexity of cause; they avoid easy generalizations and stereotypes; and, knowing that judgments about the past must often be tentative, they are ready to question "lessons of history" that are offered as quick, simple cures for complex problems in their contemporary world. They learn the importance of ideas and of individual character in history, as well as the role of accident and unreason.

None of these ways of thinking develops in a vacuum. All require a history curriculum rich in the documents, debates, and events which engage students in confronting the great developments, dilemmas, and issues of the time and in seeing those events through the eyes and mind-set of those who were there, and whose decisions were no more informed by certain

By developing historical habits of the mind, students see the past with historical empathy, grasp the interplay of change and continuity, and understand the complexity of cause.

knowledge of how they would turn out than are our decisions today. The historical context selected to develop these essential habits of the mind will necessarily be rich in controversy—controversies of the time among those caught up in these events but controversies, also, among historians as they seek to interpret the significance of events and their lasting influences upon the fortunes of people of various groups, classes, and national allegience.

SELECTION AND THE PROBLEM OF TIME

In studying both the history of the United States and the world, students will find it extremely helpful to focus their exploration and discussion of the past upon major continuing themes and habits of the mind. But as we began by saying, such a thought-provoking study of history depends upon sufficient time in the school curriculum. The two following chapters will further demonstrate the immense advantage of a curriculum that begins historical studies in the early grades, continues them throughout the middle and high school years, and provides exposure to world history as well as to the history of the United States. Such curricular reform is proceeding in several areas of the country to provide a history/geography core for the social studies throughout the school years. For teachers fortunate enough to work in these settings, the essential understandings and perspectives recommended in Chapters III and IV will be wholly practicable, provided there is careful planning by school districts of how best to sequence historical studies across the elementary, middle, and senior high school grades.

In schools that have not yet adopted the necessary curricular reforms, the chances are strong that the whole of United States history will be collapsed into a single year-long "survey course" or less at the secondary level, preceded for some but not all students by a year of United States history in the middle or junior high school, and preceded for even fewer students by an elementary school offering in United States history. For teachers of world history or Western civilization in such schools, the senior high school course, when offered at all, will likely be the first introduction most students will have had to any history of regions beyond their borders.

Given all that should be learned for a historically literate

The two following chapters demonstrate the advantage of a curriculum that begins historical studies in the early grades and continues them throughout the middle and high school years.

society, and given the absence of an adequate historical background on the part of so many students today, what are teachers in these districts to do? For them, the essential understandings set forth in Chapters III and IV will almost certainly appear to be more than can be thoughtfully developed within the short time they have for instruction. We have already argued that "coverage" is not enough by itself; it is a recipe for boredom, superficiality, and, worst of all, for serious misunderstanding of the nature of history. Racing over the 800 or so pages of a textbook simply does not allow for the active and thoughtful study of the past that results in understanding. How can teachers, then, go about the drastic kind of selection that is imposed and yet leave intact a vital narrative story line that follows significant, engaging themes and questions throughout each course?

Quite obviously, not all of the major topics and essential understandings set forth in Chapters III and IV can possibly be given equal weight or even "covered" in any single course that is built around the principles of presentation set forth in Chapter I. Teachers will therefore be compelled to select from these topics and essential understandings those that they wish to develop in depth; those that they will present in moderate detail or in a lean narrative which serves as a bridge to the next topic; and those they may leave to homework in the text, which very often amounts to leaving them out, altogether.

Racing through the 800 or so pages of a textbook simply does not allow for the active and thoughtful study of the past that results in understanding.

In practice, no such selection should be made without first answering three questions. First, is the choice made in the light of the arguments in Chapters III and IV for its significance? Second, is the choice consistent with the aims of historical study and the principles of presentation offered in Chapter I? Third, is the choice better suited than other possible choices to serve the teacher's own course design and objectives? Otherwise said, trimming and cutting may be necessary, but they should never be easy! One good test of whether decisions, to keep or to cut, have been carefully arrived at is whether they can be explained to students in ways that promote their understanding of what history is all about.

Two finals points deserve emphasis. First, it is important that study of times past be linked to the present day. Students need, and very much want, to perceive how everything they have learned possesses meaning for them and their society in the world today, and how it has deepened their understanding of all the kinds of human activity that touch their own lives.

As precious as teaching time is, a generous portion of it must be taken for the individual characters and works of real men and women whose lives deserve to be recounted whole, just as they were lived.

Second, it is important to remember that a subject as extensive and all-encompassing as history always runs the risk of inviting too many abstractions, general comparisons and contrasts, categorizations that may well be valid but are largely lifeless and unmemorable for students. As precious as teaching time is, a generous portion of it must be taken for good stories, for human adventure, for tragedy and comedy, and for the individual characters and works of real men and women whose lives must not be lost in collective abstractions or neatly relegated to one theme or another, but deserve to be recounted whole, just as they were lived.

CHAPTER THREE:
Essential Understandings in United States History

INTRODUCTION

All students graduating from high school should have a thorough understanding of their country's history—its central themes, ideals, struggles, and developments. As a diverse people without common national origins or a common religion, and as a nation continuously receiving new waves of immigrants, we need a collective understanding of our past and of the ways in which we have reached the present. Only this can give us a shared identity and a sense of common purpose. Moreover, as we seek to preserve and refine our democratic system of government, we need an active citizenry whose informed judgments are derived from their understanding of the pathways of United States history. As Montesquieu put it in Spirit of the Laws, "The tyranny of a prince in an oligarchy is not so dangerous to the public welfare as the apathy of a citizen in a democracy." Nor, we could add, so dangerous as the zeal of a citizen who is ignorant of the past.

The bulk of this chapter proceeds chronologically through successive eras of United States history from the 15th century to the present. It is a great, suspenseful story still unfolding. Its dramatic moments and turning-points, and their consequences, are best told in a narrative that is enlivened by a number of vital, continuing themes carried through from start to the present. Each period of our history has its own unique characteristics. Its problems, people, notions, and aspirations must be studied in their own setting. But students need also to be engaged across time in following significant themes and questions that mark every period of our history and are still vital to us, still unanswered, and changing in form every day.

As a diverse people without common national origins or a common religion, we need a collective understanding of our past to give us a shared identity and sense of common purpose.

Above: Celebrating the ratification of the U.S. Constitution in New York City, 1789.

Textbooks are often not helpful in setting forth and carrying through such themes and questions. But teachers should do so, choosing from among those that are obvious and finding new combinations of their own. One unending story is the **gathering of the many diverse peoples and cultures that have made up, and are still transforming American society.** Who have we been; who are we becoming? The story runs from the earliest American Indians occupying this continent, through the 15th- through 17th-century arrivals of Europeans and Africans in the "Great Convergence" of these three worlds, through the successive waves of 18th-, 19th-, and 20th-century arrivals from every part of the world, to the new immigrants of the day after tomorrow.

Another inescapable theme is the **economic transformation of the United States from pre-industrial colonial days to our highly technological, post-industrial society.** How has such change, more rapid and complex with each passing decade, affected social and family life, work, political balances, and human aspirations? A third related theme is the story of **change and continuity in American culture, in thought and education, and in religion and moral values.**

Without question, the story of **democracy's evolution in North America** should form a fourth continuing, central theme, unifying the study of the nation's history from its beginning until now. What have we aspired to and how far have we succeeded? Nowhere more than in a diverse society plunged in rapid change is understanding political ideals and acknowledging political realities essential to amity and shared purpose. On the one hand, students must grasp the American vision of liberty, equality, justice, and human dignity, and how these ideals were first defined and then redefined as time has passed. Students should follow the development of the reform impulse, which has repeatedly surfaced in our history. Just as surely, they need to follow the true story of the slow, unsteady journey of turning ideals into practices, how and where they have been applied and have been violated, the people and forces that have opened or obstructed the way.

Finally, related to the nation's political history is **our changing role in the world** from a few tiny, quarrelsome colonies in rebellion to a great power of the 20th century,

Students must grasp the American vision of liberty, equality, justice, and human dignity; just as surely, they need to follow the slow, unsteady journey of turning ideals into practices.

entangled in an interdependent world marked by breathtaking economic and political changes.

Students should see that each of these continuing stories—the gathering of our people, the transformation of our economic, social, and cultural life, the adventures of democracy in the United States, and the changes in our global role—is affected by all the others. It should also become clear to students that most questions worth asking about the history and life of the United States have no final answers and that no themes worth following have endings, happy or otherwise. The students themselves will be actors in the unfinished drama and it should burst upon them, long before the end of their studies, that they will not escape responsibility for some of its turns, any more than earlier generations have. They too will be blamed or praised, held up as bad or good examples, by historians, teachers, and students in the future.

The study of United States history should also quickly reveal to students that their own experiences of pain and conflict are not unique. They will learn that Americans in every generation have struggled to defend or extend their own and others' rights and well-being, very often at high personal cost, in peacetime as well as at war. They will learn that people here and around the world have cherished liberty and justice not because they bring affluence, efficiency, or repose—these are not, in any case, the promises of liberty and justice—but for their own surpassing value. Only historical perspective and the sympathetic understanding of men and women in the past can teach such lessons, and the many others that ought to emerge from well-conceived studies of our own history.

It should become clear to students that most questions worth asking about the history of the United States have no final answers, that students themselves will be actors in the unfinished drama.

ORGANIZATION OF CHAPTER III

To aid teachers in the work of planning their programs, each major historical era or teaching unit in Chapter III is presented under three major headings: **Significance and Teaching Goals; Major Topics;** and **Major Topics and Their Development: Essential Understandings and Related Background for Teachers**. The first, **Significance and Teaching Goals,** argues the importance of the subject at hand and some of the most worthwhile goals to be sought in teaching it. What major historical themes should be pursued?

What essential understandings should students gain from the era? What complexities and perspectives should they come to see? What about it should remain memorable to them?

The subheading **Essential Understandings** identifies the core understandings all students should have opportunity to develop before graduating from high school. These goals are presented in lists for ready reference, but draw their meaning and significance from the major historical themes they illuminate, and from the richly developed historical narrative which follows. Historical understanding must go beyond the factual knowledge implicit in these lists—*important though that knowledge is*—to the explanations of the causes and consequences of these events and the interpretations which can be drawn concerning their enduring significance. In developing their teaching objectives and lesson plans, therefore, we urge teachers to consider these lists in combination with the major themes presented at the outset of each unit, and with the interpretive narrative which follows.

Historical understanding must go beyond the factual knowledge implicit in these lists—to the explanations of the causes and consequences of these events and the interpretations which can be drawn concerning their enduring significance.

The subheading **Habits of the Mind** offers ideas about those analytical skills or habits of historical thought that may be developed particularly well by the material in question.

Under the second heading, **Major Topics**, we briefly outline those topics and sub-topics around which the larger subject may be effectively organized. Finally, under the third heading, **Major Topics and Their Development: Essential Understandings and Related Teacher Background**, there appears a more elaborate narrative, detailed and interpretive, and meant to serve as background to help teachers in framing their own interpretation and presentation. We hope that this arrangement of the material will prove useful, and also encouraging, to teachers who must always find practical means for selecting and presenting what is most worth learning from the historical record.

ACHIEVING HIGH STANDARDS AND THE CONSTRAINTS OF TIME

In their depth and detailed development, the units which follow provide a rich resource for teaching history. Teachers themselves, however, must be the final judges of what in this material is appropriately developed with their students and what is enrichment—historical background on which they themselves can draw in explaining events, deepening students' understandings, responding to students' questions, and suggesting topics for individual and cooperative learning projects which students might profitably pursue.

In Chapter I we explained the case for significantly expanding the time devoted to history in the curriculum, beginning in the elementary school and continuing in middle and high schools with no less than two years of United States history and two years of world history between grades 7 and 12. The material which follows is developed for no less than the recommended two full years of instruction, and preferably for three. Nothing less will produce students' achievement of the high standards in history vigorously sought in current proposals for curriculum reform. Teachers who are constrained by district plans that limit all study of United States history to a single year or less obviously cannot incorporate all these understandings in a single course and should not try to do so. They must, instead, decide what to select for in-depth development, what to use for small-group and individual student projects, and what to delete altogether. We trust that the major themes and the lists of Essential Understandings will identify what is most significant in each unit, and what should therefore be the core of instruction for that unit.

Nowhere will the need for adequate time—and therefore overall course planning—be more apparent than in the scope and depth of 20th-century history presented in units IX through XIV of this chapter. Typically the single-course approach to United States history leaves little time for a century that has unfolded with extraordinary importance for students' own lives. In the present curriculum reform movement, increasing numbers of school districts are lengthening the time devoted to United States history to alleviate these impossible pressures upon teachers and students, and the shallow learning that inevitably results. California's new state curriculum, for example, provides three full years for United States history, with units I through VI developed in grade 5; a retrospective on Units IV through VI plus in-depth study of Units VII and VIII developed in grade 8; and the 20th-century Units IX through XIV developed in grade 11. Some other states are

The Major Themes and Essential Understandings idenfity what is most significant in each unit and what should therefore be the core of instruction for that unit.

beginning to move in somewhat similar patterns. A number of districts follow a two-year sequence in United States history, with the Civil War and Reconstruction era the dividing watershed. The National Commission on Social Studies in the Schools recommended in 1989 a full year of United States history in grades 4-6, one year in grades 7-8, and a three-year sequence of United States and world history in grades 9-12. Florida's new Recommended K-12 Social Studies Program of Study devotes grade 3 to early world history and grades 4 and 5 to a two-year sequence in U.S. history. It then returns to the chronological study of world history through the Renaissance and Reformation in grade 9, of U.S. history to World War I in grade 10, and to modern (post 1848) U.S. and world history in grade 11, one exemplary approach to continuous learning in the high school years.

It is apparent that the renaissance in history teaching taking hold as we enter the final decade of this century carries enormous promise that more schools will be joining in the reforms required to provide teachers the time and resources to teach history well. For those teachers not yet fortunate enough to teach in such settings, the following material presents a challenge for selection but also, we trust, the historical perspectives to make those choices as wisely as possible under the constraints of limited time.

The renaissance in history-teaching taking hold as we enter the final decade of this century carries enormous promise that more schools will be joining in the reforms required to teach history well.

UNIT I
THREE WORLDS MEET
(1450-1600)

SIGNIFICANCE AND TEACHING GOALS

■ *Major Themes*

The study of American history properly begins with the first peopling of this continent some 30,000 years ago, and then proceeds to the epic events of the late 15th century when three worlds met: when Europeans, the inhabitants of North and South America, and peoples of Africa entered upon a historic convergence that was to shape much of modern history in over half the world.

These events will introduce students to two major themes in United States history. First, the great convergence which followed the arrival of Columbus in 1492 provides a human drama of epic proportions by which to launch the continuing theme, **the making of the American people**. From the beginning we, as a people, were composed of several ethnic and racial strains. And the consequences, both immediate and long-term, of that beginning were to raise issues and tensions among us that are still unresolved.

Second, these events introduce a more general theme, central to all of history: **the co-existence of forces for continuity and for change, and the impact, for good and ill, of these rival forces upon the societies they touch.** Students should see that enormous and unpredictable consequences can flow from actions whose purposes may seem quite limited and precise to those who undertake them. Columbus and his sponsors could not have foreseen the full import of the changes set in motion by his voyages: first, the redistribution

The great convergence which followed the arrival of Columbus provides a drama of epic proportions to launch the continuing theme, the making of the American people.

Above: Christopher Columbus (1451-1506) at Espanola (Haiti), the third island encountered on his first voyage to the New World.

of the world's population with several million Europeans and at least 10 million Africans relocating on the west side of the Atlantic and the indigenous population of the western hemisphere suffering catastrophic losses; second, the rise of the first global empires in world history—empires that for the next four centuries would colonize and Europeanize the world to a considerable degree and then lead to the decolonization movements of the second half of the 20th century; third, a commercial expansion in Europe that would hasten the rise of capitalism; fourth, the planting of New World English settlements where ideas of representative government would flourish and inspire similar political transformation in other parts of the world even into the 20th century; fifth, the rise of systems of forced labor in the Americas at the very time that slavery and serfdom were on the wane in Europe.

John White illustration of Native Americans making canoes, 1585.

From the above, it is clear that the **forces for continuity at the time were far less powerful than the forces for change embodied in European exploration, conquest, and emigration.** Students should seek the background causes for Europe's dynamism. What were the great changes already at work in European societies at this time? How vital were the aids to navigation developed by the Portuguese under Prince Henry the Navigator that opened once impenetrable ocean barriers to European exploration and trade? What were the effects of the "military revolution" in Europe beginning in 1500, setting off a European arms race and accelerating overseas expansion? And how did these developments combine with other forces—scientific, economic, religious, and political—to transform European societies and to propel so many Europeans overseas in search of a new life?

Students will not grasp the import of the "great convergence" without understanding the extensiveness and complexity of the societies of pre-Columbian America and West Africa.

Although the Europeans were the active forces for change at this time, students will not grasp the import of the "great convergence" without understanding **the extensiveness and complexity of the societies of pre-Columbian America and West Africa**—regions that were to be centrally involved in the events following 1492 and, like Europe, were to undergo profound changes as a consequence. Developing accurate perspectives on these pre-1492 societies will dispel stereotyped images of American Indians and Africans and prepare students for the complexity of the often violent meeting of these three worlds.

■ ESSENTIAL UNDERSTANDINGS

1. **The European background to the "Great Convergence:"** major scientific, economic, religious, and political changes in 15th-century Europe.

2. **Status and complexity of pre-Columbian societies of the Americas** and, in particular, those of the eastern seaboard and the southwestern regions of North America.

3. **Status and complexity of societies of West Africa** in the 15th century.

4. **The Columbian voyages**: their Portuguese antecedents, their intended purposes, and immediate consequences.

5. **The long-term consequences of the "Great Convergence"** when the three worlds met: redistribution of the world's population; the catastrophic losses of indigenous populations of the Americas, in large part through diseases; the rise of the Spanish and Portuguese global empires, followed by those of the English and the French; the commercial expansion of Europe and the rise of capitalism; the expansion of systems of forced labor in the Americas; and the planting of English ideas of representative government in North America.

Cultivating corn, Mexico

■ HABITS OF THE MIND

Throughout, these studies provide important opportunities to foster students' developing powers of **historical empathy, analysis, and judgment**. Understanding the consequences of 1492, for example, requires that students carefully examine and compare the changes rapidly overtaking European, American Indian, and African societies through the historic events set into motion with the Columbian voyages. Explaining these consequences and their causes requires that students think in terms of multi-causal relationships and thereby challenges their higher powers of synthesis and analytic reasoning. In what ways, for example, did European access to Chinese inventions of the compass, astrolabe, and gunpowder contribute to their exploration and colonization of the Americas? And how did the isolation of the Americas from the great

Understanding the consequences of 1492 requires that students carefully examine and compare the historic events set into motion with the Columbian voyages.

networks of trade and cultural exchange developing between China, India, the Middle East, Africa, and Europe from the 1st century B.C. onward leave American Indian populations without biological immunity to the devastating ravages of diseases which had long been endemic throughout Europe, Africa, and Asia? And how did the enormous wealth extracted by the Spanish from the gold and silver mines of South America quicken commerce in Europe, produce a price revolution on the continent that adversely affected the lower classes, and thereby increase the pressures for emigration to the New World? Weaving these networks of understanding not only deepens students' historical perspectives on this era, but fortifies their capacities for higher-order thought.

This era permits students to come to grips with one of the great ethical issues in history: the institution of slavery as an extreme violation of human rights.

Finally, this era permits students to come to grips with one of the great ethical issues in history: the institution of slavery as an extreme violation of human rights and the historical circumstances that contributed to the introduction of systems of chattel slavery into the Americas at the very time slavery and serfdom were on the wane in Europe. What explains the paradox of these contradictory developments? How did the history of slavery in Africa, sustained by Arab traders and rulers of West African states, differ from the racial and far more extensive slavery introduced into the Americas? The purpose of these comparisons should not be to exonerate fundamental violations of human rights and individual dignity but to seek explanations of why they occurred and to develop students' deeper insights into the human condition, as revealed in the long history of human tragedy as well as in the noblest reaches of the human spirit.

MAJOR TOPICS IN THE STUDY OF THE UNIT THREE WORLDS MEET

1. Background to Understanding the "Great Convergence"
   a. Europe in the 15th century
   b. Precolonization American societies
   c. African societies in the 15th century

2. Iberian Conquest and Colonization
   a. Causes and extent of Iberian colonization
   b. Effects of Iberian conquest

MAJOR TOPICS AND THEIR DEVELOPMENT: ESSENTIAL UNDERSTANDINGS AND RELATED BACKGROUND FOR TEACHERS

■ BACKGROUND TO UNDERSTANDING THE "GREAT CONVERGENCE"

Before studying Europeans in the New World, students must understand the background of those who came because their composition, their ideologies, and their motives played a large role in how the subsequent history of the Americas would develop. Whether developed in their studies of United States history or reviewed from their earlier studies in world history or Western civilization, students should understand: Europe's emergence from a long period of demographic and economic stagnation; the intellectual, commercial, and scientific consequences of the European Renaissance; the rise of the new monarchies in late 15th-century France, Aragon, and Castile; the quickening of seaborne commerce; and the "military revolution," beginning in the 16th century, that set off a European arms race and fostered national rivalries in overseas expansion. Of particular importance is comprehending the Protestant Reformation, the reform movements of Luther and Calvin with their anti-hierarchical tendencies, and the Catholic-Protestant division within Christianity that would deeply affect societies on both sides of the Atlantic down to the present day.

It is important to discuss the extensiveness and complexity of settlement in what Europeans called the "New World." Whether developed in studies of United States history or reviewed from their earlier studies of the Americas in their world history courses, students ought to know about anthropological evidence of the emigration of Asian peoples across the Bering Straits land bridge some 30,000 years ago; their further migration southward and eastward over many millennia; and the development of hundreds of linguistically distinct and culturally elaborated societies. Students should also know of American Indian beliefs concerning their origins in the Americas. Students particularly need to understand the state of American Indian societies along the eastern seaboard and in the Southwest in the late 15th century because this is where the first North American interactions occurred with the

Students must understand the background of the Europeans because their composition, ideologies, and motives played a large role in the subsequent history of the Americas.

First construction of a mariner's compass by Glavio Giova.

55

English and the Spanish explorers. Students' respect for ancient American Indian cultures can be cultivated by comparing aspects of precontact societies such as the Anasazi, the Cahokia moundbuilders, the Aztecs (whose capital city of Tenochtitlan was probably exceeded in size by only two European cities—Constantinople and Paris), the Tlingit, and the Iroquois.

Knowing the agricultural practices, the artistic creativity, the generally matrilineal family structure, and the value systems of American Indian societies will enable students to understand the social and cultural encounters that occurred when European settlers arrived. Contrary to the idea of Europeans reaching a "virgin land" or a "howling wilderness," many parts of the Americas were extensively populated, with the total hemispheric population probably amounting to 50-100 million by the time of Columbus' voyages, with some 4-7 million people north of the Rio Grande.

Awareness of the kingdoms of West Africa, their agricultural sophistication, the centrality of family, and their highly aesthetic sculpture will help students appreciate the peoples of Africa.

Students should know something of the long history of Africa where the oldest human remains have been found. Whether developed in studies of United States history or reviewed from their earlier studies of Africa in their world history courses, students need to appreciate the great ecological variations; the great cultural diversity that followed; and the cultural consequences of the early contact, dating from the 9th century, between West Africa and the Middle East, including the intellectual center established at Timbuktu. Awareness of the populousness of the kingdoms of West Africa, their agricultural sophistication, the centrality of family, and their highly aesthetic sculpture in wood, metal, and ivory will help sweep away myths about "the dark continent" that clog understanding of the African experience in the New World and help students appreciate that the peoples of Africa, who represented at least three quarters of all transatlantic immigrants from the late 15th to the early 19th century, were a great deal more than units of labor.

■ *IBERIAN CONQUEST AND COLONIZATION*

Finally, in studying how Europeans began planting permanent colonies in North and South America and in the Caribbean, it will help to explain why the Spanish and Portuguese began first and then others followed. A corollary to this is the question of why the English were among the last to establish successful colonies, more than a century after the Spanish, who by the time of the first English settlements controlled huge parts of South and Central America, the Caribbean, and the southern reaches of North America. While most students will naturally be more interested in the founding of the English colonies in North America that later formed the United States, they should also keep in mind this broader colonization by many European nations and also of the extent to which the colonies remained culturally and politically a part of the transatlantic world even as their inhabitants were profoundly influenced by the natural setting and the indigenous peoples of the Americas.

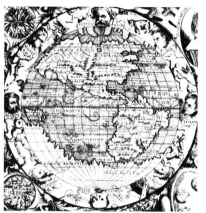

Giuseppe Rosaccio's World Map

The late 15th-century Portuguese thrust eastward around Africa to the Indian Ocean and Asia and the Spanish thrust westward to the Caribbean and Central America in the 1490s both deserve attention. The Iberian conquest of huge parts of the hemisphere in a single generation after 1492 should also receive attention (1) because it was here that the staggering effects of European diseases on native populations first became apparent; and (2) because the Spanish use of American Indian labor, and then African labor, to extract spectacular amounts of silver and gold in Peru and Mexico initiated systems of coerced labor that would greatly affect the history of the hemisphere from that time to the present day.

The Spanish thrust westward to the Caribbean and the Americas and the Iberian conquest of huge parts of the hemisphere after 1492 deserve attention.

The subsequent course of settlement—everywhere in the Western hemisphere—cannot be understood without knowledge of the destructive consequences of the confrontation of Europeans with the American Indians, especially the disastrous effect of European diseases on peoples whose isolation from other human populations had left them with no biological immunities for these diseases. This is a good place to dwell on what is inevitable and what is not in history, for the effect of disease could not have been predicted by Europeans, and neither indigenous nor settler populations could control its spread except in minor ways.

Finally, students should gain some knowledge of the changes wrought by the cultivation of sugar, first in the Portuguese Atlantic islands, then in the Caribbean and in

Students should understand how established the slave trade was before the English reached North America.

South America. Not only was the diet of Europeans transformed, but development of this cash crop triggered an intense demand for labor that was satisfied only by turning a low-level African slave trade into the largest forced migration in human history. It is important for students to understand how established this slave trade was in the hands of the Dutch, Portuguese, and Spanish before the English even reached the Caribbean and North America near the end of the 16th century.

UNIT II
THE COLONIAL ERA
(1600-1754)

SIGNIFICANCE AND TEACHING GOALS

■ *MAJOR THEMES*

The study of the colonial era in United States history is essential for all students because the foundations for many of the most critical developments in our subsequent national history were established in those years. Without an understanding of the seedtime of the American nation, it is almost impossible for students to understand such critical developments as the formation of our political institutions and values; our economic system; our multi-ethnic and culturally diverse composition; our troublesome history of slavery and the enduring problems of race that were its legacy; and the special sense of destiny or mission in the American culture— a perfectionist vision nurtured by the colonial era's strong religious ethos and by its reformist urges to rid the new American settlements of the problems of poverty, persecution, impiety, and political oppression.

The sheer scope of the nation's two hundred year colonial history requires that teachers establish a clear focus for instruction—one best found in three major continuing themes of United States history. One is to carry forward the story of **the coming together of our varied people and their cultures, ethnic and religious**. Another, vital to the colonial era, is the pre-revolutionary development of self-government, as shaped by **the European origins, transfer, and two-hundred year evolution of our basic civic values, political ideas, and institutions.** A third is the **economic development** of the colonies through agriculture and commerce.

The study of the colonial era is essential because the foundations for many of the most critical developments in our national history were established in those years.

Above: The New Dutch Church, print after a drawing by William Burgis, American, 1731.

59

Of the general historical themes applicable to nearly every time and place is **the interaction of human society and its environment**. How do differences in climate, resources, and location affect, or limit, human choice, and conversely, how do human values and culture affect the ways in which societies respond to geographic and environmental conditions? Many of the differences among the colonies may be explored along these lines.

■ *ESSENTIAL UNDERSTANDINGS*

Developing students' understanding of these major themes requires a lively narrative history, spanning two long periods of the nation's colonial past, and clarifying several critical matters:

The colonists' development of a coherent set of political and constitutional ideas established the foundations for the nation's political institutions and ideals.

1. **The main contrasts between English colonies on the one hand and Spanish, Portuguese, and French colonies on the other,** particularly in motivation and modes of control.

2. The **17th-century planting of new settlements** when small groups of English settlers struggled for a foothold on the eastern edge of North America and then, widely dispersed and often barely surviving tremendous hardships and internal tensions, established (a) the building blocks of representative government; (b) an entrepreneurial ethos incorporating values of private property and the "Protestant work ethic;" and (c) the foundations of religious freedom and denominationalism.

3. The **18th-century maturing of these colonial societies,** a time of (a) spectacular population growth with its ingathering of increasingly diverse groups of settlers; (b) dynamic economic expansion in agriculture and commerce, supporting the rise of such commercial centers as Boston, Philadelphia, and New York and a well-to-do merchant class in the North; (c) the transformation of colonial labor systems, including the rapid rise of slavery in the South; and (d) the development of a coherent set of political and constitutional ideas that established the foundations for the nation's political institutions and ideals.

■ *Habits of the Mind*

Imaginative approaches to the study of the colonial era should help students develop their **powers of historical analysis; their ability to avoid present-mindedness by seeing the past as it was experienced by people at the time; and their ability to perceive the contingency of history**, seeing that things did not have to happen as they did, that a complex of causes, including individual character, lay behind the choices people made from among their genuine options at the time.

Just as students should always be alert to the fact societies do not move teleologically to some rendezvous with destiny, and that at any stage the course of development is reversible, they should also be actively engaged in analyzing how the ideas, values, institutions, and interactions of the colonial era set the stage for later developments in the nation's history. Students should, for example, examine some of the critical documents and institutions of colonial government to analyze how they paved the way for the political system that was to evolve. How did these developments contribute to colonial experience in self-government during a time of minimal direct supervision by Britain and thus pave the way for the successful transition to political independence?

Important also is students' analysis of the foundations for such later guarantees as freedom of speech and religion in the nation's Bill of Rights. The story of the Puritans, for example, should be approached as more than the Salem witch trials or the sorry tale of religious intolerance of a people unwilling to grant others the religious freedom they sought for themselves. In order to **practice historical empathy**, students should be encouraged to put themselves in the places of Massachusetts settlers, to examine the kind of religious liberty the Puritans sought—not individual freedom from religious constraints, but the freedom to establish for their community the binding religious mores and restraints they saw as scriptural imperatives for a covenant people, living in harmony with God's will. Only by developing insights into the intensity and meaning of 17th-century religious thought, shaped by the Protestant Reformation, will students understand the historic debates of such figures as John Winthrop, John Cotton, Roger Williams, and

Students should examine some of the critical documents and institutions of colonial government to analyze how they paved the way for the political system that was to evolve.

William Penn's Treaty with the Indians, 1771, by Benjamin West.

Examining European-Indian relations during the colonial era provides students opportunity to consider what is inevitable and what is not in history.

Anne Hutchinson. Comparing the Puritan experience with the religious rivalries between Catholics and Protestants in Maryland, and with the Quaker colony's peaceful tolerance for diversity should demonstrate for students the various pathways the colonial experience took, and prepare them to appreciate the full meaning and enduring importance of the religious freedom clauses eventually incorporated into the Bill of Rights.

This era also confronts students with the fateful introduction of slavery into the American colonies, and the fundamental contradictions of this institution with the basic values and institutions paving the way toward a free and democratic republic. What forces—geographic, economic, and social— and what attitudes toward black Africans explain the acceptance of slavery in colonial America, and what transformed the limited presence of Africans in the 17th century, many of whom came as indentured servants and secured their freedom during these years, into the rapid expansion, a century later, of hereditary chattel slavery on the Caribbean model?

Examining European-Indian relations during the colonial era will again provide students opportunity to **consider what is inevitable and what is not in history, as well as the difference that individuals and their beliefs can make.** Comparing, for example, William Penn's peaceful relations with the Delaware chiefs and the Susquehannocks with the Pequot massacre in 1637 or with the wars between the colonial settlers and the Powhatans in Virginia in 1622 should dispel for students the notion that European-Indian relations necessarily followed a single inevitable course. Analyzing, also, how European wars drew the English colonists along with their Indian allies into conflict with the Indian allies of Spain and France will help students better understand the complexity of European-Indian relations of this era.

Finally, students might **hone their highest levels of analytic thinking** by inquiring into the enduring significance of the critical differences between the Spanish, Portuguese, French, and English colonies, and examine how the degree of imperial management, the presence or absence of a missionizing clergy from their homelands, and the social composition of their settlers led to distinctively different colonial societies and to legacies still observable in the different character of modern states in the hemisphere.

MAJOR TOPICS IN THE STUDY OF THE COLONIAL ERA (1600-1754)

1. The 17th-century Planting of New Societies
   a. Major differences among Spanish, Portuguese, French, and English colonies
   b. Main characteristics of different English colonies in North America

2. The 18th-century Maturing of Colonial Societies
   a. Population growth
   b. Rapid economic development
   c. British imperial policy
   d. Religious diversity, the "Great Awakening"
   e. Development of political ideas
   f. Rise of slavery and African-American culture

MAJOR TOPICS AND THEIR DEVELOPMENT: ESSENTIAL UNDERSTANDINGS AND RELATED BACKGROUND FOR TEACHERS

■ *THE PLANTING OF NEW SOCIETIES*

A sure grasp of the founding period, from the transitory Roanoke settlements in the 1580s to about 1700, can help students understand the subsequent course of United States history because in this era certain foundations were laid, sometimes unwittingly, that would profoundly influence the development of American society. Because important differences among the English colonies are noteworthy, these mainland colonies are sensibly studied in four regional groupings: New England, Mid-Atlantic, Chesapeake, and Lower South. Students should be able to understand the different recruitment of leaders and ordinary settlers in, for example, Massachusetts and Virginia in the early years and also the differing motives of the New England and Chesapeake colonists and the influence of the geographical region they settled in. For the first century of colonization it is also important that students appreciate the initial precariousness of virtually all these efforts, due both to the difficulties inherent in founding

Captain John Smith in his thirty-seventh year.

Students should understand the differing motives of the New England and Chesapeake colonists and the influence of the geographical region they settled in.

Students should appreciate the initial precariousness of virtually all these efforts, due to difficulties in founding societies in an unfamiliar setting and to tensions within those new societies.

Signing the Mayflower compact. Painting by E. Moran.

societies in an unfamiliar setting and also to the tensions within those new societies, (although the exact nature of such tensions vary, from the early struggle for survival and economic advantage in Virginia, to the religious rivalry of Catholic and Protestant in Maryland, to the difficulty in New England of balancing the intense spiritual demands of constructing a Puritan Commonwealth with the establishment of the more material world in which the settlers also had to live).

Of the 17th-century colonial developments, the following deserve special attention:

First, it is essential to understand the **imperatives of colonization;** that is, the economic, religious, intellectual, and nationalistic motives of whole peoples because the recruitment of settlers, primarily from the middling ranges of donor societies in England and Europe, made the colonies an arena for individual ambitions from the beginning. The heavy emphasis on family migration (with the early Chesapeake being an exception) also distinguished the English mainland colonies from others in the Americas.

Second, **the natural setting** that Europeans found and the manner in which they began to shape the American land are essential to understand. The shift from American Indian to European settler dominance brought a fundamental alteration of the continent's plant and animal life and introduced a concept of land as a commodity as well as a source of sustenance that has continued to transform our ecosystem ever since.

Third, **the reformist urges** of many of the settlers, especially in New England and in Pennsylvania-New Jersey, are important to understand because they established a sense of special mission in the American cultural bloodstream. The perfectionist vision saw in American settlement a historic opportunity to free society from poverty, injustice, and oppression of all kinds.

Fourth, students should study the transfer of **conceptions of English law and government** to the colonies because this laid the foundations for the political system that would evolve. Students should consider, for example, the importance of the

Massachusetts Body of Liberties, adopted by the Massachusetts Bay Colony in the 1640s to guarantee such rights as "life, liberty, and estate" and a speedy trial; limit cruel and unusual punishment; and extend equal protection of the laws to all citizens while severely restricting the holding of slaves. Special attention ought to be given to the building blocks of representative government that were laid down, such as the New England town meeting, the first elected colonial legislatures in Virginia (1619) and other colonies, the broadly participatory and representative government provided in the New Jersey "Laws, Concessions, and Agreements of 1677," the colonial manifestations of the Glorious Revolution of 1688, and the Pennsylvania Frame of Government of 1701.

Special attention ought to be given to the building blocks of representative government, such as the New England town meeting and the first elected colonial legislatures.

Fifth, the pattern of **colonial economic development before 1700** is important because the abundance of land, the periodic labor shortage, the absence of craft guilds, and the "Protestant work ethic" created or induced wider opportunities for upward mobility for many white colonists and thus nurtured a competitive, entrepreneurial ethos and a devotion to private property that grew into cardinal values in American society. Study of economic development ought to begin with the initial existence of subsistence economies and the beginning of trade within the colonies, with the Indians, and across the Atlantic. Characteristic patterns of landholding should also be understood, including the relative balance between large landholdings and the lesser ones owned by smaller farmers and the relative balance between the establishment of absolute private ownership and communal responsibilities for the land and its resources.

Sixth, the **colonial labor systems** should be understood, including how heavily the early colonial economy relied on white indentured servitude, how this harsh form of bound labor helped lead the way to slavery, and how maritime labor, the labor of artisans, and the predominant agricultural labor differed.

Lastly, it is vital for modern-day students to understand **the place of religion in early colonial society and in the lives of individuals**. Students living in a highly secularized world can understand little of the 17th-century mind (and hence little about 17th-century behavior) until they comprehend how much of early colonial life was played out within a religious ethos. Religious diversity early became a hallmark of England's mainland colonies and thus from the outset weakened the connections between church and state and laid the foundations for denominationalism—the acceptance of a variety of churches and sects and a commitment to the idea of religious freedom. Thus it is important for students to know about the major religious systems in the colonies and their key beliefs, the diversity that was from the first characteristic of religion in the colonies, the influence of religion on the larger societies (as, for example, structures of government in New England or Virginia), and its influence in private lives (the force of popular religion).

■ THE MATURING OF COLONIAL SOCIETIES (1700-1754)

If the 17th century marked the first permanent foundation of English colonies in North America, the 18th was distinguished by a remarkable growth and maturation of colonial society and political culture. Students should avoid any temptation to anticipate the American Revolution by concluding that colonists were embarked on some irreversible course toward independence. The thirteen colonies were but one part of a more numerous group of British colonies, still conscious of their separate identities and committed to common membership in the Empire. Differences among the principal regional groupings of colonies were, however, still readily apparent, and to the older coastal regions could now be added another: the vast settled hinterland that extended from the northern reaches of New England and New York through the western areas of Pennsylvania and the Southern colonies.

Two of the Mason children

The 18th century was distinguished by a remarkable growth and maturation of colonial society and political culture.

Six topics around which an exploration of the dynamic development of the 18th-century colonies can be usefully organized are: first, **the spectacular population growth,** fed by increased immigration and a rate of natural increase unprecedented in Europe, which led to territorial expansion; a huge growth in agricultural productivity in what remained a primarily agricultural society; the development of seaboard commercial and political centers such as Philadelphia, New York, and Boston; and, an expanded internal and external commerce.

Second, **periods of vigorous imperial policy**, when the home government sought to step up control over the affairs of the colonies, and when heightened European national rivalries drew the American territories of Great Britain, France, and Spain into the transatlantic world of war and diplomacy. Whenever North America became an arena of these conflicts, British colonists were also brought into confrontation with American Indian allies of France and Spain. These contests gained additional force from the land hunger of British colonists, which threatened all the interior tribes with dispossession of their lands and cultural dislocation.

Third, **the evolution of social organization** in the colonies toward more complex ranks and groupings, rural and urban, with increased ethnic diversity; the growth in the cities and towns of greater disparity in social position and wealth; and the development in the Tidewater Chesapeake, the Carolina rice coast, and the Hudson River Valley of large plantations and manors worked by large numbers of slaves, servants, or tenants.

Fourth, although seldom articulated systematically before the outbreak of the imperial crisis of the 1760s, **the coherent set of political and constitutional ideas** that took shape in North America. These ideas drew partly on the more radical strains of 17th-century English thought, embodying suspicion of all forms of political power and placing a high value on colonial political autonomy. These ideas found particular focus in the elective lower houses of assembly of each of the thirteen colonies. If these ideas were not sufficiently radical for some and were too much so for others, they nonetheless formed a broadly held perception of the British constitution that appealed to the larger number of politically active colonists and distilled much of the practical experience of more than a century of colonial development.

The coherent set of political and constitutional ideas that took shape in North America found focus in the elective lower houses of assembly of each of the thirteen colonies.

Fifth, the **growing religious diversity of the colonies**, culminating in the first major wave of revivals, the Great Awakening, which highlighted social and religious differences between more traditional Protestants and the new evangelicals. Marked religious diversity thus became a fixed feature of American life, and behind it lay, too, increasing cultural diversity, ranging from the African American culture of enslaved and free blacks to the non-English-speaking cultures of many German groups, to that of a growing Scotch-Irish population, and to the Anglo-American culture of those whose families had migrated to the colonies earlier. The Great Awakening deserves considerable attention because it weakened the hold of established churches to which all taxpayers owed support, furthered the acceptance of denominationalism, gave impetus to the founding of new colleges, and nourished the idea of the untutored individual challenging clerical authority.

Sixth, the **transformation of the colonial labor systems** which involved on the one hand the gradual decline of indentured servitude, beginning in the late 17th century in the southern colonies and after 1750 in the northern colonies; and, on the other hand, the rapid rise of racial slavery after 1690 in the South and to a lesser extent in the North. Students need to pay particular attention to two aspects of slavery because racial conflict has been a persistent problem in American history and achieving racial equality has been the thorniest of problems in our history. These are: 1) how paradoxical it was that the expansion of slavery paralleled the growth of the idea of freedom in the southern colonies, and that the freedom of some could be thought to be enhanced by the enslavement of others; and 2) how the degraded position of slaves fostered negative attitudes among whites toward those with dark skin—attitudes that have, as de Tocqueville predicted, endured for generations.

The transformation of the colonial labor systems involved the gradual decline of indentured servitude and the rapid rise of racial slavery after 1690 in the South.

Finally, in studying the rise of racial slavery, students should not only focus on the more familiar growth of the institution and its supporting legal and political apparatus but also should try to understand that, while being enslaved, Africans in America blended the culture of their various African homelands with the culture of the master class, producing a unique African American culture. This cultural evolution is best understood by delving into the topics of black religion, family life, and patterns of resistance. Black protests against slavery also show how African Americans contributed to an expanding definition of freedom, which many white Americans wanted to restrict.

UNIT III
THE REVOLUTIONARY
ERA (1754-1783)

SIGNIFICANCE AND TEACHING GOALS

■ MAJOR THEMES

The American Revolution is of signal importance in the study of United States history for the light it sheds for students upon a major theme in history: **the long human struggle for liberty, equality, justice, and dignity, and the ideas, people, and conditions that carried the struggle forward.** First (and most familiarly), the American Revolution severed the colonial relationship to England and legally created the United States. Second, the revolutionary generation formulated the political philosophy and laid the institutional foundations for the system of government under which we live. Third, the revolution was inspired by ideas concerning natural rights and political authority that were transatlantic in nature and its successful completion affected people and governments over a large part of the globe in what has been called "the age of democratic revolution." Lastly, it called into question long-established social and political relationships—between master and slave, man and woman, upper class and lower class, officeholder and constituent—and thus demarcated an agenda for reform that would preoccupy Americans down to the present day.

The revolution was inspired by ideas concerning natural rights and political authority that were transatlantic in nature.

Thus, the American Revolution was both an American and a world event. It was the first great collective step in the journey of democracy that we in the United States are still embarked upon at home. Together with the French Revolution a few years later, it proclaimed to the world's peoples that three great human aspirations were not only right but reach-

Above: "1776." Wood engraving after F.O.C. Darley.

able: national unity and independence, democratic self-government and civil equality; economic and social justice. Much of the world's history since 1800 can be taught as the complex and often violent story of people's struggles to achieve these things for themselves.

■ ESSENTIAL UNDERSTANDINGS

To understand the significance of the American Revolution and its singular place in the long human struggle for liberty, equality, justice, and dignity, students should acquire an understanding of the following:

1. **The causes and responsibilities for the outbreak of the American Revolution.**

2. **The Declaration of Independence:** its fundamental principles and their historical sources and arguments.

3. **The main stages of the Revolutionary War** and reasons for the American victory.

4. **The role of leadership** in revolution and war, from all strata of society.

5. How far **the revolutionary settlement** went to satisfy the interests and aspirations of the various groups in American society.

■ HABITS OF THE MIND

No study of revolution, our own or any other, should fail **to examine the complexity of historical cause,** to look into every sphere of human life—political, economic, social, cultural, intellectual—for the events and conditions that arouse a people's determination to overthrow an established order; to look beyond the long-range, general causes of unrest to the immediate "sparks" that set off the explosion; to grasp the role of chance and the irrational; to recognize the importance of individual activists and organizers on one side or the other. Was the Revolution justified? Was it inevitable, or were there options for England and the colonists to choose? If the latter, what explains the choice made for revolution? Such questions

Sons of Liberty force scalding tea on a tarred and feathered Tory exciseman, as a toast to the crown.

No study of revolution should fail to examine the complexity of historical cause, the events and conditions that arouse a people's determination to overthrow an established order.

can be sensibly debated only after a careful look at causes.

The same habit of historical thought must be applied to the outcome of the Revolutionary War. What factors and choices brought victory? Can students distinguish the important from the inconsequential in the usual textbook account of the war?

The revolutionary era lends itself admirably **to developing students' respect for the power of ideas in history**, how they originate and are passed along, how they are shaped over time, how they are expressed at particular moments of crisis to promote and channel the forces of change, or to guide a new order. What, for example, were the arguments of 1776 on which the patriots justified their cause and severed their allegiance to England? What explains the contemporary appeal of these same arguments to the Chinese students of Tienanmen Square and to the East Europeans who in 1989 rallied to speakers quoting phrases penned by Jefferson over two hundred years ago?

How did the legacies of Magna Carta, the Glorious Revolution, Locke's views on the social contract and consent of the governed, and the writings of Montesquieu influence the political thought of 1776 and the age of democratic revolution that followed? And how did the moral imperatives of Judaism and Christianity, derived from beliefs in the dignity of the individual before God and man and in the brotherhood of all men, justify for most colonists an imperatively persuasive case for independence?

Finally, the American Revolution offers a chance for students to **engage in the contrastive analyses of comparative history**. Why did our revolution against England result in the establishment of a stable, self-governing republic and the French revolution against their own monarch turn to civil war, terror, and military dictatorship? Once more a thoughtful analysis of forces at work in the two societies is required. How did they differ in political experience and traditions? In economic life and class relations? In religious life? In their relations with neighbors? In their internal, regional relations? It should be clear that no easy, abstract generalizations are satisfactory, that students need **to respect particularity**.

The revolutionary era lends itself admirably to developing students' understanding of the power of ideas in history, how they originate, are shaped over time, and channel the forces of change.

Announcing the signing of the Declaration of Independence.

MAJOR TOPICS IN THE STUDY OF THE REVOLUTIONARY ERA

1. The Causes of the Revolution
    a. Effects of the Seven Years' War
    b. English imperial policies
    c. Colonists' reactions and motives
    d. Roles of revolutionary leaders

2. The Establishment of Government
    a. Articles of Confederation
    b. Declaration of Independence

3. The Revolutionary War
    a. Advantages and disadvantages of contestants
    b. Central role of George Washington
    c. Impact of the French alliance.
    d. Role of Africans and American Indians
    e. The war's main stages
    f. How leaders arose from all classes
    g. War's effect on homefront

4. The Revolutionary Settlement
    a. Main provisions of the peace treaty
    b. Effects of war and its settlement
    c. Northwest Ordinance of 1787

MAJOR TOPICS AND THEIR DEVELOPMENT: ESSENTIAL UNDERSTANDINGS AND RELATED BACKGROUND FOR TEACHERS

Study of the Revolutionary era can be effectively organized around four main topics. For each, several sub-topics are denoted and illustrative events are suggested for study.

■ THE CAUSES OF THE REVOLUTION

Study of the origins of the Revolution has a natural starting point in the Seven Years' War for several reasons. First, this great contest for empire removed France from North America and thus reduced the colonists' need for the protection of the mother country. Second, the war prepared a group of political and military leaders to play roles on a larger stage.

Boston Massacre, March 5, 1770

Study of the origins of the Revolution has a natural starting point in the Seven Years' War.

Third, the war led to decisions in London that would provide the sparks of revolution, in particular the decision to leave troops in the colonies and to make the colonists pay for them.

Students should study the overhaul of English imperial policy after the Treaty of Paris in 1763 and ascertain how Americans in different locales and in different social stations interpreted and protested against these policies. They should contemplate why only thirteen of the thirty-one subordinate governments in the Americas felt compelled to resist, and consider the sources of resistance to the Stamp Act in 1765 and to the Townshend duties in 1767.

In studying the entire decade preceding the Revolution, students should also be able to trace out the political and constitutional rights invoked by colonists debating and protesting English policies and the sources of these ideas, while at the same time being able to see the connections between these ideas and the economic interests of different groups such as Virginia tobacco planters, northern merchants, and urban artisans. Some of the drama of the period can be brought to life by exploring the character, thought, and politicizing techniques of various resistance leaders—writers and theoreticians such as John Adams, Thomas Jefferson, and John Dickinson; popular polemicists such as Thomas Paine and Patrick Henry; caucus politicians such as Samuel Adams and Thomas Young; and street leaders such as Ebenezer MacIntosh and Alexander McDougall. Much of the contingency of the time will become apparent if students study the mobilization of ordinary colonists in the protests against English policies, and the divisions that appeared within the ranks of protesting colonists—divisions that would be carried into the war years.

■ *THE ESTABLISHMENT OF GOVERNMENT*

Every student should learn how the rebellious American people established new governments under which to live after casting off English authority and understand the political principles (or political theory) upon which they built government anew. They ought to know the main powers allowed the Continental Congress and the states respectively under the Articles of Confederation; the main points of the Declaration of Independence and its ideological sources, including the

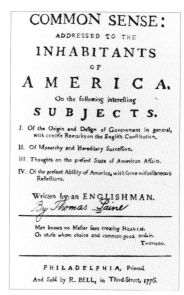

Title page of Thomas Paine's Common Sense. *Addressed to the inhabitants of America, 1776.*

Students should also be able to trace out the political and constitutional rights invoked by colonists debating and protesting English policies and the sources of these ideas.

Puritan revolutionists of the 1640s, Locke, the Scottish moral theorists, and Montesquieu; the main tenets of revolutionary "republicanism" and the disputes over its meaning. The best way to understand the political theory of republicanism and to appreciate how it was refracted differently according to place and social group is to see it in action as the people of the various states made fundamental law under which to live by constructing their state governments. It can be especially enlightening to compare several state constitutions, for example, Pennsylvania's radical constitution of 1776 and Massachusetts' moderate constitution of 1780, and to study the heated disagreements about how popular sovereignty might best be structured.

■ THE REVOLUTIONARY WAR

It is essential for students to comprehend the complexity of the revolutionary process as Americans simultaneously prosecuted the war against England and struggled internally to reconstruct their society in ways they believed were necessary to guarantee "life, liberty, and the pursuit of happiness." Study of the Revolution has a natural starting point in the military struggle for independence. Students ought to know the rudiments of how the army and navy were recruited, the difficulties of the Continental Congress in financing and prosecuting the war, the critically important role of Washington as the commander-in-chief, and the contours of the military conflict as it moved from the North in 1775-78 to the South in 1778-81, finally climaxing at Yorktown in 1781 and ending after a long period of peace negotiations in 1783. They should be able to answer the question of how the outmanned and outfinanced Americans could defeat the most powerful military force in the Western world. In studying the military aspects of the Revolution, students should learn of the critical importance of French and Dutch aid. They should also know about the response of slaves and indentured servants, including the flight of tens of thousands of slaves to the British and the contributions of many thousands to the American side; the extent and composition of the numerous American Loyalists who fought with the British or tried to remain neutral; the response of American Indians during the Revolution, including the reasons that most fought with the British; and the experience of women during the war and their contributions to

It is essential for students to comprehend the complexity of the revolutionary process as Americans simultaneously prosecuted the war against England and struggled internally to reconstruct their society.

Detail of a woodcut illustration from "A New Touch on the Times," by a Daughter of Liberty, living in Marblehead. Broadside, 1779.

the American victory.

The role of political, military, and diplomatic leaders in the war deserves attention because the crisis called forth a breathtaking array of talent. More than ordinary inspiration can be derived from studying such leaders as Benjamin Franklin, Thomas Jefferson, John and Samuel Adams, George Washington, Richard Henry Lee, and John Hancock. A study of leadership would be incomplete without also examining the flowering of leaders among people who started at the middle or bottom of society—figures such as Thomas Peters, the slave who fought for his freedom and led several thousand former slaves to a new life in Nova Scotia and then Sierra Leone after the war; Joseph Brant, the Mohawk chief who led his people through the difficult war and the more difficult postwar period when the Iroquois had to adapt to the loss of their land base and political sovereignty; Charles Willson Peale, who started as a harnessmaker and became a patriot leader and a painter who after the war helped to create a firmer sense of national identity; and Richard Allen, who purchased his freedom, hauled salt for the Continental army, and after the war became a community leader among free black Philadelphians and the founder of the first independent black denomination in America, the African Methodist Episcopal church.

The second major task in understanding the Revolution is to examine the homefront and the sometimes exhilarating and sometimes divisive efforts to create a regenerated American society. It will help if students comprehend the idealism, even millennialism, of the Revolutionary generation that led to so many calls for reformation, not all of them consistent with each other. The reformist urge, which Americans had to debate and legislate over in the midst of fighting a powerful enemy, included calls for the abolition of slavery, enlarged rights for women, free public education, "the utmost good faith" in dealing with Indian tribes, curbs on commercial profiteering and monopolizing, and the end of imprisonment for debt. To understand this era, students need to compare the contrasting revolutionary agendas that were constructed by various parts of the population, including propertied landowners and small farmers, women, slaves, merchants, artisans, and craftsmen who brought different experiences into the years of crisis with England and sought different results in

Richard Allen, founder and first bishop of the African Methodist Episcopal Church.

The role of political, military, and diplomatic leaders in the war deserves attention because the crisis called forth a breathtaking array of talent from all levels of society.

75

the revolutionary fray. Students need also to understand how people in widely varying regions and circumstances had to make difficult choices about how to involve themselves (or stay uninvolved) both in the war against England and in developing new governments and new economic and social relationships at the local and state level, for this was the first era in which the great mass of Americans were involved in public affairs.

■ THE REVOLUTIONARY SETTLEMENT

Students should understand the outcomes of the Revolution, being able to say how, beyond securing independence, it changed the ways Americans thought, acted, and arranged their institutions.

Students should have a grasp of the outcomes of the Revolution, being able to say how, beyond securing independence, the Revolution changed the ways Americans thought, acted, and arranged their institutions. They should be able to draw up a rough balance sheet that indicates to what extent different groups in society accomplished their agendas and to what extent compromises were made. This balance sheet might include entries on: a) the economic effects of the war on different regions and groups, and the continuing division of opinion about economic problems such as the proper role of government in the economy, management of the revolutionary war debt, and the advisability of paper money and banks; b) the innovations in local and state politics that broadened participation and the accountability of officeholders, such as innovations in rotation of offices, reduced suffrage and officeholding requirements, and open legislative debates and published legislative proceedings; and the political differences that continued to divide people when the war ended; c) the resolution of the western lands dispute and the system for settlement in the new territories under the Land Ordinance of 1785 and the Northwest Ordinance of 1787; and d) the effect of the Revolution on the relationship between church and state in the various states and the effect of the war on religious life.

UNIT IV
NATION BUILDING
(1783-1815)

SIGNIFICANCE AND TEACHING GOALS

■ MAJOR THEMES

Study of the era of nation building in the generation after 1783 is of unique importance for students' understanding of the central theme in the nation's constitutional history: **the creation and ratification of the United States Constitution, and the evolution of the political democracy it established**.

First, and most important, this era provides students with opportunities to examine the fundamental ideas making up the political vision of the nation's 18th-century founders, expressed in the Constitution, the debates over ratification, and the Bill of Rights. What were these ideas? Where and when did they arise? What historical conditions encouraged people to hold these views? And how were they translated into a political system of representative government that has endured over 200 years?

Second, study of this era demonstrates why the Constitution of 1787 was the culmination of the greatest and most creative era of constitutionalism in American history and perhaps of all modern Western history. During the last part of the 18th century Americans established the modern idea of a written constitution and made such written constitutions a practical and everyday part of governmental life. They showed the world not only how written constitutions could be made truly fundamental, distinguishable from ordinary legislation, but also how such constitutions could be interpreted on

Study of this era demonstrates why the Constitution was the culmination of the most creative era of constitutionalism in American history and perhaps of all modern Western history.

Above: James Madison (1751-1836), President of the United States, 1809-1817.

a regular basis and altered when necessary.

Further, they offered the world working examples of governmental institutions and modes of political action for carrying out the nation's business within the constitutional framework. It was in this period that local and state loyalties began to wane and Americans started to fabricate a national identity. In the 1790s, the embryo of the American two-party system took shape, and it was in the election of 1800 that it was legitimated. Then, during the first fifteen years of the 19th century, culminating in the War of 1812, the United States secured its place in the world by fending off both internal and external threats to nationhood.

■ ESSENTIAL UNDERSTANDINGS

To comprehend the significance of the United States Constitution and its singular place in world history, students should develop understanding of the following:

Students should develop understanding of the fundamental ideas and specific provisions of the Constitution which established the nation's federal system of representative government.

1. **The fundamental ideas and the specific provisions of the Constitution** which established the nation's federal system of representative government.

2. **The major factors leading to the Constitutional Convention**, both (a) the weakness of the Articles of Confederation in dealing with major problems confronting the nation; and (b) the rising concerns over state governments which were variously seen as unresponsive to legitimate grievances, abusive of their legislative power, or unable to control popular attacks on wealth and privilege.

3. **The principal participants of the Constitutional Convention, the major issues they debated, and the compromises they reached,** through the interplay of the political ideals and principles they believed in and the need to satisfy the deeply-rooted practical interests of the localities they represented.

4. The major arguments of <u>The Federalist Papers</u>, and **the ratification debates** in the states between the Federalists and the Anti-Federalists.

5. The significant events of the early years of the Republic which established (a) **the authority of the national government;** (b) the **Bill of Rights;** (c) the **two-party system;** (d) the **peaceful transition of government** through lawful elections; (e) the origins of **judicial review;** and (f) **the nation's commercial and banking system.**

■ *HABITS OF THE MIND*

Among the perspectives and habits of historical thinking that students may acquire from the era of nation building and constitution making, three stand out. One is to **keep in mind that it is, and has always been, natural to human life to live with unsolved problems, unfinished business that is vexing and often perilous in a world of imperfect human nature**. Great as the nation's founders were, and great as their accomplishments proved to be, they nonetheless knew very well that they were bound to leave certain problems unsolved and that their work might raise new problems for the future. It is from these perspectives that students should examine the clauses of the Constitution allowing for peaceful remedy and change; and it is in this light, also, that students can understand their pleas for vigilance and civic virtue. On these matters James Madison was most eloquent and persuasive in <u>The Federalist Papers</u>.

It follows, secondly, that students will thereby **grasp the significance of the past to their present lives and to present society**. One problem unresolved at Philadelphia was that of slavery, whose consequences afflict Americans still. Students need to confront and explain the troubling paradox of the signers' commitment to the principles of individual liberty, freedom, and justice, and their final compromises on the clauses that allowed slavery to endure: namely, the three-fifths rule of representation, the slave importation clause, and the fugitive slave clause. What were the arguments mounted on opposing sides of this issue? How close did this issue bring the convention to deadlock and what explains the concessions finally made to the southern states on this issue? What were their long-term consequences to the nation? Should compromise have been refused and the Constitution imperilled? What then would have been the

Among the habits of historical thinking that students may acquire is to keep in mind that it is, and has always been, natural to human life to live with unsolved problems.

Alexander Hamilton (1757-1804). Principal author of The Federalist Papers, signer of the Constitution.

The issues joined in the Federalist/Anti-Federalist debates and in the struggle for a national Bill of Rights have proved enduring and must be understood.

consequences? There are no quick and easy, satisfying answers.

Another problem relating to nearly every political debate in our day is the issue dividing Federalists and anti-Federalists: the tension between liberty and order, and the question of how best to resolve this tension so that the constitutional government they were creating would not be too strong (putting at risk the liberties of individuals and localities) but energetic enough to sustain stability and security, to promote commerce and the general welfare, and to safeguard the individual against the tyranny of the many or the powerful. The issues joined in the Federalist/Anti-Federalist debates and in the struggle for a national Bill of Rights have proved enduring and must be understood, for they will establish the foundations for students' thoughtful analyses of virtually every ensuing public issue and constitutional crisis confronting the nation, even into the present day.

Thirdly, students will find in the work of nation building unforgettable examples of **the importance of individuals in history, their ideas, their characters, their political experience and judgment**. The founding generation's historical achievement was not only to create a government based on the consent of the governed—a rarity in history—but to build into the Constitution and Bill of Rights provisions such as the separation of powers that would be responsive to the realities of human nature, however flawed or unpredictable. Examining both the strength and fragility of self-government will prepare students for their own individual roles as citizens in contemporary America.

Finally, and once again—as in every historical period—students must **avoid the temptation to judge people in the past solely by today's notions and beliefs**. The era under study was a time of crises and uncertainties about the future. Fear of entrenched privilege and oppressive hierarchy was real; fear of the violent character of the French Revolution was real. Students should judge the actions of Federalists and Republicans in that light (as they would wish to be judged by future historians), while at the same time appreciating the great obstacle that fear can raise to the peaceful evolution of democracy.

MAJOR TOPICS IN THE STUDY OF NATION BUILDING (1783-1800)

1. Forming a National Government
    a. Weaknesses of the Articles of Confederation
    b. Participants and interests at Philadelphia
    c. Main issues and resolutions at Philadelphia
    d. Central compromise on slavery
    e. Main arguments in ratification debates
    f. The Bill of Rights

2. Crises and Resolution
    a. The Hamilton-Jefferson debate
    b. Origins of the two-party system
    c. Impact of the French Revolution
    d. Role of presidential leadership
    e. Origins of judicial review

MAJOR TOPICS AND THEIR DEVELOPMENT: ESSENTIAL UNDERSTANDINGS AND RELATED BACKGROUND FOR TEACHERS

■ FORMING A NATIONAL GOVERNMENT

Students should capture the extraordinary originality and excitement of the constitution making era in the late 1780s. But first they need to establish a context for the formation of the Constitution of 1787 by understanding that the British viewed a constitution as unwritten and identified it with parliamentary legislation. The states had initiated written constitutions in the revolutionary era and two of them had required popular ratification.

It also needs to be understood what an unforeseen achievement the new national Constitution was. No one in 1776 anticipated creating such a strong national government as the Constitution provided for. Explaining the Constitution is therefore a major historical problem. There are two levels of explanation that require attention, one at the national level, and the other at the state level. At the national level the problem involved the weaknesses of the Articles of Confederation, principally the inability of the Confederation to deal with the Revolutionary war debts, problems of international

Students should capture the extraordinary originality and excitement of the constitution making era in the late 1780s.

trade, and boundary questions involving England and Spain. At the state level, many leaders perceived abuses of popular legislative power or saw state governments as too contaminated to control popular attacks on wealth and privilege.

Shays' Rebellion is worth attention both because it convinced many important leaders that a stronger national government was necessary and because it affords an opportunity to see how ordinary farmers (constituting the majority of households in the country) invoked revolutionary rights of petition and protest and then, as a last resort, took extralegal action when the Massachusetts government was unresponsive to what they regarded as their legitimate grievances.

The Philadelphia Convention deserves careful attention because it was distinguished by one of the greatest debates in American history and produced the Constitution under which Americans have lived for two centuries. Students should gain an understanding of the principal participants and the issues debated at the Convention, including the Virginia Plan (a strong consolidated national government with veto power over all state laws); the New Jersey Plan (retaining the equal state representation in the Articles of Confederation but creating a stronger national government); the Connecticut compromise (equal representation of states in the Senate and proportionate representation in the House); and the decisions on other institutions of the new federal government (president, electoral college, national judiciary). Students should also study the concessions made to the southern states on the issue of slavery, including the 3/5ths clause, the fugitive slave clause, and the slave trade clause.

The Philadelphia Convention was distinguished by one of the greatest debates in American history and produced the Constitution under which Americans have lived for two centuries.

Equally absorbing and important were the ratification debates in the states, marked by the Antifederalist fears of aristocratic government, by arguments for preserving the power of democratically inclined state legislatures, and by the pro-ratification arguments in <u>The Federalist Papers</u>. To study the ratification debates in just one of the major states such as Virginia, where Madison and Randolph debated Henry and Mason, is to open windows to the high level of political discourse in this era and to gain an understanding of the fluidity and uncertainty of these years, and the sharp diversity of opinion.

■ CRISES AND RESOLUTION

The first decades of the early Republic were crucial in the development of American society, politics, and culture because they saw political institutions created by the Constitution filled in and new political practices arise, such as contested presidential elections and judicial review. The population and the economy virtually exploded, with people moving westward in ever-increasing numbers. American religion in this period assumed its modern denominational character.

Students ought to catch the dynamic and explosive character of the period. Because there are impressive continuities between then and now, students should guard against anachronism—assuming that what people did then was simply an anticipation of our present. The party competition between Federalists and Republicans, for example, was not merely an early version of our two-party system. Students need to capture some sense of the crisis running through the period; otherwise the actions of the Federalists and the Republicans will seem extreme and unjustified.

Study of the Federalist era should include the organizing of national government under the first president, George Washington; the passage of the Bill of Rights; Hamilton's financial program put before the first Congress and largely ratified; and the Federalists' political program and its hierarchical tendencies. Debates over these latter two programs set the stage for the Democratic-Republican opposition that quickly developed. That opposition provides an opportunity to see how intertwined American politics became with European affairs, for the French Revolution, breaking out in 1789 just as the new government of the United States was getting underway, polarized Americans, reminding some of their unfulfilled democratic goals for the revolution and convincing others of the dangers of popular democracy.

In the heightened political contention of the period from 1794 to 1800, it is important to pay attention to the Whiskey Rebellion of 1794 and the use of the federal army to crush it; to the Alien and Sedition Acts of 1798, by which a Federalist-dominated Congress tried to restrict criticism of the government, and thus created the first crisis in civil liberties under the

George Washington (1732-1799)
President of the United States
1789-1797

Study of the Federalist era should include the organizing of national government, the passage of the Bill of Rights, and Hamilton's financial program.

Thomas Jefferson (1743-1826)
President of the United States
(1801-1809)

Jefferson's ability to convince the American people that peaceful change of government administration might take place without violence was crucial to the country's future political stability.

Constitution; and to the Virginia and Kentucky resolutions asserting states' rights.

What is sometimes called the Jeffersonian Revolution of 1800 should be of more than ordinary interest. Students should be aware of the continuing uncertainty of the American experiment in government. As Jefferson took his inaugural oath, he was confronted with a nation that was still highly fragmented, with many different state and regional loyalties that took precedence over commitment to the nation at large. Moreover, many Americans had not yet accepted the notion of a "loyal" political opposition at the time of his election, and thus his ability to convince the American people that peaceful change of government administration might take place without violence and revolution was crucial to the country's future political stability.

Other important subjects are: a) the continuing differences between Federalists and Republicans during the period 1800-1820 and the accommodations achieved between those groups; b) the reversal of Federalist programs after 1800; c) the role of the Jeffersonian Republicans in expanding the suffrage; d) the way in which important developments in the economic, social, and diplomatic spheres—for example, the opportunity to buy Louisiana, the course of westward expansion, and the beginnings of an industrial economy—forced the Jeffersonians to modify their political agenda; and e) the origins of judicial review, including the Republican attack on the judiciary, *Marbury v. Madison*, the Marshall court and its nationalizing decisions.

The War of 1812 deserves inclusion, but it ought to be studied broadly. Its military aspects are not so important as its implications for American foreign policy, which for the next century would follow principles related to an American sphere of influence set down in this era. The war also brought about the exhaustion of the Federalists after the futile Hartford Convention. And, the defeat of foreign challenges to American sovereignty serves as a symbolic point at which to close the first stage of nation building.

UNIT V
THE EXPANDING NATION:
THE NORTH (1815-1850)

SIGNIFICANCE AND TEACHING GOALS

■ MAJOR THEMES

T he study of the expanding nation prior to the Civil War is vital, for this was one of the formative eras in the nation's history—a period of dramatic territorial expansion, economic growth, and industrialization, all spurred on by the great optimism of white Americans that anything was possible with hard work, imagination, and the unleashing of the maximum freedom of the individual.

The vitality of this era, the democratic spirit and the religious faith deeply united in the 19th-century American character were reflected in nearly every sphere of American life. But developing also in this era were important sectional differences over slavery and its expansion into the West, over protective tariffs, and over states' nullification rights. Although transcended for the time being by a strong national spirit and the statesmanship of such congressional giants as Henry Clay and Daniel Webster, these deepening sectional differences were destined to reach crisis proportions in the Civil War era and must, therefore, be understood.

Three major themes in United States history are vital for helping students to understand the importance of this era. First, the era marked a major step in the **economic transformation of the nation** from preindustrial colonial days to the mighty industrial and post-industrial society of the 20th century. Between the War of 1812 and the Civil War, the northern United States and parts of the South underwent an economic

The vitality of this era, its democratic spirit, and religious faith were reflected in nearly every sphere of American life.

Above: 19th-century water mill.

85

expansion and modernization that changed the ways Americans worked, where they lived, their productivity, and their contacts with the world outside their locale, while simultaneously creating new wealth, new opportunities, and new social problems.

Second, the widespread material changes ushered in by the first stage of industrialization were accompanied by **significant developments in American society, religion, popular culture, and intellectual life**. The influx of millions of new immigrants in this period was an important stage in the **gathering of the American people**, advancing the settlement of new states and territories in the West, and contributing to the explosive growth of the nation's cities. The rise of the theater, of academies of art and music, and the first great flowering of American literature were all part of the cultural changes of this era. Religious revivals of the Second Great Awakening drew unprecedented numbers of ordinary men and women into new Protestant denominations and strengthened the foundations of community in the fast-developing territories of the nation. Together with the disquieting changes of rapid industrialization and urban overcrowding, the Second Great Awakening also contributed to a variety of reform movements, the first in the nation's history.

This era provides students an exceptionally dramatic chapter in the evolution of political democracy in the United States.

Finally, this era provides students an exceptionally dramatic chapter in **the evolution of political democracy in the United States**. The expansion of white male participation in state and national politics, the presidency of Andrew Jackson, the rise of the second party system and modern interest-group politics are all hallmarks of this age, marking the advent of modern politics in America.

■ ESSENTIAL UNDERSTANDINGS

Understanding this complex era in the nation's history and its three major themes of **economic transformation, social change,** and the **evolution of American democracy** requires that students grasp the close interrelationships among all of the following:

1. **The geographic and demographic expansion of the nation.**

2. **The entrepreneurial innovations and technological developments** that industrialized the North and led to the rapid expansion of water and rail transportation linking the nation's regions.

3. **Important advances in the American standard of living** as a result of these developments; the **growth of cities** with their new capital wealth, waves of German and Irish immigrants, and migrations of free blacks and escaping slaves from the South; **new social problems, too,** from growing industrialization, urbanization, and severe economic fluctuations as the American economy became more closely tied to international markets.

4. **Major cultural developments** of the era: the Second Great Awakening; the development of the 19th-century American character, in which strong individualism, a democratic spirit, and religious faith were deeply united; and the first great flowering of American literature.

5. **Political change** as the franchise expanded, as popular participation rose, and as new styles of political campaigning emerged—all culminating in the election of Andrew Jackson (1828), the second American party system (1832), and the advent of modern mass politics in the United States.

6. **The antebellum reform movements**, seeking through persuasion and direct action to extend public education, abolish slavery, encourage temperance, and extend women's rights.

■ *HABITS OF THE MIND*

In studying the dramatic expansion and industrialization, mainly in the North, of the antebellum years, students **should examine the complexities of cause in economic history,** taking into account: a host of inventions and technological breakthroughs; ample sources of waterpower and raw materials; rapid growth in population, making for an expanding inner market for all kinds of goods; protective tariffs; growing supplies of capital, domestic and foreign; and a new network of roads, canals, and rails.

Entrepreneurial innovations and technological developments industrialized the North and led to the rapid expansion of water and rail transportation.

All these developments were spurred by what struck foreign visitors as a particularly inventive and entrepreneurial spirit among the American people, a great optimism that individual effort in one's own self-interest would lead to abundance and prosperity, and that unleashing the maximum freedom of the individual would best serve the common good. Students will **gain insight into the power of ideas in history** by examining how these beliefs contributed to the dramatic and unprecedented economic growth and territorial expansion of these years, while evoking agendas, as well, to temper self-interest with social responsibility.

In the sphere of politics, students should **examine the coexistence** (and often the interdependence) **of change and continuity.** Well before the advent of Andrew Jackson to the White House the Marshall Court had interpreted the Constitution along conservative, federal lines to increase the power of central government over the states. And in Congress, Clay and Calhoun had led in the "national" movement of internal improvements to tie the nation together and to foster economic development.

This era also provides students opportunity to **assess the importance of the political arts of statesmanship and compromise,** especially in a rapidly changing, diverse, and regionalized society. As personified by Henry Clay in the political battles over protective tariffs, the Missouri Compromise of 1820, and in the later, lost attempts leading to the Civil War, students can examine both the great accomplishments and costs of political compromise and the sometimes heavier (even catastrophic) costs of failure to achieve it.

Finally, in the sphere of literature, the four decades preceding the Civil War offer students rich treasures of literary works to help them **see the world through other people's eyes.** This was an era marked by the first great flowering of American literature, and selected masterpieces of Emily Dickinson, Washington Irving, Nathaniel Hawthorne, James Fennimore Cooper, Henry David Thoreau, Walt Whitman, Herman Melville, and Ralph Waldo Emerson will help students grasp the spirit of the age, its optimism, its idealizing of nature and of progress, and its concerns with the nature of man and the source of evil. Oratory, tracts, docu-

A great optimism that individual effort in one's own self-interest would lead to abundance and prosperity contributed to the dramatic economic growth of these years.

*Ralph Waldo Emerson
(1803-1882)*

mentaries, and journals of the period also provide students opportunity to **examine primary sources and perceive the events and issues of the age as they were experienced by people at the time.** Important sources for students to examine are such great debates as Webster-Hayne over states' nullification rights; the abolitionist speeches of Frederick Douglass, Elizabeth Cady Stanton, Sojourner Truth, and Angelina and Sarah Grimke; and the *Seneca Falls Declaration of Sentiment*, to be compared with the Declaration of Independence.

MAJOR TOPICS IN THE STUDY OF THE EXPANDING NATION (1815-1850)

1. Geographic and Demographic Expansion
   a. The rapid expansion of settlements in the Old Northwest
   b. The development of pre-industrial towns in Ohio and Indiana

2. Market Expansion and Early Industrialization
   a. Impact of technological innovation and entrepreneurship
   b. Factory life for men, women, and children
   c. Revolution of transportation, larger markets, and enterprises
   d. Growing and changing cities
   e. Immigrants and their experiences
   f. Early struggles between capital and labor

3. Political Change
   a. Increasing popular participation in state and national politics
   b. Jacksonian Democracy: accomplishments and limits
   c. Second American party system

4. Religion and Reform
   a. Religious roots of reformers in the Second Great Awakening
   b. The several strains of reform and the role of individual leaders: temperance, public education, abolitionism, and women's rights
   c. Legacies and connections to later reform periods of the Progressive and New Deal eras

Frederick Douglass
(c. 1817-1895)

Oratory, tracts, documentaries, and journals of the period provide opportunity to examine primary sources and perceive events as they were experienced by people at the time.

MAJOR TOPICS AND THEIR DEVELOPMENT: ESSENTIAL UNDERSTANDINGS AND RELATED BACKGROUND FOR TEACHERS

■ GEOGRAPHIC AND DEMOGRAPHIC EXPANSION

To understand the significance of the changes of 1815-1850 in the Northeast and the Old Northwest, students must first have a clear sense of the rapid growth of settlement in the Ohio and Indiana territories following the ratification of the Constitution and the series of military campaigns and treaties (1787-1812) which transferred Indian title to much of the Old Northwest territory to the new American nation. With these events, Americans spilled across the Appalachian barrier in ever larger numbers until by 1815 pre-industrial towns such as Columbus and Cincinnati had been established and forests had been widely cleared for the family farms on which most settlers earned their living. This view is necessary to prevent students from assuming that American life was already mainly industrialized and urbanized before the Civil War. To the contrary, rural and village life still predominated even in large parts of the Northeast.

■ MARKET EXPANSION AND EARLY INDUSTRIALIZATION IN THE NORTHEAST AND OLD NORTHWEST

Early industrialization is an important topic because it provides an example of how technological developments and new forms of enterprise can strongly affect the course of history and profoundly affect the way people live. Students should understand the way in which technological innovations in textile and agricultural machinery and in transportation began a massive transformation of American life that continues to the present day. They should know the dramatic contributions of such individuals as Samuel Slater, Eli Whitney, John Deere, and Cyrus McCormick. Small craft shop production gradually gave way to factory production where skilled artisans were destined to become machine operators. Women and children were drawn into the industrial labor system, both through the putting out system and through factory labor. Though the numbers involved were small at first, they grew rapidly in the 19th century, transforming the lives of women and children as well as those of men.

Students should understand the way in which technological innovations in textile and agricultural machinery and in transportation transformed American life.

Work in textile mills drew women into the industrial labor system.

Students should discern the various factors that converged to produce industrialization and should be able to talk about the benefits and problems that the process entailed. They should understand how factory production stimulated the rapid development of regional, national, and international markets, which in turn increased demand for further production. They should see how market development was made possible by the spectacular "transportation revolution," which turned a nation with not so much as a road system, particularly in the West, into a nation crisscrossed with canals and inter-regional roads and railroads. The effects were spectacularly observable in the Erie Canal, which opened up the Old Northwest to rapid settlement. About the time the long-distance, inter-regional water system was completed in 1840, a national railroad system, with even more dramatic effects in moving people and goods across vast distances, began its rise. In studying the new industrial and transportation systems, students should learn of the important role played by government and law. It is especially important to understand how state governments chartered corporations to spur development and subsidized transportation; and how the law began to favor the development of transportation and manufacturing as against traditional rights of property owners.

Industrialization spurred the growth of cities, both by gathering into their folds rural people in search of work and attracting a great new wave of immigrants, primarily Irish and German, in the first half of the 19th century. It had taken Boston, New York, and Philadelphia more than a century to reach 30,000 in population, but in the 50 years after 1800 these seaboard cities attained populations of 300,000 to 600,000. The small "walking cities" of the 18th century, where class-mixed neighborhoods prevailed and residence and workplace coincided, became socially and racially divided metropoli where residence and work were typically separated.

Early industrialization provides an excellent opportunity for students to think through the positive and negative aspects of rapid change. They should consider how the transformations of life involved in industrialization brought important overall gains in the standard of living but at the same time, as regional economies became connected to national markets and as the American economy became more tightly intertwined with international markets, increasingly severe fluc-

Metal grinding

Industrialization spurred the growth of cities and attracted a great new wave of immigrants in the first half of the 19th century.

tuations in prices, production, and employment arose. The panics of 1819 and 1837, each followed by a severe depression, brought widespread misery, especially in the cities.

The rise of the cities and the accumulation of wealth by industrial capitalists brought an efflorescence of culture—classical revival architecture; the rise of theater and the establishment of academies of art and music; the first lyceums and historical societies; and a "communications revolution" in which book and newspaper publishing accelerated and urban dwellers came into much closer contact with the outside world. At the same time the volatile combination of immigration and industrialization in the fast-growing cities disrupted the social fabric on an unprecedented scale. The migration of free blacks and escaping slaves to urban centers, where they competed for jobs with immigrant Irish and Germans; the massive influx of Catholic immigrants distrusted by settled Protestant workers; and the protest of many workers against low wages, long hours, and wretched working conditions produced a period, from about 1830 to 1850, of wholesale urban disorders that led to the development of professional fire and police forces and to some of the reform movements of the antebellum period.

■ POLITICAL CHANGE

The exceptionally dynamic period of political change in the United States between about 1820 and 1860 marks the advent of modern American politics.

The exceptionally dynamic period of political change in the United States between about 1820 and 1860 marks the advent of modern American politics. Students should trace important lines of change in political thought and practice beginning in the Revolutionary era, gathering momentum during the 1790s, when the first party system emerged, and achieving dramatic new levels of popular participation during the period of the second American party system. Among the salient points are: a) increasing popular participation in both state and national politics from the 1790s to 1850s as the idea spread that political participation was the entitlement of all free adult white males, not simply property owners; b) the changing styles of political campaigning that accompanied the heightened emphasis on equality in the political process (and the importance of the West in influencing these changes); and c) the continued exclusion from the political process of women and, in many states, the new exclusion of free blacks.

Students should be familiar with the presidency of Andrew Jackson, including his tariff policy and the doctrine of nullification produced by the "tariff of abominations" in 1828; his war against the Second Bank of the United States and the depression of 1837 that followed; and his removal of the six southern Indian nations. Students should compare his presidency with earlier leadership in the new nation.

Finally, students should explore the second American party system that emerged in the mid-1830s. Students should know how these parties—Whig and Democratic—were formed by a combination of factors—sectional and cultural, as well as economic and political—because modern interest-group politics are readily identifiable in the political system emerging in this era. It should also be understood how party identification played an increasingly large part in the lives of American men, convincing them that party politics might shape their own fortunes in a changing world. It is important to know of the relationship between sectional loyalty and party allegiance; social class and party allegiance; and the differing views the parties had on the role of state and federal government in promoting economic growth.

None of these developments under Andrew Jackson and his successors can be put in sensible historical perspective without knowledge of the significant judicial decisions of the Supreme Court under Marshall from *Marbury v. Madison* (1803) onward, which gave the federal government increasing power over states' rights. Nor can they be understood without an appreciation of the great Congressional debates between the War of 1812 and Jackson's election in 1828, which dealt with the broad issues of regionalism, protectionism, and federal activism in promoting economic development.

■ **RELIGION AND REFORM**

The years between the rise of industrial capitalism in the 1820s and the outbreak of the Civil War witnessed a range of reform movements as diverse and enthusiastic as in any era of American history. Students should find excitement and relevance in exploring antebellum reform because the reformers themselves were fascinating, the issues that they addressed have contemporary resonance, and the sense of hope and

Students should be familiar with the presidency of Andrew Jackson, including his tariff policy and his removal of the southern Indian nations.

Andrew Jackson (1767-1845)

urgency expressed in the era between 1820 and 1860 would later be paralleled in the Progressive era and in the New Deal.

Two underlying concepts are important for students to understand in studying these reform movements. First, students should learn about the tension between rising individualism and the demands of social responsibility. The competing claims of self-interest and community were not new, but they became particularly intense in the antebellum era. As the visiting de Tocqueville put it in <u>Democracy in America</u>, the Americans seemed at one time "animated by the most selfish cupidity; at another by the most lively patriotism." These opposing claims operated so powerfully, and simultaneously, thought the French observer, that Americans must have them "united and mingled in some part of their character."

Students should learn about the religious roots of antebellum reform in the Second Great Awakening that brought religious revivals to large parts of the country.

Second, students should learn about the religious roots of antebellum reform. The Second Great Awakening that brought religious revivals to large parts of the country sporadically between the 1790s and 1830s is important in its own right and is indispensable to comprehending this era, for as de Tocqueville also noted, religion and the democratic spirit were deeply united in the American character. Students should learn of the role of evangelical exhorters such as Charles Finney and of their downplaying of the Calvinist precepts of predestination, original sin, and atonement. The evangelicals had faith in human ability to bring about individual salvation, but they also preached a millennialist and perfectionist collective reform. While studying this activist philosophy, students should also enter the world of the utopian communitarians who sought to create perfectionist communities at places such as Oneida, Amana, Ephrata, and New Harmony, where they offered alternatives to a world, as they saw it, characterized by factories, foreigners, flawed morals, and greedy entrepreneurship. Attention should also be paid to the Mormons—both to their particular vision, the persecution they encountered, and their trek westward in search of "the land of promise."

A camp meeting at Sing Sing, New York

In studying the reform movements of the antebellum era, students ought to learn about the problems and dilemmas of reformers who struggled, for example, against widespread public acceptance of slavery and the often violent resistance to its abolition—the alternative resorts to moral suasion, economic pressure, and political action; the use of force in order to bring about change; the role of compromise in reform. In all these regards students can deepen their insights by investigating the lives of particular reformers so as to understand the psychology and sociology of reform—as in the case, for example, of William Lloyd Garrison, Frederick Douglass, Dorothea Dix, Sojourner Truth, Arthur and Lewis Tappan, and others.

Students also need to recognize the complexities of reform and protest movements, then as now. Students should see, for example, that reformers were sometimes discredited in the eyes of the general public by the occasional zealots in their own ranks whose violent behavior could hurt the cause at issue. They should also see that in what historians call "The Age of Reform" all reformers were not innovators, looking to a new and different future. Many, offended by the effects of change, were eager to slow or reverse it, so that the society could retain, or return to, its earlier ideals and aspirations. They sought to conserve what was best in the past and feared—as de Tocqueville did—that the rush to material profits would weaken the moral and intellectual vigor of colonial and revolutionary days. Writers and artists were similarly concerned; Emerson feared that the emergence of a properly American body of independent scholarship, letters, and art would be compromised. The object of many engaged citizens was to regenerate, and to render distinct from the Old World, the American character and American culture.

While time will not permit study of every reform movement of the antebellum period, several are of special importance because they would lead to fundamental changes or have recurring relevance in later periods. One is the temperance movement, which at first emphasized moderation in the consumption of alcohol and then moved to prohibition—an example of the shift from moral suasion to political action. Another movement essential to learn about is the crusade for free public education, beginning weakly in the 1790s and gaining momentum in the 1820s. It ought to be appreciated that this movement initiated the liberation from illiteracy of large numbers of Americans who could not afford private education. Students will benefit from knowing how many

A movement essential to learn about is the crusade for free public education, beginning weakly in the 1790s and gaining momentum in the 1820s.

Sojourner Truth

Two of the most powerful, poignant, and complex reform movements, with enormous implications for later periods of American history, were antislavery and women's rights.

obstacles had to be surmounted before a system of free public education was in place, and they should also learn about the role of schools, as the reformers saw it, in Americanizing immigrants and preparing all the people for responsible citizenship.

Two of the most powerful, poignant, and complex reform movements, with enormous implications for later periods of American history, were antislavery and women's rights. Antislavery needs to be studied as a multifaceted reform movement, filled with tensions between black and white reformers and moderate and radical abolitionists, many of which are captured in the conflict between William Lloyd Garrison and Frederick Douglass. The lines running from abolitionism to women's rights are very direct and show how women linked their struggle for autonomy in a male-dominated world to the struggle of slaves for personal freedom. Excursions into the secular as well as the religious roots of women's rights; the fight against gender discrimination in the abolitionist movement; the Seneca Falls Convention of 1848 and the demand for women's suffrage; and the spread of women's rights activism in the 1850s, led by figures such as Susan B. Anthony who contended for greater legal and economic rights for women in addition to suffrage, are all topics of importance, within the larger story of antebellum reform.

UNIT VI
THE EXPANDING NATION:
THE WESTWARD MOVEMENT
(1815-1850)

SIGNIFICANCE AND TEACHING GOALS

■ MAJOR THEMES

The saga of the nation's westward expansion is in itself one of the central and most important stories in United States history, but one that also brought monumental tragedy to the American Indians. It should be told both as a great human drama, revealing numberless facets of human nature and capacities, and as a great force for change in the nation's economic, social, cultural, and political life. Indeed, **the advance of the western frontier** vitally affected all the major, continuing themes in our history: **the development of a diverse and multi-ethnic people and culture; the transformation of the American economy; the evolution of political democracy; and our changing relations with other nations of the world.**

Among the important developments of this era were the doctrine of Manifest Destiny; the vast expansion of our agricultural, mineral, and territorial resources and their effects upon the nation's resulting economic and industrial might; the emergence of slavery as a divisive political issue in the admission of new territories and states into the union; and the development of the nation's 19th-century policy toward the American Indians.

■ ESSENTIAL UNDERSTANDINGS

The basic understandings all students should develop concerning the nation's westward expansion and its important

The nation's westward expansion is one of the most important stories in United States history, but one that also brought monumental tragedy to the American Indians.

Above: Emigration to the Valley of the Mississippi

97

consequences include the following:

1. **The nation's territorial expansion** through international diplomacy (the Louisiana Territory and the Oregon Territory) and through war, justified by the doctrine of "Manifest Destiny" (the Mexican Territory).

2. **Nineteenth-century federal policy toward American Indians,** initially developed in the military campaigns and treaty negotiations which transferred Indian title to their lands in the Old Northwest and Old Southwest.

3. **The great migrations to the Far West** over the Oregon and California Overland Trails.

4. **The frontier as a zone of cultural interaction** between American Indians already in the region and new arrivals moving westward from the eastern United States, northward from Mexico, and eastward from Asia.

5. **The important role of the West** in promoting a more democratic form of politics and a more egalitarian ethic; and the critical contribution of the West to the rapid industrialization and urbanization of the East.

The West was important in promoting a more democratic form of politics and a more egalitarian ethic in the social sphere.

■ **HABITS OF THE MIND**

The stories of the westward movement should **impress upon students once more the importance of the individual in history,** not only of heroes who won fame, but the daily heroism of countless, unsung men, women, and children whose courage and fortitude made the United States a continental nation reaching from sea to sea. The dangers and grinding harshness of frontier life (and of the long ocean journey around the Horn) called forth every human capacity for good and ill. Students may find memorable accounts in the journals of sailors, pioneers, and frontier schoolteachers, as they cultivate the **habit of seeking historical insights from original sources.**

The story of Americans, black and white, moving westward, Mexicans moving northward, Asians moving eastward across the Pacific, and American Indians already on the land (or relocated from lands they had lost) reveals the co-existence of common human needs and qualities on the one hand and sharply different cultures and aspirations on the other. Students are graphically introduced to tragedy, individual and collective, in this meeting of peoples, but also to triumphs of endurance and adaptation to each other that continue to forge American pluralism today.

The period also allows for **critical analysis of important issues** debated in Congress and the press. By using records and documents of the time, students may examine the decisions and actions from several points of view. Among these issues was the federal policy of military campaigns and treaty negotiations terminating Indian title to their lands in the Old Northwest and Old Southwest, and the forced removal of the five southern nations to lands west of the Mississippi following the Indian Resettlement Act of 1830.

Because many of the long-term consequences of the War with Mexico continue into our present day, students should trace its economic, social, and political consequences for Americans and Mexicans alike.

Students can also examine the issues raised by the War with Mexico, a development that divided the nation and was debated in Congress and the press, on the one hand by such opponents of the war as Abraham Lincoln and abolitionists who feared an increase in slave states and, on the other, by Polk's supporters proclaiming the nation's "manifest destiny" in the West and by those Texans and Californians celebrating their recent independence from Mexico and seeking annexation to the United States. Because many of the long-term consequences of the War with Mexico continue into our present day, students should be able to trace its economic, social, and political consequences for Americans and Mexicans alike.

Members of the Lugo family before the War with Mexico and U.S. annexation of the Southwest.

MAJOR TOPICS IN THE STUDY OF THE WESTWARD MOVEMENT

1. The Trans-Appalachian West
   a. Population and territorial expansion
   b. Military campaigns and treaty negotiations with American Indians of the Old Northwest
   c. Jackson's Indian policy and removal of the five southern nations
   d. Role of the West in promoting more democratic politics and a more egalitarian society

2. The Trans-Mississippi West
   a. Territorial acquisitions
   b. The War with Mexico and its significance
   c. The Doctrine of Manifest Destiny
   d. The overland migrations
   e. White and black Americans, American Indians, Asians, and Mexicans in interaction
   f. Economic, social, and political impact of the West on the growing nation

MAJOR TOPICS AND THEIR DEVELOPMENT: ESSENTIAL UNDERSTANDINGS AND RELATED BACKGROUND FOR TEACHERS

■ *THE TRANS-APPALACHIAN WEST*

Much of an understanding of the nation's early national period turns on an appreciation of the enormous expansion—demographic, geographic, commercial, and cultural—that occurred in the several decades after the Constitution was ratified. The population was doubling each generation and slavery, which many revolutionary leaders thought would die after the slave trade ended in 1808, continued to grow rapidly. At the same time, free black communities took form in the North and laid down the foundations for modern, urban African American life.

Geographical expansion into the Ohio and Mississippi valleys ought to be understood. More territory was occupied by Americans than in the previous century and a half, as settlers spilled across the Appalachian mountain barrier in huge numbers. It will be instructive for students to compare the new cycle of settlement in the trans-Appalachian region with the early colonial process of migration and community formation. Special attention should be paid to the Land Ordinance of 1785, the township system it created, and the effects of the Northwest Ordinance of 1787 in setting aside land for public education.

Attention should be paid to the Land Ordinance of 1785, the township system it created, and the effects of the Northwest Ordinance of 1787.

Geographical expansion cannot be separated from conflict between the settlers and the American Indians. That, in turn, involved the prosecution of an aggressive federal policy of treaty-making with tribes west of the Appalachians, as tensions arose between the desire of white Americans on the frontier to acquire land and the determination of American Indians to defend their land base and political sovereignty. An important part of the process was the federalizing of the military campaigns against the tribes of the Ohio Valley, a policy that would extend across the continent throughout the 19th century.

The settlement of the trans-Appalachian territory needs to be understood from both sides of the cultural divide. From the Indian side the new wave of white encroachers can be usefully studied through the early 19th-century "revitalization movements" led by figures such as the Shawnee brothers Tecumseh and Elskwatawa or Black Hawk. The final defeat of the northern Indian Confederacy by General Harrison's forces at Kithtippecanoe (1811) and of the southern Creek and Cherokee nations by Andrew Jackson's forces (1814) signaled the end of organized armed Indian resistance to white settlement in the area between the Appalachians and the Mississippi River.

Students should follow the efforts of the five southern Indian nations to maintain their remaining lands against the pressures of land-hungry settlers by restricting any further sales to government agents. The crisis of 1829, following Jackson's election, should be studied, as well as the events leading to the forced removal of the five southern nations to western territories ceded to them in exchange for their southeastern lands in the Indian Removal Bill of 1830.

The role of the West in promoting a more democratic form of politics and a more egalitarian ethic in the social sphere is the other side of the frontier experience that deserves attention. Students should learn about the character of life in the frontier settlements—the intimacy and sharing among families in rural communities and small towns; the difficulties and hard work shared by men, women, and children, alike; and the changes brought with the building of roads and turnpikes, the canal-building boom, and their opening of national markets to the agricultural output of these frontier settlements. Students can also profit (while being entertained) by looking at frontier heroes such as Davy Crockett, who became a part of American folklore and a symbol of the quintessential

Sequoyah compiled Cherokee catalogue of syllables.

The settlement of the trans-Appalachian territory needs to be understood from both sides of the cultural divide.

American male character.

■ THE TRANS-MISSISSIPPI WEST

The critical starting point in the study of the trans-Mississippi West is, of course, the Louisiana Purchase, which should be understood both for the expanse of territory it added to the nation and for the Lewis and Clark Expedition (1803-1806), the most important of the ventures supported by the government to map the region, develop scientific information concerning it, and to establish official contact with the indigenous peoples of the area.

Sacajawea guiding the Lewis and Clark Expedition.

To understand the further expansion of the nation's western territories, students should consider succeeding events both from the perspective of Americans and of other governments and peoples. Comprehending the geographical character of the vast region from the Mississippi to the Pacific and the claims of England and Russia in the Northwest and of Mexico in the Southwest are starting points. Then students should study the interaction of ideas and interests: on the one hand, the growing interest of Americans in the fur trade, commerce, and land of this vast and varied region, as exemplified in the settlement of Texas; and, on the other hand, the mission-suffused character of the doctrine of Manifest Destiny. It may be helpful for students to ponder the argument that the ideas of manifest destiny have governed much of our thinking about foreign policy and America's place in the world.

Another major topic can be dealt with comparatively: the acquisition of the Oregon Territory through diplomacy (aided by declining English interest in the region) and the acquisition of the Southwest through war. In treating the War with Mexico, students should focus on its causes (significant events in Mexico and the United States); on the internal dissent and debate over the war; and on the consequences of the Treaty of Guadalupe-Hidalgo (which nearly halved the size of Mexico), including the emergence of slavery as a divisive political issue.

The early trickle of emigrants rapidly became a flood as hundreds of thousands now headed for the Far West over the Oregon and California overland trails.

With the acquisition of these western territories, the early trickle of emigrants rapidly became a flood as hundreds of thousands now headed for the Far West over the Oregon and

California overland trails. The push and pull factors in this enormous surge of Americans beyond the Mississippi needs attention, as does the social and demographic character of the overland migrations, particularly the centrality of the family (except in the case of the '49ers). The trail experience, the Indian perspective on the human flood descending upon them, and the interaction of the indigenous peoples with migrating Americans are all important and engaging topics.

It is important for students to learn about the social as well as political aspects of the westward movement. This begins with redefining the frontier as a zone of cultural contact rather than a line separating cultural groups. Although popular culture and historical accounts of the westward movement often tend to suggest that the West was either empty or settled by a few Indian tribes, students should realize the diversity of peoples and cultures in the West before 1840. Once the United States acquired new territories and migrants moved west, the region became a meeting ground for different races and cultures and a test of the American democratic creed.

Thus, the frontier experience ought to be perceived as an encounter of white and black Americans, American Indians, Mexicans, and Asians, all of them interacting in regions still in the early stages of economic, political, and cultural development. The impact of the incoming American settlers on Mexican Americans, including the dispossession of much of their land, but also their resiliency and survival as they were demographically overwhelmed, is one part of this story. A second is the relentless moving of American Indians to the margins of life, those margins being reservations. The federal Indian policy of the nation, from the removal of the five civilized nations to the Fort Laramie Council of 1851, should be understood. Alongside it, students should learn of the strategies of survival of indigenous peoples.

As they study the West, students should also be introduced to life on the farming frontier, the ranching frontier, the mining frontier, and, as one example, San Francisco as an urban frontier. They should also see less obvious ways in which the acquisition of the western half of the continent has affected our national history. The great mineral and natural resources of the West have contributed to making us one of the

James P. Beckwourth, fur trader, explorer.

The frontier experience ought to be perceived as an encounter of white and black Americans, American Indians, and Mexicans, all of them interacting in regions still in the early stages of development.

world's most prosperous nations, while a seemingly endless supply of land led to ecologically problematic agricultural practices and dispersed living patterns that are among the historical roots of contemporary urban-suburban sprawl.

UNIT VII
THE CIVIL WAR AND
RECONSTRUCTION
(1850-1877)

SIGNIFICANCE AND TEACHING GOALS

■ *MAJOR THEMES*

The American Civil War remains, in many respects, the pivotal event in American history. On its outcome depended the survival of the United States as one nation forged out of the Revolutionary War. And on its outcome depended the nation's ability to extend its struggle to bring to reality the **democratic ideals of liberty, equality, justice, and human dignity.**

The war put constitutional government to its severest test. Its outcome preserved a critically endangered Federal Union while at the same time releasing not only four million African Americans but the entire nation from the oppressive weight of slavery. The war can and should be studied as the final, violent phase in a conflict of two subcultures; as the breakdown of a democratic political system; as the climax of several decades of social reform; and as the central chapter in American racial history. Perhaps most of all, it should be studied as a national tragedy of epic proportions—one that comprised millions of personal tragedies laden with hardship, pain, grief, and death.

Union victory and Reconstruction restored the nation and put in place the constitutional amendments that opened a century-long struggle to bring equal rights to African Americans. Legacies of the era included, also, expansion of the power of the federal government and the shift of economic power to northern industrialists.

The American Civil War preserved a critically endangered Federal Union while at the same time releasing the entire nation from the oppressive weight of slavery.

Above: Abraham Lincoln, (1809-1865), President of the United States (1861-1865).

■ ESSENTIAL UNDERSTANDINGS

The extraordinary importance of this era in the nation's history compels special attention to the following essential understandings:

1. **The slave system in the Old South,** its defenders and opponents, North and South. The work and life of enslaved families and their resistance to slavery. The status and experiences of free black Americans in North, South, and West.

2. **The causes of the Civil War:** conflicting ideas and sectional interests. Attempts to compromise and their ultimate failure. The immediate causes of the war's outbreak.

The extraordinary importance of the Civil War, its sheer scope and tragedy, makes this era the ultimate test of historical empathy.

3. **The main stages in the Civil War;** the strengths and weaknesses of each side; its aims, military practices, and effects on the population.

4. **The character, words, and works of Abraham Lincoln** as President and war leader.

5. **The Emancipation Proclamation,** its circumstances and limits; **the Thirteenth, Fourteenth, and Fifteenth Amendments** to the Constitution, their significance in the short run and in the long term.

6. **The various versions of Reconstruction,** their accomplishments, limits, and failures.

■ HABITS OF THE MIND

An event so stupendous as the Civil War calls for exercise of every historical habit of thought that students are capable of, if they are to achieve the perspectives, the insights, and personal engagement the subject deserves. Its sheer scope and tragedy makes this era the ultimate test of **historical empathy.** How to put oneself in the place of those living at the time, caught up in the deep passions that tore families apart and left regional hatreds that would take generations to heal? How to understand the new hope of those who were enslaved and the perspectives of those justifying their bondage? How to recreate the temper of political leaders desperately seeking compromise and of those who saw no honorable alternative but war? How to recreate the life and death of soldiers, and their families' grief?

The war illustrates the consequences of decisions, often tentatively made, long before. The choice to use slave labor preceded a civil war that cost 600,000 lives by more than two centuries. Lincoln explained the tragedy; students should study his Cooper Union speech and his Second Inaugural Address, not only for his deep comprehension of this tragedy, but also for his Biblical appraisal of this terrible scourge upon the nation as the predictable historical consequence of the great evil of American slavery.

Soldiers waiting for orders to go into action at Marye's Heights.

The exploration of cause reveals once more the era's complexity, and the terrible significance of each factor building toward the war's coming, frustrating the efforts of statesmen straining to hold it back. It provides teachers outstanding opportunities to engage students in probing deeply into the great constitutional issues, debates, moral dilemmas, political crises, and compromises of the times. What makes these analyses so compelling is what they reveal to students about the conviction on both sides, Union and Confederacy, of the righteousness of their cause and about the unfolding of great tragedy from such mutual incomprehension.

This study provides outstanding opportunities to probe deeply into the great constitutional issues, debates, moral dilemmas, political crises, and compromises of the times.

Probing into these deep sectional differences and also into those fundamental agreements between North and South upon which final reconciliation and restoration of the Union would depend will **challenge students' growing powers of analytic thought.** Did the sectional differences that finally rent the nation prove that these two regions were fundamentally separate, two nations with differing social mores and values, economic systems, and political beliefs? Or was the nation fundamentally one in its devotion to republican principles, but possessed with critical sectional differences that got out of control with the breakdown of congressional compromise and of the restraining influences of the American two-party system? Only careful analysis of the events leading to the crisis will inform students' thinking.

In studying the war's progress, students may perceive how the most elaborate military plans go often awry under the confusions of combat, and how the factors of geography bear upon the outcome, given the weapons, transport, and communications of those days. Students can measure the effect of disease and infection, given the primitive nature of medical care.

In studying the period of Reconstruction, students can **strengthen their historical perspectives** by comparing the economic plight of the freed slaves with the Russian counterpart of their emancipation—the freeing of the Russian serfs in 1861, accompanied by Czarist long-term economic planning and allocation of lands to the free serfs. Why was no similar provision made in the case of the freed slaves, despite the promise of "40 acres and a mule?" What was the economic condition of the nation following the devastation of the war? And what accounts for the waning of the Radical Republicans' idealism?

Students should examine how the hopes of black Americans for full equality remained the unfinished business of the nation for another hundred years.

How much change and how much continuity was there in the lives of the freed slaves? How much did war and the Reconstruction accomplish for them and how much was unfinished? Students should confront and discuss de Tocqueville's grim prediction of 30 years before, observing that though slavery might be abolished, "the prejudice to which it has given birth is immovable." Perhaps the most significant of the issues that students should examine is how the hopes of black Americans for full equality, constitutionally raised with the 13th, 14th, and 15th Amendments to the Constitution, were subsequently undermined by the courts and by political interests, and so remained the unfinished business of the nation for another hundred years.

MAJOR TOPICS IN THE STUDY OF THE CIVIL WAR AND RECONSTRUCTION

1. Slavery and the Old South
   a. Origins and growth of the slave system
   b. Impact of technology
   c. Westward migration and new slave states
   d. The economic and social structure of the southern society

e. Slave life: work, family, religion, laws, and resistance.

f. Justifications offered by slaveholders for the slave system

2. The Coming of the Civil War
   a. Exploring cause in history
   b. North and South: likenesses and differences of the two regions
   c. Impact of westward expansion
   d. Why attempts at compromise failed
   e. Coalescing of anti-slavery interests in the Republican Party
   f. How Lincoln's election led to secession and war

Robert E. Lee

3. "The War of the Rebellion"
   a. The importance of leadership: Lincoln, Davis, Lee, Grant
   b. The two sides: strengths and weaknesses
   c. The major stages and campaigns
   d. Life and death of the soldier
   e. Life and disruption on the home front
   f. Emancipation; promise and limits
   g. Lincoln the leader and "narrator:" Gettysburg and the Second Inaugural Address

A full knowledge of slavery in the 19th century is necessary in order to understand the persistent problem of race in American society.

4. Reconstruction
   a. The consequences of the assassination of Lincoln
   b. Reconstruction amendments and legacy
   c. Postwar conditions in the South
   d. Economic conditions of the freed slaves
   e. Retreat from Reconstruction
   f. Achievements of Reconstruction
   g. Overall effects and legacy of the Civil War and Reconstruction

MAJOR TOPICS AND THEIR DEVELOPMENT: ESSENTIAL UNDERSTANDINGS AND RELATED BACKGROUND FOR TEACHERS

The history of the Civil War era can usefully be divided into four units: a) The South and the institution of slavery; b) the sectional controversy; c) the military conflict; and d) the aftermath called Reconstruction.

James Hopkinson's Plantation, Edisto Island, South Carolina. Planting Sweet Potatoes.

■ **SLAVERY AND THE OLD SOUTH**

African slavery as it developed in an expanding South in the 19th century is a difficult and often sensitive subject that must nevertheless be thoroughly studied. A full knowledge of slavery is necessary in order to understand not only the Civil War and Reconstruction but also the persistent and divisive problem of race, which has so profoundly affected American society throughout its entire history.

Students should understand that in spite of the Revolutionary generation's acknowledgment that slavery was incompatible with a republican system of government, and in spite of the gradual abolition of slavery in the North, slavery spread rapidly throughout the piedmont and trans-Appalachian South, especially after Eli Whitney's technological breakthrough made it possible to grow "short staple" cotton in most parts of the South. The South's slave population increased tenfold between 1780 and 1860. The great westward migration of southerners and those held in slavery, together with the sale of slaves from the older South to the newly developed regions, often brought out the worst features of the brutal system of coerced labor, for it involved not only the extremely hard working conditions typical on new frontiers but also the breaking up of slave families. Students should be able to describe the geographical distribution of the plantation system, the regional distribution of the different staple crops, and the new slave states that entered the Union.

Students should understand that three-quarters of all southern white families owned no slaves; far more numerous were the southern yeomen and the "poor whites."

Students need to understand that the South was not simply made up of large plantations and that although agriculture dominated the southern economy, the South also underwent some industrialization and had many commercial centers. Students should understand that three-quarters of all southern white families owned no slaves; that the typical slaveowner worked a family farm with fewer than ten slaves, and that only about 10,000 families owned 50 or more slaves. Far more numerous were the southern yeomen, who lived on small farms in modest circumstances, and the "poor whites" who scratched a living in the pine barrens and foothills as herdsmen, lumberers, and mixed-crop farmers. The Old South had a class structure as varied as the North's and poverty held many southern whites in its thrall. In studying southern society, students should also learn that there was a sizeable free black population which occupied an anomalous position in the South's social structure.

It is important that students learn about slavery from both sides of the racial divide. First, they need to understand the system of law that undergirded slavery. Next, they should fathom what the experience of slavery was like for field hands, house servants, and artisans. Students should study the confinements of slavery and also the ways that slaves shaped their own lives, including their attempts to create and maintain families; the role of religion in their lives and their creation of an African Christianity; and their resistance to the system of bondage.

Students should learn about the motivations and behavior of the white masters and mistresses: about their justifications of the slave system, about the troubied consciences of some southerners, and about the effect of slavery on gender relations, both black and white. In the end, students should be able to perceive the Old South not as an aberration from the genuinely American experience but as an integral part of the historical development of the United States.

■ THE COMING OF THE CIVIL WAR

Students should learn how the Civil War was precipitated by southern secession, and how secession grew out of sectional differences, principally over slavery, that dated back to the founding of the nation. Earlier confrontations between North and South had been resolved by congressional compromise. The key question is how this long-standing quarrel got so much beyond political control by 1860 that it disrupted the Union.

Examining the great debates between the three congressional giants, Webster, Clay, and Calhoun, over the Compromise of 1850, and between Lincoln and Douglas on issues of slavery, will open students' thinking to the compelling interests of the time. That historians should still be debating whether the war was inevitable or not should convince students of the tentative nature of judgments about the past.

It is important to understand that the two sections, North and South, were not monolithic but internally varied and that

Examining the great debates between Webster, Clay, and Calhoun over the Compromise of 1850 and between Lincoln and Douglas over slavery will open the compelling interests of the time.

they shared important characteristics, such as devotion to republican principles and democratic government. At the same time, students need to know that the sectional conflict extended beyond the problem of slavery to cultural differences, conflicting economic interests, and opposing constitutional perspectives.

After reviewing what they already know about the origins and nature of abolitionism, students should learn how westward expansion caused an increasing emphasis on slavery in the territories and broadened the antislavery movement to include free-soilers as well as abolitionists. They should also come to understand the political path to disunion—that is, how the American party system of Democrats and Whigs, which had acted as a restraint on sectionalism, broke down under a variety of pressures in the early 1850s, and how various antislavery elements then coalesced as the Republican party, posing a new threat to southern security over maintaining slavery.

A battery on drill from a photograph of the Civil War.

Students should reflect upon the question of why Lincoln's victory led so promptly to disruption of the Union.

Secession was precipitated in 1860 by a normal American political event, the election of a president, and students should be encouraged to reflect upon the question why Lincoln's victory led so promptly to disruption of the Union. It is important to note that southerners, although united in their hostility to the Republican party, were divided on the question of immediate secession; consequently, only seven of the fifteen slave states responded to the election by seceding and forming a new Southern Confederacy. Four more states eventually joined them but only after the outbreak of war. Students should also learn something about the last-minute efforts at compromise, the policy of the incoming Lincoln administration, and the reasons why Fort Sumter became the point of transition from crisis to conflict.

■ *"THE WAR OF THE REBELLION"*

The Civil War, according to the official northern definition, was a war fought to repress rebellion and preserve the Union, but it should also be examined from the Confederate perspective as a war for independence and from the black perspective as a war of liberation. It was a military conflict that reshaped a constitutional system and had social consequences amounting to revolution. Well-organized accounts of the war may be informative, but they can be misleading as well. Students should be encouraged to recapture some sense of the confusion and uncertainty, the rumor and alternating hope and despair with which Americans lived through the four years from Fort Sumter to Appomattox.

More than earlier American conflicts, the Civil War tended to be a total war in its stated purposes, its military practices, and its effect upon the entire American population. Students should learn something about each of the following: the opposing forces and their respective advantages; the problem of disloyalty and its suppression; the recruitment and organization of troops, including 186,000 black troops in the North; the war as a logistical contest; the life of the common soldier; the naval war; the diplomatic front and the Confederacy's vain hope of European intervention.

A young black man in his Union uniform after the Emancipation Proclamation.

The many campaigns and battles can best be understood as occurring in two major theaters. There was the intensive and indecisive war in the East (Peninsular campaign, Union defeats, Lee's two offensives, Grant's movement toward Richmond); and there was the extensive and decisive war in the West (Union progress up the Tennessee and down the Mississippi; capture of New Orleans and Vicksburg; the Chattanooga campaign, which set the stage for Sherman's invasion of Georgia). Students should learn how the war constricted and eventually exhausted the Confederacy and how it came to an end at Appomattox.

Emancipation is a major topic to be discussed in any consideration of the Civil War. One needs to begin by considering how vulnerable slavery was to the disturbing effects of civil war. Like their ancestors during the American Revolution, slaves in large numbers seized the opportunity to free themselves. Thus self-liberation was the beginning of emancipation. Students should understand the political and constitutional barriers to universal emancipation, and they should learn how self-liberation by slaves themselves, military policies, and congressional legislation foreshadowed Lincoln's famous Emancipation Proclamation and the Thirteenth Amendment. The sequel to emancipation was the enlistment of freed slaves in the Union army. Attention should

Students should understand how self-liberation by slaves themselves, military policies, and congressional legislation foreshadowed Lincoln's Emancipation Proclamation and the Thirteenth Amendment.

Women filling cartridges at the Watertown, Mass. arsenal during the Civil War. Woodcut, 1861.

Students should understand the economic effort behind the military effort; life on the home front; the many roles of women during the war; and the extensive devastation in the invaded and occupied South.

also be given to the experience of blacks as soldiers.

Finally, the war on the homefront is worthy of attention. It should be emphasized that party politics continued in the North, though not in the South, and that the war could have had a political ending. The Democratic party made a strong recovery in the state elections of 1862, and if it had captured the presidency in 1864, the result might have been a negotiated peace and an independent Confederacy. Students should understand the consolidating effect of the war in both North and South. They should know something about the economic effort behind the military effort; about life on the home front and especially the many roles of women during the war; and about the extensive devastation in the invaded and occupied South. They should also be introduced to the lively, continuing controversy about why the North won and why the South lost.

■ **RECONSTRUCTION**

Students should be made aware of how much the interpretation of the Reconstruction era has changed in the second half of the 20th century, and they should understand the relation of that change to the modern civil rights movement. It should be emphasized that Reconstruction was a double aftermath of both civil war *and* emancipation. The principal problem posed by the ending of the war was the status of the Confederate states and the treatment of their conquered white population. The principal problem posed by emancipation was the status of the liberated southern black population and its future in a reunited nation. Much of the complexity of Reconstruction resulted from the connections between these two sets of problems. A crucial question is to what extent policies for the aid and protection of the freedmen were actually designed with the problem of the conquered white South primarily in mind.

Presidential Reconstruction is the first topic for students to learn about. The first steps toward restoration of the southern states were taken during the war under military supervision and as a result of presidential initiative. Students should learn how the Lincoln-Johnson Reconstruction governments came into existence and how growing congressional opposition resulted in the rejection of presidential Reconstruction in a historic confrontation between the president and Congress.

Next, students ought to learn about congressional Reconstruction, which can be divided into two phases. First, Congress triumphed in its struggle with President Andrew Johnson and drafted the Fourteenth Amendment as the principal basis for Reconstruction, but ten of the eleven seceded states refused to ratify the amendment and thus rejected the terms of reconciliation offered them. In the second phase, a Congress made more radical by the election of 1866 imposed a system of military Reconstruction which produced state governments in which blacks participated fully as voters and officeholders. This change was eventually formalized in the Fifteenth Amendment. Students should study the content of the Reconstruction amendments and understand that their significance extends far beyond the Reconstruction period.

Reconstruction was a complex and confused process, difficult to summarize. Students should learn something about its economic and social aspects, including the impoverishment of the South by the war; the uneasy relationship between the races; the efforts of the Freedmen's Bureau to aid the transition from slavery to freedom through education for freed slaves and many other forms of assistance (the first comprehensive intervention of the federal government in social problems); the inadequacy of economic aid to freed slaves; and the development of share-cropping and the crop lien system that kept most black farmers in peonage. Students should also learn something of the role of blacks in the Reconstruction governments of the South and in the U. S. Congress, and something of the social and political advances credited to southern Reconstruction governments. Most important was the establishment for the first time of systems of public education in the South for whites and blacks alike.

Students should learn something of the role of blacks in the Reconstruction governments of the South and in the U. S. Congress, and of the social and political advances credited to southern Reconstruction governments.

The retreat from Reconstruction is an important topic that should be of concern to all students. They should learn how southern white resistance and the withdrawal of federal supervision resulted in the "redemption" of the South through the disfranchisement of blacks, the end of the role of blacks in Reconstruction legislatures, the development of racial segre-

The achievements of Reconstruction should not be ignored. For blacks especially, it was a revolution aborted but never forgotten.

gation, the rise of the Ku Klux Klan with its policies of intimidation and violence, and the creation of an economic system of black peonage. As a sequel to emancipation Reconstruction was a failure, and the reasons for that failure ought to be pondered. First, one must consider racism, both as a stimulant of southern resistance and as a limitation on northern will. Second, there was the restraining effect of constitutional conservatism in Congress and the Supreme Court. Third, there was the increasing association of Radical Reconstruction with public corruption. Lastly, there was eventually a diversion of public attention to other pressing problems, such as the economic depression beginning in 1873. At the same time, the achievements of Reconstruction should not be ignored. For blacks especially, it was a revolution aborted but never forgotten.

A natural conclusion to the study of Civil War and Reconstruction is a consideration of the legacies of the era. Students can easily be confused by the complex mix of change and continuity. Too much stress on the "unfinished agenda" of the period can obscure the great changes actually wrought. Notable among them are the following: the expansion of the power of the federal government; the shift of economic power toward northern industrialists and away from southern planters; the effect of the war and Reconstruction on race relations in an era of growing conservatism in the courts and in Congress; and the impact of the war on America's position in the world.

UNIT VIII
THE SECOND INDUSTRIAL
REVOLUTION (1865-1900)

SIGNIFICANCE AND TEACHING GOALS

■ *MAJOR THEMES*

From the era of Reconstruction to the end of the 19th century, the United States experienced an economic transformation that students must understand if they are to comprehend the origins of modern American life and the legacies of an era that still shapes our lives. It was an era in which the explosive growth of the economy, fed by the 19th-century technological revolution and the advance of heavy industry, changed the United States from what had been a "developing nation" before the Civil War to an economic giant by 1914.

Understanding the dynamics of this era will cast important light for students on two of the central themes in American history: the many forces behind **the development of the American economy** and **the impact of economic and technological changes on social, political, and cultural developments in the nation**.

A third theme, arising from the enormous increase in immigration from southern and eastern Europe and from Asia and Mexico throughout this period, is the **changing nature of American society.** Related to this theme was the search for ways to nurture **national unity amidst growing cultural diversity**, as the nation responded to the need for a people of many racial, ethnic, linguistic, and cultural heritages to live together in mutual respect within a political system whose foundations were largely English and western European.

The 19th-century Industrial Revolution changed the United States from a developing nation before the Civil War to an economic giant by 1914.

Above: An American Factory

■ **ESSENTIAL UNDERSTANDINGS**

Students' grasp of the economic and social development of the nation in this era will require understanding of the close interrelationships among the following developments:

1. **The technological revolution of the late 19th century,** bringing with it heavy industry and big business.

2. **Changes in the work place** that brought about the labor union movement, and the obstacles raised to it by business and government.

3. **Mass immigration** that fed the demands for labor and changed the ethnic and religious makeup of the nation.

4. **The resulting growth of American cities** as industrial centers with ethnic enclaves of increasingly diverse cultures and nationalities.

5. **The importance of public schools** in advancing literacy and forging a national culture amid increasing ethnic diversity; contrasting opportunities for black American youth under segregated schools.

6. **The mechanization of agriculture,** the economic hardships of many farmers, and the rise of Populism.

7. **The Second Great Removal of the American Indians,** opening the West to large-scale agriculture, ranching, and mining, and resulting in the disintegration of the American Indians' traditional way of life.

■ **HABITS OF THE MIND**

Among the habits of the mind that should be developed through study of this era, three stand out: **the search for the multiple causes explaining the great technological and economic changes that profoundly altered the lives, work, and prospects of millions of Americans after the Civil War; respect for the particularities and historical context of the age, as antidotes against excessively abstract generalizations that fail to account for the many contingencies**

Mass immigration changed the ethnic and religious makeup of the nation and created the need to develop national unity amid growing cultural diversity.

of the time; and recognition of the importance of individuals and of human choice. These are essential insights for students to acquire, for it is easy for adolescents to assume that the enormous complexity of the economic, social, and political world into which they are stepping is wholly beyond the influence of individuals like themselves. Studying this era which so much helped to shape the world in which they now live should help students better grasp the dynamics of change and the many contingencies on which economic and social developments turn—many of them influenced by men and women from many walks of life whose actions helped to shape the course of events and the society in which they lived.

Edison with phonograph. Its musical potential evolved later.

The importance of individual talent and character can hardly be overemphasized in the study of this era. The technological and entrepreneurial inventiveness, the "Yankee ingenuity" recognized by the world of that day, was broadly represented in the American people and found its most dramatic expression in such gifted individuals as Bell, Edison, Westinghouse, Singer, Sears, and Ford who became household words in the fullest sense. Their contributions, together with those of countless others, quite literally raised the comfort and living standards of millions.

The importance of individual talent and character can hardly be overemphasized in the study of this era.

Other vivid examples may be found in the lives of the railroad-builders and business giants such as Andrew Carnegie, John D. Rockefeller, and J. P. Morgan, who grasped the importance to their enterprises of a critical amount of predictability (limiting the risks of a pure free-market economy) and took the steps that concentrated more and more stages of production in highly successful large corporations that enhanced the predictability of prices, labor costs, and access to markets while also reducing competition and its risks.

Students can also observe the actions of individuals among farmers and labor organizations who sought to counter the power of the railroads, corporations, and banks and, though only partly successful at the time, laid foundations for the Progressive agenda of the early 20th century and for the 20th-century labor movement. Biographies of such labor organizers as Samuel Gompers, founder of the American Federation of Labor (AFL); such reformers as Jane Addams and Lillian Wald of the settlement house movement; black leaders such as Booker T. Washington and W. E. B. Du Bois; Protestant ministers and lay workers of the Social Gospel movement who tied Christian teachings of individual salvation to good works for social betterment in the urban slums; and such historical novels as Willa Cather's My Antonia and O. E. Rolvaag's Giants in the Earth will demonstrate to students the many avenues of active human response to the social costs of industrial capitalism.

It is critical that students analyze the many interrelated causes for the spectacular expansion of the American economy before 1914.

Because economic growth and modernization are prime concerns in today's world, it is critical that students **analyze the many interrelated causes for the spectacular expansion of the American economy before 1914.** Several questions leap forth in analyzing the causes of economic growth, then and now. To what extent did the society enjoy abundant sources of energy, at low—or at least predictable—prices? Raw materials? A productive, efficient agriculture? An ample and able labor supply? Ample and dependable sources of capital? Governmental policies friendly to enterprise? Technological and managerial prowess? An entrepreneuring spirit both patient and adventurous? Pride in the quality of its products? A widely accessible market for its products at home and abroad? A high level of social peace and civic order at home, and of security from foreign threats? An ideology of individualism and equal opportunity?

Students' powers of historical empathy and their grasp of the complexity of historical causation should also be enhanced by following the story of the Second Great Removal of the Plains Indians and the cultural disorganization of the tribes. Students will better understand the human tragedy of those years by considering the point of view of the nomadic Plains Indians who found the ideas of settled life and land ownership meaningless, just as most westward-bound Americans found barbarous and primitive the Indians' nomadic way of life. Could alternative decisions to those made by the army and Congress between 1851 and 1890 have altered the course of history in the West? Students should be encouraged to develop the historical imagination to recreate the (genuine, not wishful) options people had at the time. Reading from annals and such documents as the view of Indian affairs by Chief Joseph of the Nez Percé will provide students needed perspectives on these events.

MAJOR TOPICS IN THE STUDY OF THE SECOND INDUSTRIAL REVOLUTION

1. Transformation of the Economy in the Late 19th Century: inventions, advent of heavy industry, and consolidation of large-scale corporations

2. A Changing Society
    a. Immigration: its sources, motives, and consequences
    b. Education: its role in advancing literacy and a national culture
    c. Urbanization and its social and cultural effects
    d. Labor: changes in the work place and rise of the union movement

3. The Modernization of Agriculture
    a. Mechanization and increased farm productivity.
    b. The disruptive effects of modernization on farm families and communities
    c. The plight of many farmers and the rise of the Populist movement

4. The Development of the Trans-Mississippi West
    a. The Homestead Act of 1866 and expanded migration to the Plains
    b. The Second Great Removal of the American Indians
    c. Development of the western ranching and mining frontiers

5. Politics in the Gilded Age
    a. Corruption
    b. Urban "bossism" and mass politics
    c. The civil service system

Chief Joseph (c. 1840-1904)
[Hinmaton-Yalakit]
Nez Percé Indian chief

MAJOR TOPICS AND THEIR DEVELOPMENT: ESSENTIAL UNDERSTANDINGS AND RELATED BACKGROUND FOR TEACHERS

In what can be thought of as the second industrial revolution, the nation's productive capacities were reorganized by large-scale, national, bureaucratic corporations; urbanization proceeded rapidly; much of agriculture moved from family farms to large-scale operations; immigration increased; and

Students' historical empathy should be engaged by examining the Second Great Removal of the American Indians and its consequences.

121

labor organization and protest entered its most dynamic and violent phase. While interrelated, these developments can each be studied in turn.

■ TRANSFORMATION OF THE ECONOMY

Students should study how the American economy was transformed by the advent of heavy industry and large corporations in the late 19th century. Led by the steel industry, powered by the conversion to steam and then electrical power, and facilitated by the completion of a national railroad system, American industry achieved international significance by the early 20th century. In studying this process, it is best to modify the old "robber baron" image and attempt first to understand what the industrialists believed in and what they thought they were accomplishing. With that beginning students can then study how farmers and workers responded to the attempts to reorganize the free enterprise system in the United States. They should understand that the new business leaders rejected in practice (but not in rhetoric) the ideology of laissez-faire capitalism with its notion of the self-regulating market; that they wanted predictability in large units of production for sale of products over a vast terrain; that they believed they could bring rationality to a chaotic economic system both through vertical integration that combined various stages of production and through horizontal integration that aimed at eliminating competition and stabilizing prices. As J. P. Morgan expressed the new ideology: "I like a little competition but I like combination a lot better." The era saw a tremendous increase in economic productivity combined with a momentous concentration of the nation's productive capacities in a much smaller number of businesses. In steel, for example, some 808 American producers in 1870 had dwindled to less than 70 by 1900, while output jumped from 77,000 to 11.4 million tons in the same period.

The Carnegie Steel Company's enormous plant at Homestead, Pennsylvania, in the 1890s.

Learning about Social Darwinism will enable students to understand how a new social ideology, derived from biological theory, was used to justify the new industrial order.

Learning about Social Darwinism will enable students to understand how a new social ideology, derived from biological theory, was used to justify the new industrial order. They should learn how the theories of Charles Darwin (who argued that the plant and animal world evolved through constant struggle in a long process of "natural selection" in which only the fittest survived) were adapted to explain how human societies progressed by the strong forging ahead and the weak falling aside. Such a theory justified aggressive business practices and promoted the idea that government should never interfere to protect the weak because this, as William G. Sumner, the nation's leading Social Darwinist, put it, would only insure "the survival of the unfittest."

■ A CHANGING SOCIETY

Students should learn that one of the most important accompaniments of this Second Industrial Revolution and the opportunities it presented was mass immigration from southern and eastern Europe and significant immigration from Asia and Mexico—all of which changed the ethnic and religious makeup of the country, leaving it less Protestant and northern European in composition than before the Civil War. Given the present-day flow of immigration in American society and the unprecedented influx of people from Asia and Central America, it is imperative that students develop a more sophisticated understanding of the late 19th-century immigrant experience. After learning about the size of the immigrant tide (14 million in the forty years after 1860 as against 5 million in the forty years preceding 1860), the focus here ought to be on the motives, expectations, and experiences of different immigrant groups as they attempted to preserve the culture of their homelands while responding to the requirements of American citizenship, urban living, and industrial work in a new country. In that era, as more recently, the United States welcomed those fleeing poverty or oppression. But students need also to understand the current of nativist hostility to newcomers, fed by fears that, coming by the millions and competing for employment, they would displace or undercut the wages of other workers. Such opposition created barriers to advancement for immigrants and fed their desires to preserve ethnic enclaves, churches, and even schools in the large cities where they congregated.

Special attention should be given to the role of public schools in extending literacy among the millions of new immigrants and in forging an American nation during a period of rapidly increasing ethnic and cultural diversity. The growth of "land grant" colleges and privately endowed institutions of higher education opened further opportunities for millions of

One of the most important accompaniments of this Second Industrial Revolution was mass immigration from southern and eastern Europe and significant immigration from Asia and Mexico.

Immigrants entering the United States.

Americans. Students should also examine the educational consequences of the "separate but equal" ruling of *Plessy v. Ferguson* (1896) for African Americans and the importance of Tuskegee Institute, founded in 1881 by Booker T. Washington to provide vocational training for black youth.

The rise of the American city from 1875 to 1925 (at the end of which time more than half of all Americans lived in cities as compared with only 7 percent in 1860) is closely connected to the rise of industrial America and is an important topic for today's city-dwelling students to understand. Among noteworthy topics to study are the movement of farm families to towns and cities, which became the major industrial arenas; city growth and urban architecture; the advent of mechanized mass transportation, from horse cars to subways; the development of suburbs to which the rapidly growing middle class began to migrate; the development of modern urban services such as fire and police protection and social aid; and the long history of cultural mixing in American cities. Related, too, were new modes in the use of leisure, from spectator sports to the motion pictures, from museums to public libraries.

Large-scale industrialization required a different organization and employment of labor, and students should comprehend the historic changes that took place in this aspect of life in the late 19th century and how workers responded. On the positive side were a gradually shortened workday, the new material comforts that fully-employed workers could earn, a standard of living and a rate of home ownership not paralleled in any industrialized European country. On the other hand, rewards were unevenly distributed, and greater material benefits for many contrasted with great hardship for others, induced by low wages in some sectors, by high accident rates, unhealthy working conditions, frequent depression, and average annual unemployment exceeding 10 percent in both the 1870s and 1890s. Time needs to be given also to a study of the union movement beginning with the Knights of Labor (1869) and the American Federation of Labor (1886). An understanding of the attempts of American workers to organize includes labor's resistance to the transformation from craft to mechanized labor, the imposition of formalized work rules, and notions of scientific management. In the struggle between capital and labor, attention ought to be given to the interven-

Students should examine the educational consequences of the "separate but equal" ruling of Plessy v. Ferguson (1896) for African Americans and the importance of Tuskegee Institute.

Booker T. Washington, founder of Tuskegee Institute (1906).

tion of state and federal government against strikes from the late 1870s through the 1890s.

■ THE MODERNIZATION OF AGRICULTURE

Farming evolved toward a modern business in the late 19th century through mechanization, which greatly increased average farm size and productivity and turned the United States into the world's premier producer of food—a position it has never surrendered. Students need to recognize the plight of farmers large and small as they faced an industrializing country where transportation and storage facilities were controlled by powerful corporations. The farmers' attempts in the Populist movement to organize against falling prices during depression years in the 1870s and against unfair railroad and storage rates need to be studied for a number of reasons. It was the most sustained example of farmer radicalism in our history, it was a root cause of Progressivism, it led to the first intervention of government into business practices affecting the nation's food supply, and it initiated the federal government's special protection of farmers, especially through the Interstate Commerce Act of 1887.

■ THE DEVELOPMENT OF THE TRANS-MISSISSIPPI WEST

In studying the experience of farmers from Reconstruction to the early 20th century, it is useful to focus on the trans-Mississippi experience because the Great Plains and Pacific coast areas were important new zones in which the development of agriculture was accompanied by the continuing conflict of white and Indian societies. Especially important were the expanded migration on the Great Plains fueled by the Homestead Act of 1862 and the Second Great Removal of the American Indians, with the federal army playing the leading role in the displacement and destruction of many western tribes. The Dawes Severalty Act of 1887, which ended the traditional policy of respecting tribal bonds and allocated acreage to individuals while promising them citizenship, set the course for federal Indian policy until the New Deal. The Indian attempts to maintain their culture after removal to reservations during the heavy migration of farmers and ranchers west of the Mississippi is most dramatically—and tragically—revealed in the Ghost Dance movement of 1889-90,

Especially important were the expanded migration on the Great Plains fueled by the Homestead Act of 1862 and the Second Great Removal of the American Indians.

Chinese laborers during building of Northern Pacific Railroad. 1,500 Chinese were involved in the project. Photograph taken in Western Montana Rockies along Clark Fork River.

This era saw the maturation of the two-party system, and the alignment in both parties of interests and regional groups that were to remain influential through much of the 20th century.

which ended with the Wounded Knee massacre of 1890. Attached to the topic of agriculture is that of western ranching and mining. The latter, apart from providing the nation with most of the gold and silver that supported industrial expansion, brought together Mexican, Chinese, and European immigrants and native-born American settlers in a colorful and often tension-filled set of exchanges.

■ POLITICS IN THE GILDED AGE

Students, like historians, may not find great excitement on the surface of national politics during what Mark Twain dubbed the Gilded Age, for it was a period of lackluster leaders and few disputed principles to distinguish the Republican and Democratic parties. It was also an era of widespread corruption in state and federal government, both in the legislative and executive branches. On the other hand, students should learn that local politics involved citizens at a high level of participation, partially because urban political bosses attracted large numbers of immigrants to their local political machines. Students should also learn why urban "bossism" offended the older middle class and how reformers set about to strip power from machine bosses and turn municipal government over to expert city managers.

On the national scene, beneath the unexciting surface, important developments were taking place. Students should be able to trace the Farmers' Alliance movement, the creation of the Populist Party in 1892, and the debate over the unlimited coinage of silver that became a crucial issue in the election of 1896. The creation of the Civil Service Commission ushered in a merit-based system of government employment. The Interstate Commerce Act presaged federal regulation of egregious malpractices in economic affairs. The aftermath of the Civil War also saw the maturation of the two-party system, and the alignment in both parties of interests and regional groups that were to remain influential through much of the 20th century.

UNIT IX
THE PROGRESSIVE ERA
(1900-1914)

SIGNIFICANCE AND TEACHING GOALS

■ *MAJOR THEMES*

The Progressive Era deserves study because it included the nation's most vibrant set of reform ideas and campaigns in the 100 years between the reforms of the 1830-40s and the New Deal. Progressives, whether holding liberal or conservative points of view, or a mixture of both, tried to respond to problems arising from rapid industrialization, urbanization, waves of immigration, and business and political corruption of the late 19th century. With varying results they set out broad agendas for reform, addressing issues the nation would turn to again and again, down to the present.

Students can best understand the significance of this era if they approach it as a chapter in **the evolution of democracy in the United States,** when the nation confronted a new dilemma of the industrial age: could the political vision of the nation's democratic ideals, formed in a simpler agrarian era, be maintained in a vast industrialized society harboring problems undreamed of by Jefferson, Madison, Locke, or Montesquieu? Would the great "middle ground," on which Jefferson counted for the survival of democracy, endure in an industrialized age with its unprecedented concentrations of wealth and economic power in the great railway, banking, commercial, and industrial monopolies and trusts, and with the ever larger gaps between the rich and the poor?

The central dilemma confronting Americans of this era,

Progressives tried to respond to problems arising from rapid industrialization, urbanization, waves of immigration, and business and political corruption of the late 19th century.

Above: Frances Willard (on bicycle), turned the National Women's Christian Temperance Union into the country's largest women's organization.

The central dilemma of this era was how to maintain the great material benefits flowing from the Industrial Revolution while ensuring economic opportunity for all Americans.

and still central in our own day, was how to maintain the great material benefits flowing from the Industrial Revolution while bringing the powerful forces creating those benefits under democratic control, to ensure economic opportunity for all Americans. How successfully this dilemma was resolved by the Progressives is a much-debated subject among historians. This is partly so because the story of reforms then called progressive was but one of several important stories to be told about the era: important, also, were **the continuing, and massive, expansion of the economy; the expanding population; striking changes in popular culture; and the rise of the United States to world power.**

Each of these developments brought significant changes to American life, with effects complicating the conventional picture of a simple struggle between reformers to be applauded and opponents to be decried, or between those who believed only in change and others who sought only continuity. The two central figures of this era, Theodore Roosevelt and Woodrow Wilson, dramatically exemplify the co-existence of liberal and conservative impulses, of tastes for both activism and patience, for daring and prudence. Since the same is true of so many influential figures of the time, students must take into account the complications of circumstance and personality as different historians have perceived them since. And they should understand the often underplayed significance of the nation's participation in World War I as it crossed and interrupted an era of democratic self-examination and self-correction.

■ **ESSENTIAL UNDERSTANDINGS**

1. **Who the Progressives were, their central aims and ideals,** the sources of their zeal, and the nature of their limitations.

2. **Their major rivals and obstacles, their major allies and supporting forces.**

3. **Their major accomplishments and setbacks** in the states and on the national level, including the roles of Theodore Roosevelt, William Howard Taft, and Woodrow Wilson.

4. **The weakness and evasions of the Progressives** on the issues of race and labor in the United States.

5. **The impact of World War I** in halting much of the Progressive movement.

■ *HABITS OF THE MIND*

The Progressive Era provides students a wealth of opportunities to exercise the habits of historical thought, most importantly the predisposition **to tolerate complexity in the interplay of multiple forces in human affairs, and to accommodate such complexity in their thinking about the causes and consequences of major events** in the United States of the 20th century. Students should analyze the Progressive movement as a multifaceted agenda committed both to improving people's lives and working conditions under industrial capitalism and to greater scientific order and efficiency in a society that had grown vastly more complex, beset with inequities and with corruption in local governments and in big business. In a common aspiration to progress and human welfare, liberals could stress social justice and conservatives, scientific and economic efficiency. Both could decry corruption, fraud, and waste of resources, but would naturally differ on allocating blame and contriving remedies.

The Progressives also offer an opportunity for students **to learn about paradox in history and to see that all movements for reform take twists and turns that could not have been anticipated**. The Progressives, for example, in their multiple agendas pushed for the adoption of "direct democracy" measures such as the initiative, referendum, and recall in order to "return goverment to the people" while simultaneously installing experts at the controls of new regulatory agencies that in effect restricted the direct participation of the urban and rural masses. Students might analyze the effects of the increased role of government Progressives created in order to accomplish their ends: through legislation and increased regulatory controls; through judicial activism in the courts, led by Louis Brandeis and Oliver Wendell Holmes; and through expanded executive powers under the active presidencies of Theodore Roosevelt and Woodrow Wilson. What explains these measures and the anachronism between Wilson's

Students should analyze the Progressives' agenda, committed both to improving people's lives and working conditions under industrial capitalism and to greater scientific order and efficiency.

intentions to liberate the nation from big government and the expanded federal role he created?

The era also offers students many chances **to evaluate primary sources.** The era is rich in novels (Upton Sinclair, Theodore Dreiser, Frank Norris) and documentaries such as those of Jacob Riis (How the Other Half Lives), Lincoln Steffens (The Shame of the Cities), W. E. B. Du Bois (The Souls of Black Folk), and Jane Addams (Twenty Years at Hull House) that provide students opportunities **to perceive past events as they were experienced by people at the time, and thus develop historical empathy** in dealing with the past.

Students should ask themselves why the Progressives gave so little attention, beyond anti-lynching legislation, to equal-opportunity needs of black Americans.

Students should ask themselves why, unlike the reform movement of the 1830-1840s in which Abolitionists were at the very center of the fray, the Progressives gave so little attention, beyond anti-lynching legislation, to equal-opportunity needs of black Americans, and to the enduring problems of discrimination in every sphere of public life—jobs, housing, education, and access to the ballot box. Examining the bitter rivalry in these years between the accommodationist strategy of Booker T. Washington and the more radical strategies of W. E. B. Du Bois will cast this issue in larger perspective, as will examining the forces for strict separation of the races, confirmed in *Plessy v. Ferguson,* the "separate but equal" ruling of the Supreme Court in 1896. Students will **sharpen their own historical perspectives, and quickly recognize the significance of the past to their own lives**, as they confront the long-term effects of this neglect by the Progressives of what would become a central challenge to the nation's unity by the mid-20th century.

W. E. B. Du Bois, Founder of NAACP and noted black historian and essayist.

MAJOR TOPICS IN THE STUDY OF THE PROGRESSIVE ERA

1. The Social Justice Movement

2. Reform in the Cities and the States

3. Progressivism and National Politics in the White House, Congress, and Supreme Court

4. War and the Waning of the Progressive Era

MAJOR TOPICS AND THEIR DEVELOPMENT: ESSENTIAL UNDERSTANDINGS AND RELATED BACKGROUND FOR TEACHERS

■ *THE SOCIAL JUSTICE MOVEMENT*

Students should know who the Progressives were—mainly middle-class, native-born, educated Americans—and what were their main concerns. They should know that the Progressives' goals included ending child labor; passing protective legislation for women workers; relieving abysmal housing, especially in urban tenements; improving public school systems; attacking consumption of alcohol and drugs; ending prostitution; obtaining decent wages and working conditions for workers; passing anti-lynching legislation; and initiating a set of reforms for women that included gaining the suffrage and legalizing birth control.

The journalists whom Theodore Roosevelt called "muckrakers" emerged as the publicists of the Progressives' concerns. They exposed corruption, fraud, and exploitation through the new mass-circulation press and magazines that widely distributed their exposés. In the writings of Lincoln Steffens and Ida M. Tarbell—talented journalists and forerunners of today's investigative reporters—students will find the burst of energy that brought the call for reform to the attention of the American people.

Individuals from all walks of life came forth to serve the cause of reform in those years, from the settlement house workers of Hull and Henry streets and innumerable church-related social welfare projects to reform-minded academics such as John Dewey, conservationists like John Muir, and the mixed group of white and black reformers who organized the NAACP in 1909. Protestant leaders preached the "social gospel" and Catholics found inspiration in the declarations of the reform-minded Pope Leo XIII.

The social justice movement also provides opportunity to consider the role of women in American life between 1865 and the 1920s. Students should learn about the declining importance of the ideal of domesticity in this period and the increasing involvement of women outside the home. The

Child labor. Oyster shuckers, Port Royal, South Carolina.

The journalists whom Theodore Roosevelt called "muckrakers" emerged as the publicists of the Progressives' concerns.

latter took two forms: first, the growth of the female wage labor force, primarily in domestic service, clerical and retail work, and industrial manufacturing; second, the movement of middle and upper-class women into higher education, beginning in the 1870s, and from there in substantial numbers into vocations such as teaching, social work, and, as was especially important among African American women, into club work devoted to "the lifting of the race." An upsurge of suffragism brought about state suffrage laws as early as 1910-11 in Washington and California and a constitutional amendment a few years later; the rise of feminism was directed at the amelioration of the conditions of wage-earning women through the organization of such groups as the Women's Trade Union League.

An upsurge of suffragism brought about state suffrage laws as early as 1910-11 in Washington and California and a constitutional amendment a few years later.

Women's suffrage in Wyoming Territory. Scene at the election polls in Cheyenne, Engraving, 1888.

■ REFORM IN THE CITIES AND STATES

Students should understand how Progressive reform usually started at the local level and worked its way upward to the state and then to the national level. At the city level, the reformers were mostly middle-class professionals and businessmen who sought to reduce corruption and inefficiency and limit the power of the political bosses and their immigrant allies, usually by instituting a commission form of government, municipal administration by nonpartisan experts, and municipal ownership of utilities and public transportation. At the state level, the Progressives attempted to regulate railroads and utilities; to initiate "direct democracy" by giving the people new powers of initiative, referendum, and recall; and to pass social legislation.

Today's students have little idea of the primitive conditions in American cities at the turn of the century. Most were suffering from the effects of opportunism, profiteering, and sheer confusion endemic to rapid growth at a time of governmental "laissez-faire." Nearly every one of the services necessary to a decent life for people packed densely together was absent or inadequate. City reformers attacked the obvious needs—sewage, water, street paving and lighting, transport, police and fire protection, utilities, and open spaces. Almost everyone believed that these services should be municipally-run, dedicated to everyone's welfare. Cities had, for example, legal authority to obtain rights-of-way for transportation, in particular for building the popular streetcar networks that crisscrossed American cities for fifty years, until their disappearance in favor of subway systems and buses after World War II. Almost all cities had serious bridge problems, and solved them during the Progressive era by building huge steel bridges that, like the early subways, have lasted for a century.

Students will find interest in reform mayors like the colorful Tom Johnson of Cleveland, but many would-be city reformers found their hands tied by the power of entrenched interests at their state capitols. As Progressive forces grew, reform governors appeared—Hiram Johnson in California, Robert M. LaFollette in Wisconsin, Woodrow Wilson in New Jersey among them—who, together with their supporters, presided over the passage of fairer tax laws, control of railroads and utilities, child labor laws, improved working conditions, and (in a number of western states) women's suffrage.

■ *PROGRESSIVISM AND NATIONAL POLITICS*

Students should see that just as city reform could not be sustained without supportive action—or, at least, toleration—by state officials, so state reforms would be short-lived or of limited effect without the cooperation of the federal government. Critical to the prospects for reform at the federal level was the accidental arrival of Theodore Roosevelt to the White House, upon the assassination of McKinley. Roosevelt's programs on conservation, public health, and business regulation were important to state and local reformers but hardly revolutionary. In the coal miners' strike of 1902 he took labor's side against the owners, a first for American presidents; he denounced the "corruption and fraud" of "malefactors of great wealth."

It can be instructive for students to consider Taft's administration, his reasons for distrusting the "direct democracy" programs of the Progressives, and his loss of their support by favoring the Payne-Aldrich Tariff (which failed to reduce traiffs as they anticipated) and by supporting the sale of public coal lands in Alaska to mining interests. Although Taft added a million acres of Appalachian forests to the public lands, supported the 8-hour work day, and vigorously indicted more trusts and monopolies than Roosevelt, Progressive Re-

Theodore Roosevelt (1858-1919) President of the United States (1901-1909)

Critical to the prospects for reform at the federal level was the accidental arrival of Theodore Roosevelt to the White House upon the assassination of McKinley.

publicans turned again to Roosevelt whose Bull Moose platform of 1912 included women's suffrage, unemployment insurance, and the minimum wage. Its implementation would have put the United States in the lead of the world's reform democracies. But with the split in the Republican leadership, Roosevelt, like Taft, was defeated in the election of Woodrow Wilson.

Wilson's sometimes populist rhetoric gave encouragement, as had Roosevelt's, to Progressives everywhere. And although he was by no means ready to go as far as the Bull Moose program, Wilson's achievements in advancing his agenda were considerable.

■ THE WANING OF PROGRESSIVISM AND ITS LEGACY

American participation in World War I is often called a watershed between the Progressive era and the decade of the 1920s. Historians can never know what added changes might have ensued if war had not intervened to divert national attention from domestic to foreign affairs. Two qualifications, however, are in order. First, certain reforms of business regulation were passed as late as 1920 and two quite spectacular reforms favored by many Progressives, the 18th and 19th Amendments, were ratified in 1919 and 1920, respectively. The first, Prohibition, proved ill-advised and ephemeral; the second, Women's Suffrage, has been universally accepted as fundamental to the evolution of political democracy.

American participation in World War I is often called a watershed between the Progressive era and the decade of the 1920s.

In considering the legacy of Progressivism, its exclusionary aspects must be taken into account: its failure to address the problems of black Americans in an era of rising tensions, its suspicion of many new immigrant nationalities, its fears of activist labor and of mass politics in the cities. During the 1920s Progressive activists such as George Norris, Burton K. Wheeler, and Robert M. LaFollette fought on, largely unsuccessfully and without broad popular support, with their reform agendas. These last were among the precursors of the New Deal, whose program partly revived several aspects of the Progressive agenda under the exigencies of the Great Depression.

UNIT X
THE EMERGENCE OF THE UNITED STATES AS A WORLD POWER
(1890-1920)

SIGNIFICANCE AND TEACHING GOALS

■ *MAJOR THEMES*

All issues of American foreign policy in the 20th century—and in the world today's students will live in as adults—have their origins in the emergence of the United States as a major world power in the years just before and after 1900. For decades following the Civil War the United States had been preoccupied with internal affairs and the development of its vast resources at home. Toward the end of the century, however, a combination of economic interests and international developments came together to change the foreign policy outlook of the nation. Within three decades the United States was to enter the Spanish American War, acquire overseas territories in the Caribbean, Central America, and the Pacific, and become deeply engaged in a world war that would leave Europe exhausted—with wrenching consequences to follow—and the United States as a major world power.

How did it all come about? To understand these years, and their long-term significance for the world in which they now live, students must first grasp the 19th-century imperial expansion of the major European nations into Africa and Asia—a scramble for overseas empires in which the United States finally became involved through its annexation of Hawaii and its acquisition of the Spanish territories of Puerto Rico, Guam, and the Philippines, following the Spanish-American War. Students need also to understand the nature of American interventions in the Pacific, Central America, and the Caribbean just before World War I, and the "Open Door"

All issues of American foreign policy in the 20th century have their origins in the emergence of the United States as a major world power in the years just before and after 1900.

Above: Versailles Treaty: Lloyd George, Clemenceau and Wilson in Paris during peace negotiations, 1919.

No less for Americans than for Europeans who went to war that summer, the 20th century began in August 1914.

Woodrow Wilson (1856-1924). President of the United States (1913-1921)

policy for commerce that the nation sought to establish in the Far East. Finally, students need to understand the extraordinary importance of the first World War and of American participation in it, for it was this war that, historically speaking, opened the contemporary era and shaped the modern world. No less for Americans than for Europeans who went to war that summer, the 20th century began in August 1914.

The central historical theme unifying all these events is, of course, **the nation's changing role in world affairs.** Following its massive economic and military intervention in the war, the nation turned to a leading part in shaping the Versailles Treaty and the League of Nations. But Woodrow Wilson's commitments to the Allies and the League were sharply defeated by the Senate at home and following that defeat, the nation's leadership recoiled from any further international obligations requiring collective action in the interests of international security. This defeat of Wilson's plan did not, however, preclude a good number of later initiatives of our own in the international economic and financial sphere, or in political and military matters directly affecting American interests. But only the coming of the Second World War would bring the United States back to a foreign policy of commitment to collective security.

Other significant themes of this period include the **effects of the great war on American political, economic, social, and cultural life, and the deeper repercussions of the war**—rarely perceived at the time—that would shape the rest of the century for most of the world: the revolution in Russia; the seeds of inflation and depression; the origins of Nazism; the disarray and disillusion among the victors that presaged the policy of appeasement; the changing balance of forces in the Far East; in sum, all of the major sources of the Second World War and the subsequent Cold War.

■ ESSENTIAL UNDERSTANDINGS

1. **American expansion at the turn of the century:** the context of European imperialism; American motives; major events and their consequences.

2. **The European causes of World War I** and the reasons behind the entry of the United States.

3. **The impact of the war** upon
    a. the foreign policies of the United States.
    b. the domestic affairs of the United States.
    c. the wider world in the long run.

4. **The process of peacemaking** and the tragedy of Woodrow Wilson.

■ *HABITS OF THE MIND*

As they study the changing role of the United States in the world, students need to develop a special version of **historical empathy: the ability to see ourselves as others see us.** What other peoples believe of us, however true or untrue it may be, is a force to be reckoned with in foreign affairs. To ignore it is to live with illusions and to be repeatedly surprised when others do not share our self-image. The effects of American action, and inaction, on people from Manila to the Caribbean, and from France to Japan are well remembered by them to this day, nearly a century later.

Equally important is the **realization by students that events happening far away can have greater, more lasting effects on American life than many domestic events** featured in the usual textbook account of history. Nothing comparable in importance to the future of the United States happened at home in 1905, when the Japanese humbled the forces of Czarist Russia, or in 1914, when the assassination of Franz Ferdinand at Sarajevo was allowed to precipitate a general European war. The interconnection of 20th-century global events means that the history of the United States must constantly be viewed against the international background.

Few historical events offer better chances for students **to confront and debate complex causation** than the new expansionism of the late 19th century and the Great War of 1914-18. What factors drove the United States to annex the Philippines, halfway across the world, so far from the American sphere of influence mapped by the Monroe Doctrine? What were the causes of the World War in general, and the American entry in particular? How are students to analyze critically—well beyond the simple formulas of textbooks—

Few historical events offer better chances for students to debate complex causation than 19th-century expansionism and the Great War of 1914-18.

137

the failure of the statesmen at to forge a lasting peace? Students must, for example, outgrow the myth of selfish, vengeful Europeans riding roughshod over American altruism and impartiality.

Several other **habits of critical thinking** in the historical mode can be practiced in this unit of United States history. For one example, the implications of geography are ever-present and should be analyzed: the proximity of the Philippines to Japan and China; the proximity of Cuba to the American mainland; the invaluable asset of the Panama Canal; the false sense of insulation from Europe engendered by the breadth of the Atlantic Ocean.

The implications of geography are ever-present and should be analyzed: the proximity of the Philippines to Japan and China; the invaluable asset of the Panama Canal.

Students will also recognize, both in the outbreak of the Spanish-American War and in the coming of World War I, **the importance of chance** in history and, even more surely, **the role of individuals and personal character** in bringing about events: Theodore Roosevelt, Franz Ferdinand, Kaiser Wilhelm II, Lloyd George, Georges Clemenceau, Woodrow Wilson. Students will understand how their intentions mattered but also how their means—and circumstances beyond their control—shaped subsequent events in ways they did not foresee.

Finally, as students proceed to their later study of the origins of World War II, they will see that the "lessons" learned from the failed diplomacy of 1914 were largely inapplicable to the very different international crisis taking shape in the 1930s—insights that will reveal that historical analogy can be treacherous and that **the particularity of each time and place must be respected.**

MAJOR TOPICS IN THE STUDY OF THE EMERGENCE OF THE UNITED STATES AS A WORLD POWER

1. The American Version of Imperialism.
   a. Causes of the new imperialism.
   c. Debating imperialism: the Philippines.
   d. Expansion and intervention in the Far East and Latin America.

2. The United States in World War I.
   a. Causes and responsibilities for the war.

b. Factors in United States' entry in 1917.

c. The military side of World War I.

d. The war's impact on the home front.

e. Postwar peacemaking: American role.

MAJOR TOPICS AND THEIR DEVELOPMENT: ESSENTIAL UNDERSTANDINGS AND RELATED BACKGROUND FOR TEACHERS

■ *AMERICAN VERSION OF IMPERIALISM*

Causes and motives for the new European imperialism of the late 19th century deserve study. They are usually presented as: a) the need for new markets and raw materials for the enormously productive Western industrial economies; b) the desire to achieve national greatness; c) the race for strategic bases and supply routes in the search for a military balance of power; d) the missionary impulse to carry Christianity, medicine, and modernization of all kinds to people who were seen as backward. Students should understand how American versions of these motives combined to bring about American involvement in the Spanish-American War and the annexation of Guam, Hawaii, Samoa, and the Philippines; how they became manifest in Theodore Roosevelt's energetic diplomacy that brought about a police role in the Caribbean, intervention in Central America that led to building the Panama Canal, and new attempts to obtain commercial rights in China; and how the aim of bringing other nations into conformity with American ideals, often called "missionary diplomacy," brought about the intervention in the Mexican Revolution under Woodrow Wilson.

Causes and motives for the new European imperialism of the late 19th century deserve study as do American versions of these motives.

Theodore Roosevelt and the Panama Canal—a triumph for TR's "big stick" imperialism.

Students should explore the particular causes of the Spanish-American War. Here several factors were at work, including the American investment in Cuban sugar, the largest of our overseas investments at that time. A second factor was reaction to the prolonged violence and suffering endured by the Cubans in their struggle for independence, a result of Spain's unwillingness to give up Cuba but inability to place an effective army on the island to subdue the revolt. Last among the precipitating causes was the still-unsolved sinking of the American battleship *Maine* in Havana harbor, and the anti-Spanish feeling whipped up by the popular press. Despite Spanish readiness to meet all American demands and to free Cuba, McKinley did not find a way to stay out of war.

The conduct of the war in Cuba deserves attention, not least because Theodore Roosevelt made himself a national hero at San Juan Hill. More significant was his order, as Assistant Secretary of the Navy, to Commodore Dewey to attack the Spanish fleet in the Philippines. Dewey's victory forced the divisive issue of annexation, which launched one of the most dramatic debates on basic constitutional questions ever held in the Congress. Students should be introduced to the main arguments as well as the main proponents and opponents of the American plunge into imperialism—a move that was to involve the brutal suppression of the Filipino independence movement in fighting that lasted until 1902.

John Hay's Open Door policy of freedom for all nations to trade in China on an equal basis also came directly out of American possession of the Philippine Islands. The Open Door was no more than a formula by which the United States hoped to obtain consent to free and equal trade from the European powers in China and to preserve China as a free market against the increasing ambitions of Japan. But some of the seeds of the Pacific side of World War II were planted in this policy that aimed to restrict Japan.

Two companies of First D.C. Regiment infantry volunteers leave May 14, 1898 for Camp Alger, for the Spanish-American conflict.

American activism in the Far East was accompanied by interventions in the Caribbean and Central America. The Panamanian revolution of 1903 provided the opportunity for the administration of President Theodore Roosevelt to extract the rights to build a canal across the Isthmus of Panama and to take possession of a zone in which Americans were promised virtual sovereignty. Under the Roosevelt Corollary, the United States intervened in the Dominican Republic in 1904 and, under terms of the Platt Amendment, in Cuba in 1906. Under "Dollar Diplomacy" the Taft administration forced Nicaragua to accept an American-dominated government and, under Wilson, U.S. Marines landed in Haiti, the Dominican Republic, and Nicaragua once more. Wilson's well-intentioned use of force in the Mexican Revolution and the ensuing disorders only increased Latin Americans' distrust of the United States.

■ THE UNITED STATES IN WORLD WAR I

The most important expression of the United States' emergence as a world power was its intervention in World War I. Students should understand the European origins of that war, and the events through which it became a world war. They should understand the frightful human and physical losses of World War I, and the bitterness over those losses which made a new war so likely. It is important for students to understand why real neutrality, Wilson's proclaimed policy, was so difficult to maintain and why the needs to trade and to be a player in the outcome led the United States into the war by 1917. Students should also understand the domestic opposition to the war, which fed postwar isolationist sentiment and later peace movements.

The most important expression of the United States' emergence as a world power was its intervention in World War I.

The domestic impact of the war is of signal importance because it prompted new manufacturing and business techniques and, in creating the need to mobilize the nation's resources, expanded central authority in Washington while forging a new relationship between business and government that had large implications for the future. The War Industries Board demonstrated the potential of federal intervention in the economy, as the government sought to protect and extend the rights of organized labor (though at the same time suppressing radical labor leaders and organizations). The war also needs to be understood for its effects on women and African Americans. Both were brought into industrial work to an unprecedented degree, for the war, by cutting off the European immigration that had supplied the labor needs of a rapidly growing industrial economy, expanded employment opportunities and vastly accelerated the movement of rural African Americans from the South into northern cities. Moreover, patriotic African Americans answered the call to arms despite the white political consensus that denied them rights guaranteed by the Constitution. Students should see that the war which started as a patriotic crusade became also the occasion for xenophobia and attacks on freedom of speech and press. Wartime vigilantism, together with hostilities against foreigners, minorities, and labor unions, carried into the 1920s.

Yanks in French Renault tanks advance in Marne region.

141

The Paris Peace Conference needs considerable discussion. It is an excellent way to show the concerns and problems of war-ravaged Europeans, problems which, left unsolved, would bring another world war (with much larger American involvement). It also shows how American attitudes, mostly from the 19th century, discouraged American participation in the work of peace-keeping in the 1920s and 1930s, down to World War II. Students should understand how the constitution of the League of Nations, the Covenant, stood in opposition to American tradition, and also to very practical American national reasons for avoiding international structures and obligations. The people of the United States—this point deserves stressing—removed themselves again, as they had in the past, from European concerns, and sought to believe that those concerns were not their own. Woodrow Wilson struggled in vain against the American mainstream (and his own personal and political weaknesses) in the losing cause of a new, organized internationalism. Americans believed that World War I had added further support for their traditional view that alliances and other long-term foreign commitments were dangerous. It took a second world war to demonstrate that avoiding commitments could be equally dangerous.

The Paris Peace Conference needs considerable discussion to show the concerns and problems which, left unsolved, would bring another world war.

Terms of peace treaty submitted to German delegation, May 1919.

UNIT XI
THE 1920s: A DECADE OF PROS-
PERITY AND PROBLEMS

SIGNIFICANCE AND TEACHING GOALS

■ *MAJOR THEMES*

With the end of World War I the United States embarked on a decade of industrial productivity, economic growth, and national affluence unrivaled anywhere in the world and unprecedented in all of history. This was also a decade of internal tensions rising from the war and of significant social and political change. It would culminate sharply and disastrously in the economic crash of 1929. To understand this decade, students need to dig beneath the popular image of the "roaring Twenties," a carefree "Jazz Age" of boosters, flappers, speakeasies, and "normalcy". By so doing, they will discover a much more complicated—and more interesting—range of currents and counter-currents in American society.

Students should examine the decade for its part in the **continuing transformation of the economy, and the impact of economic changes on social and cultural life.** By the mid-twenties the basic foundations of the nation's modern economy were established. Vast economic expansion created a new level of prosperity for millions of Americans and by mid-decade the nation's economic system was hailed as the new consumer paradise, the triumph of capitalism, American style. But the subsequent depression revealed that the prosperity of the time had not been deeply or broadly enough rooted to withstand the world-wide economic problems of the decade's end. The system was more vulnerable to economic problems abroad than generally realized, and it had few

To understand this decade, students need to dig beneath the popular image of the "roaring Twenties," a carefree "Jazz Age" of boosters, flappers, speakeasies, and "normalcy."

Above: "Chicago" (1923). Oil on canvas, 22 x 17 1/2, by Louis Lozowick.

143

safeguards against abuses and economic fluctuations at home.

In the sphere of **political life, the decade saw both an advance and a retreat for democracy.** The Nineteenth Amendment, ratified in 1920, doubled the electorate by establishing women's right to vote. But the war's unhappy effects on democracy in the United States were deep and harmful, and the opening years of the decade were also marked by the tensions of postwar adjustments, the anti-radical fears aroused by the Bolshevik revolution in Russia, and the various anti-union, anti-black, and anti-immigrant sentiments in the society that found expression in the Red Scare, legislation restraining individual privacy and freedom of expression, the Sacco-Vanzetti trial, the rise of the Ku Klux Klan as a national organization, and federal immigration quotas.

In **foreign affairs, students should follow the theme of America's changing role in the world,** which in this decade was by fits and starts alternately isolationist and interventionist. The great damage done by World War I to the world economy, to European societies, politics, and morale was not well understood, or acknowledged, even by Europeans. It is hardly surprising that Americans should assume that the world had been made safe enough to pursue the foreign policies that seemed appropriate at the moment. But under the surface of this inattentive decade were developing the seeds of World War II, most especially in Germany.

■ **ESSENTIAL UNDERSTANDINGS**

Students' understanding of the 1920s will require insight into the major currents and counter-currents of change in every sphere of activity:

1. **The vast expansion and prosperity of the nation's economy;** effects in widespread prosperity, public confidence, and optimism; changes in American urban and suburban living, increased mobility, and popular culture. By contrast, the postwar downturn in the farming economy as European agriculture recovered and American farmers lost their overseas markets.

2. **Progress and retreats of democracy:** the Nineteenth

The decade saw both an advance and a retreat for democracy. The Nineteenth Amendment established women's right to vote. But the war's unhappy effects were deep and harmful.

Amendment; effects of the war and of fears raised by the Bolshevik Revolution (legislative restrictions on civil liberties, Red Scare, Sacco-Vanzetti trial); effects of revived nativism and racial tensions (rise of Ku Klux Klan, black nationalism, and immigration quotas.)

3. **America's postwar role in the world, alternately isolationist and interventionist:** international policy of nonaggression and arms control (Washington Naval Arms Conference and Kellogg-Briand Treaty); U. S. repayment policy on wartime loans to Allies and its contributions to Germany's economic collapse.

■ *HABITS OF THE MIND*

From the study of the 1920s, whose conventional image is frivolity, students can reinforce many of their healthy habits of historical thought. They will see that the frivolous "Jazz Age" activities so much celebrated by the press, radio, movies, and popular novels were inconsequential to the vast majority of Americans and need to be subordinated to what was really important to most people, then and later. This may help them to take less seriously, and to discern daily reality behind, the over-publicized "happenings" and personalities of their own day. Another good habit would be instinctively to reject the breezy labels pinned to each decade as it passes and to wait for deeper understanding of its undercurrents, of the decade's relation to what happened before and after.

In the 1920s, auto makers advertised their products with photos like this one.

By insisting that the lives of all kinds of people be examined before accepting easy generalizations about an era, students will **realize once more that progress, stagnation, and even regression often co-exist in a given society at a given moment.** This was evident in the uneven distribution of the benefits derived from economic modernization in the 1920s. Tariffs that enriched certain sectors of the economy and their workers resulted in losses for others. Automobiles both enhanced people's lives and brought new problems. Radio and movies offered treasures and trash, as did the popular newspapers and magazines, combining education and miseducation as they do today. It should not be difficult for students to step backward into that time and to see it from several points of view.

By examining the lives of all kinds of people, students will realize that progress, stagnation, even regression often co-exist at a given moment.

The period should **suggest to students that even the best-informed observers may incompletely grasp the realities of their own time.** In the case of the 1920s, these would include the deeper, half-hidden economic, social, and psychological effects of the Great War, its direct links to American farm problems and to the ensuing Depression. The war had indeed changed the world. Students will perceive the danger of ignoring that central fact, but also see how people at the time could not appreciate the depth of that change, as we now can. Harding's appeal to nostalgia, promising a return to the "normalcy" of a simpler past, was understandably attractive to war-weary Americans. But quite apart from the fact that the United States had always grown and changed too fast ever to have had a time of "normalcy" were the unprecedented forces, both happy and unhappy, that postwar leaders might have taken into account. An interdependent global economy ravaged by war was not safe for the nostrums of the previous century, especially as the United States had become a creditor, not a debtor, nation.

To see the world through others' eyes, students should become acquainted with the novels of Fitzgerald, Hemingway, Lewis, and the black writers of the Harlem Renaissance.

Finally, the decade of the 1920s offers a compelling range of imaginative literature, memoirs, and biographies to help students **see that world through other people's eyes.** Without assuming they were typical, students should become acquainted with the literary characters of the "lost generation" in the novels of Fitzgerald and Hemingway, and of small-town America in the novels of Sinclair Lewis. But healthy correctives are also needed, in excerpts from the biographies of real people.

Students should explore the origins and developments of jazz, a black American contribution to the world's music. Attention should also be given to the black writers associated with the Harlem Renaissance: the stories and autobiographies of Zora Neale Hurston and James Weldon Johnson, the poetry of Langston Hughes and Countee Cullen, the political writing of Marcus Garvey. In all of these, students will find powerful examples of the changes and continuities from that day to this in the lives of African Americans.

MAJOR TOPICS IN THE STUDY OF THE 1920s

1. Economic Change and Ramifications.

2.   The Social and Cultural Scene.

3.   Domestic Politics and Foreign Relations.

MAJOR TOPICS AND THEIR DEVELOPMENT: ESSENTIAL UNDERSTANDINGS AND RELATED BACKGROUND FOR TEACHERS

The 1920s were a decade in which Americans established several of the foundations for the nation's modern political economy and culture, while wrestling with important postwar problems in the nation's internal and international affairs.

■ *ECONOMIC CHANGE AND ITS RAMIFICATIONS*

The enormous industrial expansion of the 1920s, caused by more efficient manufacturing methods, innovative advertising, installment buying, new technology and products, brought changes of great significance that have ever since characterized modern American life: clusters of urban skyscrapers in all the major cities; suburbanization; electrification of industry; a communications revolution in which telephones and radios became a part of everyday life; the growth of white collar jobs for women; and, perhaps most important, the advent of automobility. As cars came within reach of the middle class, registered motor vehicles increased from 2.5 million in 1915 to 26 million in 1930. This accelerated the move to the suburbs earlier spurred by trolley lines, created a road building boom and countless new jobs in auto maintenance and tourism, and transformed the uses of leisure time.

No public figure better demonstrated the American faith in voluntary public service and rationally organized free enterprise than Herbert Hoover. As Secretary of Commerce under both Harding and Coolidge, Hoover pressed for action on standardization of manufactured goods, trade associations, regulation of new enterprises such as radio and airlines, conservation of resources, and control of pollution. Some historians credit him with envisaging a national economic system of open information, business cooperation, and coordination to mitigate the harsher, more wasteful effects of laissez-faire. Hoover's election as president in 1928 marked the high-water mark of the decade's prosperity and optimism.

The enormous industrial expansion of the 1920s brought changes of great significance that have ever since characterized modern American life.

*Herbert Clark Hoover
(1874-1964)
President of the United States
(1929-1933)*

147

Students need to understand, however, that large parts of the United States were left outside of this era of opportunity and advancement. The real income of farmers and many workers actually declined from their wartime levels. African Americans, American Indians, and Mexican Americans benefitted hardly at all, and one-third of the American people lived in poverty as late as 1929, according to national income statistics.

The onset of the Great Depression after 1929 not only meant a tragic interruption of economic security for millions of Americans but also demonstrated that the economic system of the 1920s had serious weaknesses. Farmers' purchasing power never recovered from the post-war downturn in food prices, brought on by the recovery of European agriculture following the war and the resulting market competition with American farm products. Although generous by pre-war standards, industrial wages were modest compared with those of post-World War II and the purchasing power of workers was weakened by periodic layoffs and technological unemployment. European markets for American exports were limited, and the rising flood of speculation on Wall Street diverted funds from new productive investment.

■ THE SOCIAL AND CULTURAL SCENE: PROGRESS AND CONFLICT

For many Americans the 1920s were a confident time of rising standards of living and even higher expectations for the future. A great many Americans felt that their future was opening into a warless world and that they themselves could decide the courses of their lives. For them, the era was carefree in this sense—not, as popular books were to relate, in a sense of wild abandon.

Here the teacher must add that all that glittered was not reality. The foundations of modern popular culture were indeed laid, in the sense of liberation from Victorian ways, even of encouragement of eccentric behavior that could turn into faddism, of glorification of spectator sports, and of countless heroes who did the new and difficult, such as flying a monoplane across the Atlantic or swimming the English Channel. Most Americans, however, lived far more staid

Charles Lindbergh, who flew solo across the Atlantic, in 1927.

For many Americans the 1920s were a confident time of rising standards of living and even higher expectations for the future.

lives, had nothing to do with the flapper culture, and spent their years in work and schooling and hope, as would the generations yet to come.

The new age of science and technology, urban life, and increased geographical mobility was not universally welcomed, and students need to study the cultural and political clashes of the 1920s because their echoes are still heard today and because they indicate how Americans have tried to work out their differences. Important among these was the Scopes trial in 1925 over the teaching of evolutionary theory in public schools, which seemed to pit urban modernism against rural traditionalism. Important also was the victory of prohibition (along with the profits of organized crime in bootlegging alcohol).

This era may also be interpreted as a time in which the recent war's threat to democracy had itself created a counter-threat. Certainly some of the decade's excesses arose from the war or events that surrounded it, such as anti-radical fears inspired by the Bolshevik revolution in Russia, resulting in the Red Scare. The suspicions aroused by the Sacco-Vanzetti trial; the second rise to prominence of the Ku Klux Klan, not only in the South, but in the Midwest and West as well; the imposition of federal immigration quotas that especially restricted the inflow of Asians and southern and eastern Europeans: all these were new expressions of American nativism, especially strong in groups and classes feeling threatened by economic or social change. The latter had appeared nearly a century earlier, at the time of Irish immigration after the potato famine. The huge wave of immigration after 1880 had continued through the Progressive era and was halted only by American entrance into the World War. It gave indication of beginning again in the early 1920s. This prospect, together with the inner migrations of black Americans, revived nativism and racial tension throughout the country.

The rise of the NAACP as a reform organization dedicated to the fuller realization of American democracy can be counterposed against these renewed racial tensions. So too can the impact of Marcus Garvey and the ideology of black nationalism, which can be studied profitably alongside the Harlem Renaissance as an alternate form of black aspiration.

The Passion of Sacco and Vanzetti as painted by Ben Shahn.

This era may also be interpreted as a time in which the recent war's threat to democracy had itself created a counter-threat.

■ DOMESTIC POLITICS AND FOREIGN RELATIONS IN THE 1920s

The cultural, racial, and ethnic conflicts just summarized occurred in an era of generally conservative politics, when political leaders in the Harding and Coolidge administrations were mainly concerned with promoting industrial, commercial, and financial interests as the best way to prosperity for all. "The business of America is business," were Coolidge's oft-quoted words. The consensus of the press and of political leaders, whether Republicans or Democrats, was that the American capitalist system was the best hope for peace and progress at home and abroad. Overwhelming electoral victories by Coolidge in 1924 and Hoover in 1928 demonstrated that the voting public agreed.

Disillusioned with war and wary of entangling commitments, the nation turned to isolationism but also to a policy of "moral cooperation" in arms control.

Disillusioned with the outcomes of the war, and wary of commitments that could entangle the nation in another conflict, the public supported both a return to isolationism and a foreign policy of "moral cooperation" in the cause of international arms control. The Washington Naval Arms Conference of 1921 is important because it averted a naval-arms race and actually reduced battleship tonnage of the major powers—the first significant arms limitation agreement in history. The Kellogg-Briand Treaty of 1928 pledged 62 nations to outlaw war and aggression; however, lacking any enforcement mechanisms, it did not avert the rise of militarism in the 1930s. More important was the isolationist sentiment that led to the United States' insistence that its wartime allies repay their huge wartime loans while at the same time making such repayment more difficult by maintaining the high tariff barriers that limited the ability of the Allies to earn American dollars. Such policies contributed to the economic collapse of Germany in the 1920s, which in turn contributed to the rise of Hitler and Nazism.

UNIT XII
THE DEPRESSION AND
THE NEW DEAL (1929-1941)

SIGNIFICANCE AND TEACHING GOALS

■ *Major Themes*

The Depression that began in 1929 and lasted until World War II deserves careful study because it was the greatest economic crisis in American history and because it wrought deep changes in people's attitudes toward government's responsibilities, gave new rights to organized labor, and set in place legislation that helped shape modern American capitalism. Students can benefit from studying the responses of government to massive economic dislocation by comparing the American case to that of Germany, where a dictator came to power who led the nation not to recovery but to ruin.

Two major themes run through this twelve-year period. The first is **the struggle to maintain and to extend political democracy.** The Great Depression, born of economic dislocations brought on by World War I, the worldwide economic problems of the 1920s, and governments' failure to confront them, shook the institutions of political democracy as never before. The Weimar Republic in Germany could not survive the strain, with terrible consequences for much of the rest of the world. By 1932 some Americans expected revolution and dictatorship, but instead the following years saw the nation take vigorous, lawful action to meet the economic, social, and psychological crisis. What factors made it possible for democracy to survive in the United States, Britain, and elsewhere in Europe? What changes and costs had to be accepted in order that democratic leaders might restore a measure of

The Depression that began in 1929 was the greatest economic crisis in American history and set in place legislation that helped shape modern American capitalism.

Above: Bread line during the Depression.

151

public confidence in self-government and free enterprise?

The second major theme must be the effect of the Great Depression on people's lives, **how disaster in the economic sphere of life brought with it deep social and personal problems, and new strains of thought and culture**. This was, after all, one of the great shaping experiences of American history, ranking with the Revolution, the Civil War, and the Second World War, for it endowed three generations with memories and values never to be erased, and altered our central political and economic institutions in ways that have lasted to the present. The Depression, far more than the Progressive era, was a time of substantial change in the American political economy, with repercussions that reached into almost every American home.

The Great Depression was one of the major shaping experiences of American history, ranking with the Revolution, the Civil War, and the Second World War.

Students will face once more the ever-challenging question of cause. What brought the Depression about, and what forces made it so long and severe, as contrasted to depressions and recessions experienced before and since? A clear focus on causes is indispensable to students. Otherwise they will have little chance of understanding the New Deal's attempted cures and no way to evaluate the overall approach of the Roosevelt administration to the crisis. Only by relating likely causes and attempted cures will students also acquire some bases for evaluating what is said (or not said) in current debates over economic problems afflicting the United States.

Finally, no study of the Depression and New Deal can ignore their effects on American foreign policy as the war clouds darkened over the world of the 1930s. Although democracies survived economic and social turmoil in Britain, France, and the United States, they were greatly distracted by domestic crises, weakened and unable to rebuild effective means of collective security against aggression.

■ ESSENTIAL UNDERSTANDINGS

1. **The causes of the Great Depression,** of its severity and duration.

2. **Its effects upon people and society,** upon culture, ideas, and politics.

3. **The New Deal** as response to the causes of economic crisis.

4. **Successes, failures, and overall significance of the New Deal** to the society and politics of the United States.

■ *HABITS OF THE MIND*

Whatever the historical event or period, students' chances to comprehend its essential facts and concepts usually depend upon their personal engagement in the questions, the drama, or the people on the scene. Of all the historical habits of mind we seek to develop, **empathy—the ability to see the past as it was lived and thought about by people at the time—is perhaps the surest path to engagement and thereby to acquiring other habits of critical thought and perspective.** Nowhere is historical empathy more vital than in studying the Great Depression. But it is no longer easy for Americans to sense the deep despair that arose from the near collapse of the American economy beginning with the stockmarket crash of 1929. People who remember the Depression are now in their late sixties, seventies, and eighties, and no longer have school-age children. Even the biographies and memoirs only partly convey the feelings of that time. Nor do they clearly show how much it meant to have a new American president in 1933, a charismatic, ebullient leader who was confident and eager to take action. Teachers should use every resource at hand—novels, letters, film, photographs, and eyewitnesses—to convey the bewilderment, suffering, and fear of the 1930s. At the same time, students will find in the popular culture of the period—radio, movies, song, and dance—sources and signs of that generation's resilience and humor, even a certain confidence in long-run improvement.

Once engaged, students may move on to other perspectives and historical insights. How best may the causes of the Depression be analyzed? How far back in time and how far across the world should they look? The topic is ideal for students to learn basic concepts from the discipline of economics in a dramatic historical context. Sociology and psychology have contributions to make as well; social classes, ethnic and racial groups, the young and the old, women and

Franklin D. Roosevelt addressing the nation over the radio in one of his "fireside chats."

Teachers should use every resource at hand—novels, letters, film, photographs, and eyewitnesses—to convey the bewilderment, suffering, and fear of the 1930s.

153

men—all had different experiences of the Depression and the New Deal. Inclusiveness is all-important to understanding that time.

Very few students are without fears, or plans, or aspirations that have to do with earning money and building careers. The significance of the economic sphere to their own lives will be evident, but so also should be the differences between American problems then and now. Discussing them will open up **the habit of looking for both change and continuity in human life.** It will also force students to confront the difficulty of choosing which lessons and cures from the past continue to be relevant and which may not. One lesson, always relevant, to be learned again from the Depression and the New Deal is **that amelioration of the human condition is immensely difficult, that the voices of despair and resignation will resound repeatedly, but that improvement has nonetheless been achieved**, that both the endurance and strivings of individuals can make a difference.

The era of the Great Depression and the New Deal is close enough to be still subject to intense partisan disagreement in our political debates. In coming to their own evaluation of the New Deal—and of the larger question of the proper relationship between government and business—students need **to cultivate the ability to distinguish between facts and assertions, between evidence and opinion.**

In coming to their own evaluation of the New Deal students need to cultivate the ability to distinguish between facts and assertions, between evidence and opinion.

MAJOR TOPICS IN THE STUDY OF THE DEPRESSION AND THE NEW DEAL, 1929-41

1. Origins of the Great Depression.
   a. Economic dislocations of World War I.
   b. Governmental policies of the 1920s.
   c. The stock market Crash of '29.

2. Effects of the Depression on people and society.

3. The New Deal: Major approaches and programs.

4. Evaluation of the New Deal
   a. Successes and failures.
   b. The continuing debate.

MAJOR TOPICS AND THEIR DEVELOPMENT: ESSENTIAL UNDERSTANDINGS AND RELATED BACKGROUND FOR TEACHERS

■ *ORIGINS OF THE GREAT DEPRESSION*

It is important for students to understand the special severity of the Great Depression, which cut much deeper into the social fabric and lasted much longer than any of the other economic dislocations that had preceded it reaching back to 1819; and it is important for them to understand some of the main explanations of its origins, about which historians still disagree. At the very least, students should know of the great impact of World War I on the global economy, and on that of the United States in particular. Thus they will have a base from which to compare and contrast the economic consequences of the two world wars, and to see the sharp contrasts in American postwar economic policies of the 1920s and the 1940s—a case of historical lessons very well learned, to everyone's benefit, at home and abroad.

Among the first war's early economic legacies was the American farm depression, set off when postwar food prices plummeted as production resumed in war-torn countries. War-inflated prices for all U.S. goods fell and Europe, deeply in debt, tried to limit imports of all kinds by tariffs and quotas. Rounds of recriminations over war debts, the mirage of reparations, the uncertainties of American loans and rising American tariffs, all contributed to clogging international trade.

Policies of governments in Europe and the United States in the 1920s helped bring depression and, after 1929, helped to deepen and prolong it. Tariffs rose, quotas sank, American loans were cut off, further shrinking American markets overseas. Behind the Crash of '29 on Wall Street also lay excessive speculation and abuses left unregulated; but most important was the fact that by 1929 securities prices far outstripped their earning power. Given the fever of speculators, large and small, and reckless borrowing without collateral, an orderly "adjustment" downward was not possible. Panic brought collapse and cold fear throughout the business community. Retrenchment, closings, and layoffs were as hasty as expan-

Policies of governments in Europe and the United States in the 1920s helped bring depression and, after 1929, helped to deepen and prolong it.

155

sion had earlier been.

Students should learn about President Hoover's attempts to use the power of the federal government to deal with economic crisis (public works, the Reconstruction Finance Corporation, and the Federal Home Loan Bank) but also about his deeply held commitment to local voluntarism and self-reliance and his fear of a large federal bureaucracy that limited how much he was willing to do. He was also convinced that the problems were global and needed action on an international scale.

■ EFFECTS OF THE DEPRESSION

As suggested above, every effort should be made to place students in the shoes of all kinds of Americans in the Depression years. Readings, photos, and eyewitnesses may communicate to students what it meant for families in cities and in the country to see their economic livelihoods threatened and disappear. In the cities, jobs ended and people did not know what to do, where to go. In the country, the cash crops that had driven American agriculture ever since it had become a business in the Civil War era no longer brought cash; farmers did not feel so abandoned as did city dwellers, because they could rely on garden plots and farm animals, but they too were badly disheartened, their lives disarranged. And because many farmers had mortgaged their farms heavily (to expand production for wartime prices), they suffered widespread foreclosures. Dust storms, too, were partly a price of overcultivation. On the human effects of the Depression, Steinbeck's The Grapes of Wrath provides scenes never to be forgotten as do the photographs of Dorothea Lange and Walker Evans.

A mother and child on the road to California, from a classic photograph by Dorothea Lange.

Roosevelt's success in restoring people's faith in constitutional government and free enterprise defeated those who sought a revolutionary end to the system.

Roosevelt's landslide victories of 1932 and 1936 were accomplished through a new coalition of urban workers and African Americans, together with the still traditionally solid white South that would keep the Republicans out of the White House until 1953. Roosevelt's success in restoring people's faith in constitutional government and free enterprise also defeated those who sought a revolutionary end to the system. Prophets of direct action and drastic economic change were many, ranging from American Nazis to Louisiana's fiery populist Governor Huey Long to the Communist Party USA. Each enjoyed local successes and newsworthy moments, but no extremist group, whether of the right or left, won a broad national following even in the depths of the Depression. Still, students will gain valuable insights into the clashing world ideologies of the 1930s by reviewing their American versions.

Students will also be engaged by the lively popular culture of the Depression years. This was the golden age of radio and the downtown movie palace. Broadcasts and films, which students should hear and see for themselves, both depicted the realities of life and offered endless modes of amusement and escape. So did a veritable industry of song and dance, embracing jazz, the blues, Tin Pan Alley, and the new Swing era of big bands. Folk and country music often depicted the harsher side of Depression life, as did proletarian and populist novels and plays, and the work of many painters and photographers.

■ THE NEW DEAL

To those Americans who had feared or hoped for salvation-by-dictatorship Franklin Roosevelt's New Deal seemed moderate indeed. And it was, in most respects. Students should see it first through Roosevelt's pragmatic approach to providing relief and stimulating a recovery of the economy, at the heart of which was the idea that he might superimpose relief measures on the capitalist system, leaving free enterprise and the profit motive undisturbed. It is important to describe the relief and recovery efforts called forth as the unemployment rate reached 25 percent in 1933: greater federal control over banking, the stock market, and financial transactions; the federal government as the employer of the last resort through programs such as the Public Works Administration and Civil Works Administration; support for farmers and the beginning of crop subsidies; and guarantees of labor's right to bargain collectively. Among the so-called second New Deal programs created in 1935 and after, those particularly deserving of study because of their long-range impact are the Works Progress Administration—the first massive attempt to deal with unemployment; the rescue of the elderly by Social Security; minimum wage legislation; and rural electrification (the REA) that brought cheap electricity to remote

Students will gain valuable insights into the clashing world ideologies of the 1930s by reviewing their American versions.

157

The Roosevelt program aimed at restoring public confidence in banks and the stock market by opening new markets for consumer goods and reviving international trade.

areas and lightened the bleak lives of so many farm families. Students will readily see that the main thrust of the New Deal was to restore and to increase the purchasing power of as many Americans as possible: farmers, workers, and the elderly. In addition to stimulating the economy, the Roosevelt program aimed at restoring public confidence in banks and the stock market by deposit insurance and securities regulation; at opening new markets for consumer goods (by rural electrification, for example); and at reviving international trade.

■ EVALUATION OF THE NEW DEAL

The New Deal alone cannot be credited with bringing the United States out of the Depression; only World War II restored full employment and allowed the nation to emerge into a new era of prosperity. But Roosevelt achieved two of his central goals. Like the Progressives, and his distant cousin Theodore Roosevelt, he believed that capitalism could be saved only by reforming itself. The New Deal did much of that. Secondly, Roosevelt proved that the answer to economic dislocation was not an abandonment of political democracy. Once again, students will appreciate these accomplishments only by grasping for themselves the despair people felt in 1932, their slipping faith in both free enterprise and free government.

Mrs. Roosevelt visits children in Puerto Rico in 1934.

As for specific instances of success and shortcomings, teachers will not lack for a broad range of examples. Against the evident successes of New Deal programs such as Social Security, the Federal Deposit Insurance Corporation, the Civilian Conservation Corps, the Fair Labor Standards Act and the like, critics point out the contradictory and wasteful farm programs, the growth of the federal bureaucracy, the muddle of the NRA, and the explosion in government spending. Roosevelt's attempt to "pack" the Supreme Court in 1937 was widely condemned as dictatorial. The experience of America's minorities under the New Deal also requires attention, including the aid to African Americans, who continued to suffer discrimination in all parts of the country; the repatriation of thousands of Mexican Americans; and the new federal Indian policy that reversed the land policy established by the Dawes Act in 1887 and recognized the importance of Indian culture, language, and ritual.

For lively portrayals of the issues as they appeared at the time, students should examine the platforms and debates of the Republican and Democratic parties in the presidential campaigns of 1936, 1940, and 1944. Roosevelt put together a new coalition of Democratic voters from the lower middle class, the industrial working classes, farmers, and African Americans (who had earlier tended to vote Republican, in those locales where they could vote at all). In this, he was much aided by the initiatives and activities of his wife Eleanor, who took up the causes of women, children, the poor, and the ill; and of equal rights for African Americans and American Indians. Roosevelt appointed the first woman to a cabinet post, Frances Perkins as Secretary of Labor, and more than a hundred women to senior administrative positions. Among the latter was Mary McLeod Bethune who, along with Robert Weaver, was among the leading spirits of the "black cabinet," composed of some fifty African Americans who served in the Roosevelt administrative agencies.

The New Deal continues to be the subject of debate in American political campaigns. From the mid-1930s to the present, critics on the right have freely used words like "socialistic" and "communistic," but even if all of the New Deal initiatives had passed and survived, the outcome could hardly be described even as a "middle way" as the world understands the term. The balance of power shifted only slightly away from capital to labor, from laissez-faire to regulation, as subsequent developments have repeatedly proved. Liberal critics contend that the New Deal did too little to raise blacks, migrant workers, the urban poor, and many farmers above the poverty level because it failed to confront structural problems in the American economic system. Critics on the far left deny that any middle ground was, or is, possible between laissez-faire, free-market capitalism and a socialized command economy. Before taking sides, students should recognize their responsibility to seek out and weigh the evidence available, and to measure the actual results of major economic choices, not only those made by government, but by the business world itself since most significant choices remained in business hands.

Students will recognize that current debates are but new variations of quarrels that go back before 1900 over the

Mary McLeod Bethune

Roosevelt appointed the first woman to a cabinet post and more than a hundred women to senior administrative positions, among them Mary McLeod Bethune.

proper role of government in business and of business in government. It should not escape their notice that behind the often lively disputes, both liberals and conservatives, labor and business consider certain aspects of the New Deal to be relevant to our time—conservation, tax reform, securities regulation, youth programs, the re-building of long-neglected roads, bridges, and other public facilities; in sum, long-term investment for the future rather than instant winnings for the moment, a platform upon which both liberals and conservatives can meet.

UNIT XIII
WORLD WAR II AND THE COLD WAR (1939-1961)

SIGNIFICANCE AND TEACHING GOALS

■ *MAJOR THEMES*

The German invasion of Poland in September 1939 led to the most destructive war in human annals, a war in which the United States joined with full mobilization after the Japanese attack on Pearl Harbor on December 7, 1941. The first major question to explore is the same as it would be in the national history courses of any country caught up in that dreadful conflict: how did it all happen? **The causes of World War II** must be traced through the prior actions—and inactions—of all the major powers of Europe, the Soviet Union, China, Japan, and the United States as well. Students need at least a rudimentary knowledge of European and Asian history in the interwar period, especially the rise of Fascism and Communism in Europe and the expansionist drive of Japan in Asia.

The second major topic is **the course and conduct of the war** itself. Military history has long been out of favor in our schools and colleges. Land, sea, and air actions, campaigns and turning points are virtually ignored in favor of events on the home front and the changes—economic, social, cultural, political—wrought by war upon societies. For most wars, this is an intellectual and pedagogical error, for the length, the course, and the character of combat strongly affect what changes war will bring, and how extensive they will be. It is as true of the Second World War as it was of the First.

These two topics, the causes and the course of the war,

The German invasion of Poland in September 1939 led to the most destructive war in human annals.

Above: The conference of the leaders of the three Allied Powers: Churchill, Roosevelt, and Stalin among their military advisors.

Production for war ended the Great Depression; the American economy grew by leaps and bounds, and unemployment virtually disappeared.

provide students important insights into **the nation's changing role in the world**—one of the major themes in the study of United States history. A second major theme to follow is **the enormous impact of World War II on the American home front.** Production for war ended the Great Depression; the American economy grew by leaps and bounds, and unemployment virtually disappeared; women took the places of the absent men; the continuing quest for equality by African Americans obtained a Fair Employment Practices Commission in 1941, but they failed to avoid discrimination in the armed forces, where racial segregation was still the order of the day. Overall, the war provided the American economy a worldwide near-monopoly through the late 1940s and 1950s; a windfall at the time, it encouraged practices that would weaken our competitiveness in the last third of the century.

The postwar period is again best understood in terms of these same two major themes of United States history: **the nation's changing role in international affairs** and **the transformation of the nation's economy** and its effects on **social and cultural developments at home.** Regarding the first of these themes, students should understand the state of the world following World War II, the wartime planning for peace, the creation of the United Nations, the new American policy of containment of militant international communism, and the Cold War—its origins, development, and consequences through the Truman and Eisenhower administrations. Students should be aware of the great contrasts between the postwar foreign policies of the United States after World War I and those following World War II such as the Marshall Plan, debt relief, and NATO. Many, though not all, of the differences can be traced to the pressures of the Cold War. Students should also be aware of the distinctions between the Cold War in Europe and its manifestations in Asia.

Finally, the two decades from 1939 to 1961 deserve study for the **economic transformations continuing at home, and the deep social and cultural changes that the war had either originated or hurried along.** Like the 1920s, the period after World War II saw widespread alterations of human expectations. New technologies, new products, new amusements, and new patterns of production and consumption emerged. Unlike the 1920s, prosperity was more widely enjoyed and the good times lasted. Students should be knowledgeable enough to debate the reasons for this contrast, and also to recognize the continuing presence of poverty in sectors of the population, most obvious in rural areas and among migrant laborers, African Americans, and other minority groups.

■ ESSENTIAL UNDERSTANDINGS

1. **The origins of World War II** in Europe and Asia; the sources of aggression and appeasement; the debates over responsibilities for war.

2. **The main stages and turning points** in the European and Asian theaters of war; plans, weapons, and actions behind the turning-points.

3. **World War II on the American home-front;** economic and social changes; internment of Japanese Americans.

4. **Major agreements and alliances for peace, their motivations, terms, and their consequences:** the Tehran, Yalta, and Potsdam agreements; the formation of the United Nations; the Truman Doctrine, Marshall Plan, Berlin airlift, and NATO.

5. **Origins and conduct of the Cold War;** the rejection of isolationism and the United States as superpower.

6. **Domestic developments in the postwar era;** change and continuity in the society and its culture; the impact and limits of prosperity; campaigns for women's and minorities' rights.

■ HABITS OF THE MIND

If the main use of history to the citizen is the **nurture of political wisdom,** then no era puts more sharply into perspective the long human struggle for liberty and decency, and what that struggle has cost, than World War II and the Cold War. Students should readily see the significance to their own lives of the defeat of Nazism in Germany and of militarism in Japan.

No era puts more sharply into perspective the long human struggle for liberty and decency, and what that struggle has cost, than World War II and the Cold War.

The democracies were not blameless for the rise of either movement—a vital lesson in itself about facing the consequences of one's actions—but war seemed the only way to reopen the world's path to a future in which people could hope for justice.

In studying the Second World War, **students should examine how the consequences of human aims are shaped by the means used to carry them out.** Nazi Germany could probably not have been defeated, or soon enough, without the Soviet Union's full partnership. The price was to be Soviet military and economic control of most of Eastern and Central Europe. Only half a century later, after the enormous expenditures, human and material, of the Cold War, are paths reopening to self-determination and political democracy in the former Soviet spheres. In examining the retreat of Soviet power in Eastern Europe and steps to liberalize the Soviet regime itself, students wise in history should be ready to consider new obstacles to world peace and progress, and to observe that as always we must live with unfinished business and perilous uncertainties.

Students' appreciation for the complexity of historical cause will be enhanced by analyzing the forces behind Axis aggression and the complex sources of passivity among the Western democracies. They should see why the easy condemnation of "appeasement" is far too simple and of little help to political intelligence. In studying the military history of the war, they will perceive the fascinating interplay between the individual and the new technologies of warfare, and grasp the abiding, and probably increasing, importance of the human being on the scene, making vital choices in what Churchill called "the wizard war," and then dealing with the consequences. Democratic citizens also need to know how often the best of military plans and preparations are undone by the pressures and confusions of combat, how often the turning points are unpredictable and arise out of error, chance, unforeseen conditions, or (again) out of remarkable individual acts.

Students' appreciation for the complexity of historical cause will be enhanced by analyzing the forces behind Axis aggression and the passivity among the Western democracies.

Finally, the human experiences of the Second World War should powerfully **exercise students' talent for historical empathy.** That era of death and destruction, of terror, torture, surrender, resistance, folly, heroism, and daily endurance, has an entire generation of survivors from whom students can learn a more complicated reality than popular movies portray. In this regard, American students are especially fortunate because so many survivors found their way over here, from Nanking and Hiroshima as well as from the Nazis' first concentration camps, from the bombings of Rotterdam, London, Berlin, and Dresden, from the fighting at Leningrad, Anzio, and the Bulge, and from the hardly imaginable scenes of the Holocaust.

MAJOR TOPICS IN THE STUDY OF WORLD WAR II AND THE COLD WAR

1. The Origins of World War II.
    a. The rise of Fascism and Nazism.
    b. Militarism and imperialism in Japan.
    c. Aggression and appeasement.
    d. The American entry into war.

2. World War II: The Military Side.
    a. Period of intense danger.
    b. The turnaround.
    c. The elements of victory.

3. World War II on the American Home Front.
    a. Economic changes and effects.
    b. Social changes.
    c. Internment of Japanese-Americans.

4. Wartime Planning for Postwar International Cooperation and Peace.
    a. Atlantic Charter
    b. Bretton Woods Conference
    c. Tehran and Yalta agreements

5. The United States as a Superpower.
    a. Origins of the Cold War.
    b. Superpower competition in Europe and Asia.

6. The Immediate Postwar Era.
    a. Postwar prosperity
    b. Anti-Communism at home.
    c. The Truman and Eisenhower years.

The human experiences of the Second World War should powerfully exercise students' talent for historical empathy.

These gaunt survivors of the Nazi concentration camp at Evensee, Austria, greeted their liberators from the U.S. Third Army on May 7, 1945.

MAJOR TOPICS AND THEIR DEVELOPMENT: ESSENTIAL UNDERSTANDINGS AND RELATED BACKGROUND FOR TEACHERS

■ *THE ORIGINS OF WORLD WAR II*

Students should review the outcome and effects of World War I on Italy and Germany to see the reasons for their turn to Fascism and Nazism. Students should grasp some of the main principles of Nazi ideology: in particular, racism, militarism, expansionism, totalitarianism under a single leader, the rejection of religion, democracy, and the equality and dignity of the individual. They should understand the weaknesses and failures of the Weimar Republic, especially its inability to counter the destructive effects of inflation and depression—an object lesson of liberal democracy under siege, with many of its people in despair.

Students should understand the weaknesses and failures of the Weimar Republic, an object lesson of liberal democracy under siege.

Likewise, students need to see the forces behind the rise in Japan of military expansionism. They should not neglect Japanese ill-feeling toward the United States, dating back to the Open Door, to our annexation of the Philippines, and to our exclusion of Japanese emigrants. Dating back to the Paris peace conference were quarrels and mutual incomprehension among the British, French, and American allies of the first war, who were further pulled apart and distracted by the worsening economic problems of the 1920s and 1930s. Depression forced their attentions inward, so that Italian and German aggression was met by avoidance of action. Students should have examined the sources of British and French appeasement in their world history courses. And they should understand that our former allies were hardly encouraged by the strident American neutralism of the 1930s. Despite rising outrage over Nazi and Fascist behavior, despite the fall of France and the siege of Britain, it took the Japanese attack on Pearl Harbor to send the United States to war.

General Douglas MacArthur wades ashore at Leyte, P.I. during initial landings, Oct. 1944, during World War II.

■ *WORLD WAR II: THE MILITARY SIDE*

It is difficult for teachers to convey briefly to students the American military experience from 1941 to 1945. The best approach, perhaps, is not to divide World War II into theaters, Europe and the Pacific, but into periods, of which there were three that applied to both theaters. First was the period of intense danger (1939-42), when it looked as if the Axis powers might win. In the second period (1943-44) both theaters of war began to turn around. American forces in the Atlantic were winning the war against Nazi submarines, and they entered the Continent with the invasion of France in June 1944. On the German-Russian front, the turnaround came with the German defeat at Stalingrad and the increasingly powerful Russian offensive all along the Eastern front. In the Far East it was the American movement north from Australia and the navy's campaigns to the west of Hawaii, both converging on the forces of Japan. In the war's third period, 1944-45, came victory in both theaters but also, as became evident shortly after V-E Day, the falling out of the British and the Americans with the Russians. Attention should be given to the development of the atomic bomb and the controversy over its use in 1945.

In the war's third period, 1944-45, came victory in both theaters but also the falling out of the British and the Americans with the Russians.

■ WORLD WAR II ON THE AMERICAN HOME FRONT

In studying the war on the home front, students should examine the war's effects on the economy. They should recognize that the war ended the Depression in the United States, created nearly full employment, but also greatly distorted the balance and workings of the economy, as large-scale war is bound to do. They should also strive to understand some of the most important human and social events and changes of these years: a) the internment of Japanese-Americans in 1942 and the debate over its necessity; b) the attempts of African Americans to obtain desegregation of the armed forces and the end of discriminatory hiring; c) the massive influx of women into previously male job roles; d) the large shifts in population to war-production centers.

Finally, students should recognize the vast expansion of governmental power that war also brings, with general public acceptance. In this era, the habits of hot war carried over into cold war. The powers of the President were extended, especially in military and foreign affairs, while those of Congress were weakened; the United States maintained a permanent, large-scale military establishment closely linked to the arms industries, as well as a worldwide network of agencies for information, espionage, and covert action.

"Catship Burner," Wilmington, California, 1943. Painting by Edna Reindel. (Woman factory worker during WWII.)

■ WARTIME PLANNING FOR PEACE

Even during the conduct of the war, allied leaders had initiated planning for postwar international cooperation and peace. Students should become acquainted with these major initiatives and the purposes that inspired them: Roosevelt's broad goals of the "Four Freedoms," proclaimed in the Atlantic Charter drawn up by Roosevelt and Churchill; the 1944 Bretton Woods Conference to develop a plan for stabilizing postwar international monetary transactions; and the formation of the United Nations in June 1945. Students should also examine the wartime meetings of Roosevelt, Stalin, and Churchill at Tehran (1943) and Yalta (1945) in relation to Roosevelt's peacetime ends: to maintain the Anglo-American alliance and to insure international security. His success, Roosevelt perceived, depended upon guarantees for Soviet security in Europe and Asia—a Germany stripped of power to make war, a Soviet sphere of influence on its western borders, from Poland south to Turkey and Greece, and territories and facilities in North Korea, Manchuria, and outer Mongolia. Five months later, in the Potsdam conference between Truman and Stalin, tensions between the Soviet Union and the United States had increased to the point no common ground could be found, and each settled for influence in the territories it then held.

Even during the conduct of the war, allied leaders had initiated planning for postwar international cooperation and peace.

■ THE UNITED STATES AS A SUPERPOWER

American isolationism had, in practice, ended with Roosevelt's destroyer deal to Britain in 1940 and Lend-Lease in 1941, prior to Pearl Harbor. Through the war years, bipartisan support grew for reversing the policies of post-World War I; the United Nations was shaped by American leadership and won Senate approval before the defeat of Japan. The war over, the reversal continued. Students should see the Marshall Plan, for example, as an act of enlightened self-interest, an investment to aid war-torn allies and democracies in danger, but also to promote our export trade and to avoid unemployment and another farm depression like that of the 1920s. Stalinism was being exported to Eastern and Central Europe, where rival parties were everywhere crushed by the massive presence of the Red Army after 1945. As large Communist parties also pressed for power in Western Europe, the continent seemed in danger of falling to a second totalitarian conquest. In response, the United States launched its containment policy, supported by moderate and liberal Democrats and Republicans in a centrist bipartisan coalition that turned back the remaining domestic impulses toward isolationism.

The Cold War between the Soviet Union and the United States so influenced our domestic politics, the conduct of foreign affairs, and the role of the government in the economy after 1945 that it is obligatory for students to examine the debate over its origins and the forces behind its continuation into the late 20th century. They should understand how the American and European antipathy to Leninist-Stalinism predated 1945, and was rooted in the messianic nature of Soviet Communism during the interwar years, in the horror of Stalin's collectivization of agriculture, in the great purges of the 1930s, the Nazi-Soviet pacts, and the betrayal of the Warsaw uprising of 1944. Students should also consider the Soviet Union's goals following World War II. Its catastrophic losses in the war and fear of rapid German recovery were factors in Soviet demands for a sphere of influence on its western borders, achieved through the establishment of governments under Soviet military and political control. Students should also know how the United States' policy of containment was successfully conducted in Europe: the Truman Doctrine; the Marshall Plan; the Berlin airlift; NATO and the maintenance of American forces in Europe under what was called the nuclear "balance of terror." They should also recognize that the American anti-Communist strategy of containment in Asia confronted very different circumstances and would involve the United States in the bloody, costly wars of Korea and Vietnam.

The Berlin Airlift, 1948-49, brought supplies to the blockaded city of West Berlin.

The Cold War so influenced our domestic politics and foreign affairs that students should examine its origins and its continuation into the late 20th century.

■ THE UNITED STATES IN THE IMMEDIATE POSTWAR ERA

At home, the Cold War brought about, for the first time in American history, a permanently fixed military-industrial complex of vast proportions and a semi-wartime economy that—together with pent-up demand for consumer goods, rising agricultural and industrial productivity, the impact of New Deal reforms, and the United States' near-monopoly of world trade—sustained a high level of purchasing power through the 1950s. Here students should be aware of the far-reaching effects of the GI Bill, a gigantic widening of access to higher education, and of low-interest home mortgages. The first spurred the most significant burst of college and university building in the nation's history; the latter fueled a home construction boom and led to a sharp increase in the rate of homeownership, a significant part of the American dream.

The Truman and Eisenhower years saw American confidence in the future mixed with fears of another, even more destructive war and deep divisions at home over the extent of the Soviet threat. Students need some time to analyze the domestic anti-Communist crusade of the 1950s when McCarthyism threatened to stifle dissent, and such developments as the Soviet acquisition of the atomic bomb in 1949, the atomic spy cases, the Chinese Communist Revolution, and the outbreak of the Korean War.

The Truman and Eisenhower years saw American confidence in the future mixed with fears of another, even more destructive war.

All the while the civil rights of African Americans were beginning to win more federal recognition and protection. The basic change came during the Truman administration when Roosevelt's successor publicly took a stand in favor of civil rights, well before the presidential election of 1948, resulting in the Dixiecrat party that vainly sought to deny his candidacy and then his election. The president was already desegregating the armed forces before the outbreak of the Korean War. In 1954, Chief Justice Earl Warren announced the Supreme Court's epochal *Brown v. Board of Education* decision, declaring "separate but equal" schools unconstitutional. In 1957, President Eisenhower used federal troops to enforce school desegregation in Little Rock, Arkansas.

Integration at Central High School, Little Rock, Arkansas, Sept. 4, 1957.

In retrospect, from the viewpoint of the troubled 1960s and 1970s, the decade of the 1950s was described by the press and popular writers as placid and complacent. Students will see that this was an over-simplification. Beneath the surface of events and headlines, forces were building for further changes in American life, especially those affecting women, minorities, and the poor. And decisions by the Eisenhower administration affecting events in Cuba, Central America, the Middle East, and Vietnam that appeared at the time to be of limited importance were to have immense consequences in the years to come.

UNIT XIV
THE RECENT UNITED
STATES (1961-PRESENT)

SIGNIFICANCE AND TEACHING GOALS

■ *MAJOR THEMES*

As they approach the end of the 20th century in their studies of United States history, students should be challenged to locate themselves in relation to the several main, continuing themes of the unfinished American story. What changes have developed in technology and economic life? How have these affected society, culture, and politics and the prospects and aspirations of students themselves? What have been the critical events of our changing role in the world since the 1950s? How have our diverse peoples and cultures been further shaped by immigration in the last few decades? Who are we becoming and what difference will it make in students' lives? How shall we proceed to unite ourselves around those aspirations of liberty, equality, and justice that are especially vital if a multicultural society is to live in peace and mutual respect?

In every sphere of national life—social, political, economic, and international—students will see profound changes underway, some enormously hopeful, others filled with challenges and uncertainty for the future. All must be placed in their historical context to be understood, and their significance assessed. **The profound social changes** in American life brought about by the Civil Rights Movement of the 1960s, the women's revolution that sprang from it, and the associated civil rights movements of Hispanic Americans and American Indians merit special attention. Associated with these changes have been those emanating from the Immigration Act of 1965

The profound changes underway in every sphere of national life must be placed in their historical context to be understood and their significance assessed.

Above: Martin Luther King who, opposed to violence, became its victim.

that ended immigration quotas and opened America's doors to people everywhere in the world. The consequences for the nation's ethnic, cultural, and linguistic diversity have been profound, creating what has been called the "first universal nation," robust and growing, immeasurably enriched, but fraught, too, with the strains of achieving national unity amidst growing ethnic, cultural, and religious diversity. Students will do well to compare the social changes of the past forty years, transforming the makeup of the nation and creating a society in which progress against racism, ethnic prejudice, and gender discrimination—however deep the remaining problems—has nevertheless been real and dramatic.

Related to these social changes have been important **developments in the political sphere,** as well. It is too early to judge whether the "Reagan Revolution" and the rise of the "New Conservatism" of the 1980s has been a lasting realignment in American political life equal to that accomplished by Roosevelt and his New Deal of the 1930s, but the question merits consideration by students. Worth examination, also, are the effects of the deeply unpopular and divisive Vietnam War; the civil protests that erupted at home; their effects on the presidency of Lyndon Johnson; and the events leading to the first resignation of a sitting president, Richard Nixon. To focus students' attention on what appear from the short-run, at least, to have been of greatest historic significance in these events, it is important to emphasize the major constitutional issues they raised concerning the proper conduct of the presidency, separation of powers, and the conflict between "the people's right to know" and the proper limitations on disclosure and freedom of the press in matters of national security and the public interest. From these perspectives students can most profitably examine the controversies surrounding such events as the release of the Pentagon Papers, Watergate, and the Iran-Contra Affair.

The economic and technological transformations of these years have been dramatic, led by the scientific and "high tech" revolutions that have redefined the nation's economic strength.

The economic and technological transformations of these years have been dramatic, led by the scientific and "high tech" revolutions that have redefined the base of the nation's economic strength, revolutionized medical science, raised new moral issues of genetic engineering, and opened the way to the "information revolution" that is changing the world. This is a unit in which basic issues of macro-economic and fiscal policy should also be examined, for within these forty years the nation changed course from its commitment to Keynesian economics, developed in the New Deal era, to an endorsement of principles advanced by such leading conservative economists as Milton Friedman. In this unit, too, students should examine new global economic realignments, the ramifications of changes in international trade and banking, the rise of multinational corporations, and their immediate consequences in the employment opportunities (and losses) for Americans of all walks of life, students themselves included.

Finally, time must be devoted to what has been among the most important issues of the past 40 years, **the nation's changing relationships in the world.** The end of the Cold War can most profitably be assessed in relationship to the policy of containment of international communism forged in the Truman years by George Kennan, W. Averell Harriman, and Dean Acheson and maintained for forty years by Democratic and Republican administrations alike; the policy of multilateral diplomacy and detente introduced by Nixon and Kissinger; and the Reagan policy of negotiating through strength with a massive arms build-up credited by some analysts with the final collapse of the already weakening Soviet economy in their effort to keep up .

The end of the Cold War can most profitably be assessed in relation to the policy of containment of international communism forged in the Truman years.

Within the context of these basic policy directives, students can best examine the causes and outcomes of such events as the Cuban missile crisis; the Vietnam War; United States' recognition of China; the Camp David accords; the United States' intervention in El Salvador, Panama, Grenada, and Nicaragua; and the Gulf War and its aftermath in the Middle East. How did the direction and fortunes of U. S. policies abroad influence domestic response at home, and how did domestic challenges, in turn, cut across and influence the conduct of the nation's foreign policy and the fortunes of the presidencies of Lyndon Johnson and Richard Nixon?

Chou En-lai and President Nixon on the plane carrying the President from Peking to Hangchow.

As they survey the contemporary world scene, students should also consider important developments in the Middle East, in American leadership in the Gulf War, and in efforts toward a Middle Eastern peace agreement. Important also have been creation of the 1992 European Economic Community; Western assistance to East European and Soviet republics in support of their transition to market economies; and the fortunes of the free-trade arrangements between the United States and its neighbors in the western hemisphere. These have been heady years, rich with promise for the future, but harboring new crises, too, emerging from unfinished agendas in the nation's domestic affairs and regional global politics of the years ahead. No less than generations before will today's students face a world full of problems and of challenges to come. Only a sure understanding of their historical antecedents will bring the wisdom required to analyze and soundly judge policy alternatives for the years ahead.

Only a sure understanding of their historical antecedents will bring students the wisdom required to analyze and soundly judge policy alternatives for the years ahead.

■ ESSENTIAL UNDERSTANDINGS

1. **Social changes in American society** brought about by the Civil Rights movements, the women's movement, and the Immigration Act of 1965.

2. **"Great Society" Program of the Johnson Administration:** purposes and consequences of his "war on poverty."

3. **"New Federalism" of the Nixon Administration:** purposes and effects in reversing aspects of the Johnson program, returning responsibilities to the states.

4. **Major foreign policy developments** of the past 50 years, their bipartisan support and results: Truman's containment policy of international communism; Kennedy's "flexible response" policy; Nixon/Kissinger policies of multilateral diplomacy and detente; Reagan's policy of "negotiating through strength."

5. **Major developments in the world role of the United States** and their major effects at home and abroad: the Vietnam War, the opening to China, relaxation of the Cold War, the Gulf War, and initiatives for peace in the Middle East.

6. **Technological and economic changes:** their scope and effects on the global realignment of economic relationships, and on economies of the U.S. and other nations.

■ HABITS OF THE MIND

The study and discussion of recent history and current affairs will present the ultimate test of how well students have cultivated their powers of judgment, the helpful habits of mind that their study of history should have nourished. Under the bombardment of "messages" on current issues, will they be able to pause and reflect upon how each issue has its roots in the past? Will they remember that by reviewing past versions of each issue they may gain perspective and ways of judging the claims of partisan interests?

If so, they will **recognize once again the complexity of cause,** for example in the loss of American competitiveness in foreign trade, in the tragic problems of drug traffic and addiction, or in the breakup of the Soviet empire. They will realize that legal equality for minorities and women will have less meaning without favorable economic opportunities, that poverty and prejudice are not curable by law alone. And they will see that each foreign crisis solved or softened is likely to be followed by a new crisis elsewhere; hence the need for a constant flow of reliable information from the world over, unclouded by wishful thinking.

In recent United States history, students will again observe **the importance of the extraordinary individual**. Recent decades have seen many kinds of Americans make a difference, heroes and heroines of their chosen work, who have taught and heartened others, and served as models for all ages: Martin Luther King, Jr., Thurgood Marshall, General Colin Powell, Jonas Salk, Sally Ride, Sandra Day O'Connor, Jeanne Kirkpatrick, Leontyne Price, Rachel Carson, Betty Friedan, Jim Henson, Sam Irvine, Elie Wiesel, Bayard Rustin, Cesar Chávez, Armstrong and Aldrin landing on the moon, and the thousands who labored to put them there. And students should also realize that leaders, like any others, need not be heroes in all respects to deserve honorable places in history for their greater achievements: for example, Kennedy in the Cuban missile crisis; Johnson with civil rights; Nixon on China; Carter at Camp David; Reagan at Helsinki.

Finally, students will recognize the **importance of ideas and principles in history**, that the political sphere of a

Astronaut Edwin M. Aldrin walking near the Lunar Module during Apollo II extravehicular activity, July 20, 1969.

Recent decades have seen many kinds of Americans make a difference, heroes and heroines of their chosen work, who have served as models for all ages.

175

Students should understand that the first need of a society aspiring to justice is to develop a shared conscience, grounded in democratic principles.

nation's life in particular must constantly be judged and renewed by a people's common understanding of their civic ideals. Students should come to the end of their school studies of United States history with several centuries of proof that the first need of a society aspiring to justice is to develop a shared "conscience," grounded in democratic principles, that enables people to be moved to action, whether to promote change or to safeguard continuity, by the problems and hopes of others, even those very different from themselves.

MAJOR TOPICS IN THE STUDY OF THE RECENT UNITED STATES

1. Domestic Programs of Kennedy and Johnson

2. The Civil Rights and Women's Movements of the 1960s

3. Foreign Policy in the Kennedy and Johnson Administrations

4. New Immigration Policies

5. Religion in America: Diversity and Issues

6. Nixon and the "New Federalism"

7. The Watergate Affair

8. Changing Economic Relationships in the Post-Vietnam Years

9. United States' Foreign Policy Since the Vietnman War

10. American Civilization in the Contemporary World

MAJOR TOPICS AND THEIR DEVELOPMENT: ESSENIAL UNDERSTANDINGS AND RELATED BACKGROUND FOR TEACHERS

■ *DOMESTIC PROGRAMS OF KENNEDY AND JOHNSON*

Students should study the domestic programs of the Kennedy and Johnson administrations as attempts to extend New Deal legislation through federal aid to education; medical care for the elderly; renewal of cities through subsidies for redevelopment and transportation systems; housing support; job training; and direct payments to the poor. They should study reasons for opposition to these programs but see how some were accepted by Republicans under Nixon and Ford as well as Democrats under Carter and have become part of what is described as welfare capitalism. In analyzing the ongoing debate between liberals and conservatives over the best means to economic and social well-being, students should be ready to take into account a wide range of factors at work: for example, the extent to which the massive costs of the Vietnam War affected the federal effort to wage the "war on poverty" and to create what Lyndon Johnson called the "Great Society;" and, on the other hand, the extent to which the programs themselves were flawed by mistaken approaches or inflexibility.

Students should analyze the economic and social interests behind the words and policies of the major partisan actors on the domestic scene, and how such interests combined with their personal ideas of the good society to shape their decisions on critical issues such as taxes, regulation of financial institutions, health-care programs, trade policies, public works, labor and social legislation, investment and monetary planning, ecology, and budgetary priorities. As far as possible, students should have access to the facts concerning the actual effects on people and institutions (public and private) of the major policies of the White House and Congress in the Kennedy and the Johnson years.

President Johnson signed into law the new civil rights-open housing bill during a ceremony in the White House East Room, April 11, 1968.

■ THE CIVIL RIGHTS AND WOMEN'S MOVEMENTS OF THE 1960S

The civil rights movement reversed the late 19th-century policy of black disenfranchisement and racial separation upheld in *Plessy v. Ferguson,* and marked the longest step taken toward ending discrimination against a minority in America since passage of the Fourteenth Amendment. The integration of schools after *Brown v. Board of Education,* desegregation of public transportation and accommodations (culminating in the Civil Rights Act of 1964), and, most important, voting rights (culminating in the Voting Rights Act

The civil rights movement marked the longest step toward ending discrimination against a minority in America since passage of the Fourteenth Amendment.

177

of 1965, which led to registration of one million black American citizens in the South within three years) should all be examined. Also worthy of study are the alternative means of protest under a new generation of black leaders, from nonviolent civil disobedience to Black Power confrontations to massive marches on Washington.

NOW members march down New York City's 5th Avenue in a women's liberation parade.

The increasing importance of American feminism requires exploration because it proceeded faster and farther than in any other part of the world, and because it has changed gender relations and roles of women in ways not likely to be reversed.

It is important to follow a study of the black civil rights movement with parallel civil rights movements of Hispanic Americans and American Indians. A useful focus for the former is the rise of the United Farm Workers and campaigns among the increasing numbers of Hispanic Americans for political representation and nondiscriminatory treatment. The study of American Indian protests is best centered on struggles for restoration of land and water rights won under early treaties that had later been broken.

The increasing importance of American feminism is also a topic that requires exploration because it proceeded faster and farther than in any other part of the world, and because it has changed gender relations and roles of women in ways that affect men and children, as well as adult women, in ways not likely to be reversed. Students should examine the major issues confronted by the women's movement in the 1960s, including economic issues of equal pay and equal job opportunities, addressed in the Equal Pay Act of 1963 and the Civil Rights Act of 1964; reproductive issues culminating in *Roe v. Wade* in 1973; and political rights invoked in seeking greater access to public office. The broad appeal of the women's movement in all regions in recent decades has resulted in their stronger presence in politics and their entry into the professions and into dozens of previously male strongholds in the work force. While considering these changes, students should also consider the increasing dissolution of the American family, the increase in single parent households, the "feminization of poverty," and the political and economic issues related to these developments.

■ FOREIGN POLICY IN THE KENNEDY AND JOHNSON ADMINISTRATIONS

The Kennedy administration saw the intensification of the Cold War in Berlin and in the Cuban missile crisis, and the origins of what would become the longest and most divisive overseas war in the nation's history. To put these events into historical perspective, students should review the containment policy forged in the Truman administration, its success in Europe and, at the price of war, in Korea. Students should be introduced to Kennedy's extension of the containment policy through "flexible response"—a policy designed for military assistance to friendly regimes in the Third World threatened by local insurgents led by revolutionary elites supported by the Soviet Union, China, and Cuba. Recognizing that Third World poverty was frequently the root factor in popular support of these movements, Kennedy also created the Peace Corps, the Alliance for Progress with Latin American governments, and the Agency for International Development.

Students should review the containment policy forged in the Truman administration; its success in Europe and, at the price of war, in Korea; and its extension through Kennedy's policy of "flexible response."

The Vietnam War

To understand Kennedy's commitment of military assistance to Vietnam, it is necessary for students to grasp some of the history of French colonialism in Indochina, the division of Vietnam into a communist North and pro-American South following the French defeat in 1956, and the outbreak of civil war in South Vietnam by insurgents supported by Ho Chi Minh and, indirectly, by China and the Soviet Union.

Students should understand Johnson's escalation of the American commitment to full military intervention in 1964 to stave off the collapse of South Vietnam. They should also analyze the growing frustration of Americans in maintaining a costly and expanding war to defeat a movement that had effectively infiltrated the South Vietnamese population. The influence of American public opinion on foreign policy in an era when the war, in televised form, reached into nearly every American household is worth studying, for it was public opinion turning against the war that denied President Johnson the possibility of reelection in 1968 and provoked widespread turmoil in the society.

American soldier in South Vietnam

The growing protests, combined with reactions against the drug culture of the 1960s and the counter-culture's rejection of authority and "Establishment" values, contributed to the election of Richard Nixon. Negotiations undertaken by

Henry Kissinger culminated in the 1973 Paris accords but a successful North Vietnamese offensive brought the fall of Saigon.

The effects of the Vietnam War are crucial, including the bitterness it stirred among opponents and proponents alike and the growth of skepticism about military intervention in countries undergoing civil war. The plight of the Vietnamese boat people and of Laotians, Cambodians, and other refugees from the continuing turmoil in Southeast Asia—as China now invaded Vietnam and the totalitarian Khmer Rouge seized power in Cambodia, destroying a third of the population in one of history's most appalling genocides—helped to forge this nation's postwar resettlement program.

■ NEW IMMIGRATION POLICIES AND THEIR CONSEQUENCES

An important part of the American scene in recent years has been the renewed flow of new peoples who have chosen to stake their children's future upon the American promise of economic opportunity, freedom, and justice. Students should know that the Immigration Act of 1965 brought an enormous change in the number and origins of immigrants. (Los Angeles airport now receives more immigrants annually than Ellis Island did in its heyday). They should see how the Civil Rights Movement created an atmosphere in which the preferential quota system of the 1920s no longer seemed justifiable, and how foreign policy in the 1960s opened doors to Asian immigrants—who had always been less favored than those of Western Europe—and to the immigration of Cubans, Haitians, Salvadorans, Jamaicans, and Russian Jews as well. Students should also sort out the issues involved in illegal immigration through our borders with Mexico and in recent provisions for amnesty. Great numbers of new and diverse citizens pose a challenge equivalent to that of the late 1800s and early 1900s, when immigrants arrived by the millions. Students should discuss how the United States can welcome, and draw new strength from, an increasingly multicultural population, all the while preserving the commonly shared vision of liberal democracy that alone can allow so many different kinds of people to live together in a just and peaceful society.

Students should discuss how the United States can welcome, and draw new strength from, an increasingly multicultural population, while preserving the commonly shared vision of liberal democracy.

■ RELIGION IN AMERICA: DIVERSITY AND ISSUES

In examining America's growing diversity, students should also give attention to the changing profile of the nation's religious faiths, rapidly expanding since 1965 to include rising populations holding to Buddhist, other Eastern, and Muslim beliefs, for example; and the dramatic rise in fundamental and evangelical Christianity in the United States— perhaps the greatest religious revival since the Second Great Awakening of the 19th century— and its growing influence in national affairs. In this area, students should consider the basic constitutional guarantees of freedom of religion under the First Amendment; the controversies surrounding the constitutional interpretations of the courts concerning separation of church and state on such matters as prayer in schools and public financing of educational programs in private denominational schools; and the protection the Constitution guarantees citizens from governmental intrusion into the free exercise of their faith and its free expression in public policy forums at every level of civic discourse.

■ NIXON AND THE "NEW FEDERALISM"

Students familiar with their nation's 20th-century history will be able to trace recurrent shifts in public mood and policy following major wars and dislocations: the 1920s search for "normalcy" following World War I and the changes wrought by Progressivism; the Eisenhower conservatism following World War II. In not dissimilar fashion the nation responded to the profound changes of the civil rights and women's movements and the turmoil unleashed by the Vietnam War and, in 5 of the next 6 national elections beginning with 1968, elected Republican presidents whose national platforms called for a new era of conservatism in fiscal and social policy.

Students should understand something of the growing strength of the neoconservative intellectual movement which challenged many of the policies of the Johnson program by criticizing federal welfare programs for perpetuating a culture of dependency; by calling for a sharp reduction in the expanded bureacracy and regulatory powers of the federal government; and by reaffirming the principles of the market economy, competition, and private enterprise.

Students should consider the basic constitutional guarantees of freedom of religion under the First Amendment and the protection the Constitution guarantees citizens from governmental intrusion into the free exercise of their faith and its free expression in public policy forums at every level of civic discourse.

Students will gain valuable insights into the politics of moderation and compromise in Nixon's first term of office by noting how many of Johnson's Great Society programs were kept alive and even advanced in these years: for example, expansion of Social Security, *Roe v. Wade,* establishment of the Environmental Protection Agency and the Occupational Safety and Health Administration, and deficit spending to stimulate the economy. But to reverse the flow of power and resources to Washington, Nixon also initiated his "New Federalism" and with it, the cutting off of funds to support such programs as federal job training, urban renewal, and federal support for education, programs at the heart of Johnson's "war on poverty."

Because the debates over public policy in these years have continued to the present, students should examine the major issues evoked by these policies, as well as those of the "Great Society:" debates, for example, over state vs. federal fiscal responsibilities on problems that are national in scope and, in some cases, the outgrowth of federal policy; and debates over "group rights" to a fair share vs. "individual rights" to equal treatment—in short, the nature of "rights" themselves under the Constitution. This is also the time to confront the great constitutional issues of separation of powers and presidential responsibility to uphold the law that came to a head in Watergate.

Watergate merits attention because it represents constitutional democracy under attack but also demonstrates the ability of the democratic system to defend itself.

■ THE WATERGATE AFFAIR

Watergate requires attention because it represents constitutional democracy under attack but also demonstrates the ability of the democratic system to defend itself. Attempts of officials in high places, including not least the president of the United States, to obstruct justice were involved in a series of Watergate-related hearings and trials and in the ultimate resignation of President Nixon. At the center of the Watergate affair were the increasingly autonomous operations of the American presidency, avoiding those Congressional restraints and delays inherent in our system of checks and balances. Students should be reminded that although the Watergate affair ended with a presidential resignation and a decline of trust in executive credibility, it did not prevent the covert actions of a decade later in the Iran-Contra affair, which again

Senate Watergate Committee Chairman Sam Ervin (left) confers with some of his committee and staff members during the hearings, July 18, 1973, in Washington.

challenged the authority of Congress and the constitutional principle of separation of powers.

■ CHANGING ECONOMIC RELATIONSHIPS IN THE POST-VIETNAM YEARS

To understand the fortunes of the national economy and therefore of students' own prospects in the years ahead, it is important to understand the major economic developments since the Vietnam War. Among these have been the great shocks to the economy caused by OPEC's cutting off of oil shipments to nations supporting Israel in the Yom Kippur War, and raising oil prices by 400 percent in 1973 and again in 1979. Added to the costs of the Vietnam War and the Great Society programs, these increases brought on severe economic stagnation combined with runaway inflation in Carter's administration and contributed to public awareness of the nation's energy dependence.

In this context, students can also examine the growing national tax revolt and opposition to federal spending. Reagan's promise to restore the nation's economic health through "supply side" economics, and the consequences of the steps undertaken by his administration should also be understood: the dramatic recovery of the economy by 1983, the drop in inflation and unemployment, but also record federal deficits resulting in part from a massive increase in military expenditures and from heavy tax cuts to stimulate the economy and force cuts in domestic spending.

Students should understand the far-reaching changes in the nation's economy with the increased competition it has faced in the world market, for these changes, too, directly influence their own job opportunities and future planning. With competition from abroad, the nation's trade deficits have soared and such basic industries as automobiles and steel, traditionally providing employment for a large sector of the nation's work force, have been hard hit. Significant population movements to the suburbs and the Sunbelt followed new employment opportunities in the aerospace, computer, research, and information industries resulting from the "high tech" revolution transforming the post-industrial world. Problems confronting the nation's cities, however, with their

To understand the fortunes of the national economy and of students' own prospects in the years ahead, it is important to understand the major economic developments since the Vietnam War.

declining tax bases and growing numbers of urban poor are the other side of this story and need to be understood.

All signs as the final decade of the 20th century got underway was for a global realignment of economic as well as political relationships among nations, a realignment holding enormous implications for the world in which students will live out their lives. Time must be given to the changing shape of economic alliances and relationships in the world and to their implications for students' prospects ahead. Students can be sure that what happens at home will be partly determined by the role of the United States in the world economy; by changing patterns of world trade and of credit, commodity, and labor costs; by multinational business; by the directions taken in the giant economies of Japan and the European community; by the expansion of free trade between nations in the Western hemisphere during the Bush administration; and by the ability of nations to collaborate in meeting long-term economic and environmental problems.

U.S. President George Bush and Mexican President Carlos Salinas de Gortari at the Museum of Nuevo Leon in Monterey November 27, 1990, during the second day of President Bush's visit to Monterey.

■ **UNITED STATES FOREIGN POLICY SINCE THE VIETNAM WAR**

Today's students live in a much more interdependent world and therefore ought to be cognizant of the main outlines of American foreign policy in their own and their parents' lifetimes. Especially important to understand are Nixon's detente with the People's Republic of China; Carter's human rights campaign and the Camp David accords; and Reagan's diplomacy with the Soviet Union, "negotiating from strength," which by the late 1980s seemed to signal the end of nearly half a century of Cold War.

Living in a much more interdependent world, students should examine the main outlines of American foreign policy in the postwar era.

All three presidents—Nixon, Carter, and Reagan—carried on, as had their predecessors, the policies of containment crafted in the Truman administration by George Kennan, W. Averell Harriman, and Dean Acheson. Each of these presidents sought to maintain a strong military establishment, to keep alliances intact, to foster the economic health of the Western democracies. Each took strong anti-Soviet stances when such seemed called for, even at substantial political costs at home, as in the case of Carter's grain embargo in response to the Soviet invasion of Afghanistan.

The end of the Cold War and the liberation of Eastern Europe was the first astonishing change in the realm of foreign affairs in half a century. Even more profound was the rapid sequence of events following the aborted Soviet coup of August 1991 and the dissolution of the Soviet Union. Partly responsible for these results were American moves and counter-moves in foreign policy, though their effects are difficult to measure as yet. The huge defense expenditures for American military readiness, particularly during the Reagan administration, helped undermine the collapsing Soviet economy, which could not keep up.

Also a likely factor was the great prosperity of Western Europe and its political freedoms, originally sustained by the Marshall Plan and NATO. What seems to have set off the discontent of Soviet and East European citizens also was travel to the West, including the United States, and visions of Western consumer goods offered by television. The communications revolution may have done much to bring down the Soviet colossus. Certainly there was a yearning for freedom, disclosed in speeches, mass rallies, and calls for democracy. But whatever the reasons, it represented a triumph for the Western powers, led since 1945 by the United States, and for the idea of democratic politics and for more reliance on private property and enterprise.

Carter, Sadat, and Begin after signing of the Egyptian-Israeli Peace Treaty.

■ AMERICAN CIVILIZATION IN THE CONTEMPORARY WORLD

To enrich their understanding of their nation's role in the contemporary world, it is important, finally, that students consider the major currents of American thought and culture in the late 20th century, as influential on Western thought and values as those of Italy during the Renaissance, France in the 17th century, or England during the Industrial Revolution. Important among the forces contributing to the nation's intellectual and scientific accomplishments have been the success of American universities and the emergence of powerful centers of scientific research and innovation—accomplishments students will see reflected in the first landings on the moon and the nation's non-manned space probes of the galaxy; advances in electronic digital computer research; recombinant DNA research and genetic engineering; and

Important among the forces contributing to the nation's intellectual and scientific accomplishments have been the success of American universities and the emergence of powerful centers of scientific research and innovation.

associated advances in medical science and health care.

While students will be well-acquainted with the popular culture America has exported to much of the world, they should also be introduced to the contributions of American arts and letters in the 20th century, including motion pictures, the nation's most distinctive art form. Mature students should appreciate how a nation's art and literature reflect upon and give expression to the hopes, fears, anxieties, and aspirations of a people, and thereby provide indispensable insights into a society in rapid change. Composers such as Leonard Bernstein and Aaron Copeland; architects like Frank Lloyd Wright, Buckminster Fuller, I. M. Pei; artists like Jackson Pollack, Fritz Scholder, David Siquieros, Willem de Kooning, and Georgia O'Keefe; writers such as J.D. Salinger, Richard Wright, and Lorraine Hansberry; and playwrights such as Thornton Wilder, Eugene O'Neill, and Tennessee Williams are among those whose work can help students to measure the impact of this age on modern life.

Chinese born American architect I. M. Pei, (left) at a ceremony to present Pei's vision of the renovation of the Louvre to the press.

In assessing the growing sense of public urgency for global environmental concerns, for the humane uses of technology, and for the protection of human rights at home and abroad students should appreciate the values that drive the commitment to address and resolve these problems: the values of respect for the individual, of basic human rights of all peoples, and of equality of opportunity for all. Students should be able to assess to what extent these goals, derived from the nation's core democratic values, have today achieved broad-based constituencies at home and abroad, and have emerged, in an increasing number of nations, as the dominant goals of modern, 20th-century societies.

Students should assess to what extent the nation's core democratic values have emerged as the dominant goals of modern, 20th-century societies.

A closing word about the importance of historical perspectives on contemporary issues is in order. If students see that they themselves are part of a grand historical procession, they will better grasp one major purpose of historical study, which is to bring the perspectives and knowledge gleaned from such study to the reasoned analysis of questions of obvious significance to themselves and their society—questions whose historical dimensions must be taken into account if they are to be intelligently thought about and resolved in the months and years ahead.

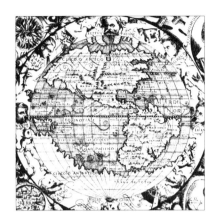

CHAPTER FOUR:
Essential Understandings
in World History

INTRODUCTION

To prepare for an increasingly interdependent world, to sharpen analytical skills, and to enrich their education, American students must learn about the major cultures and civilizations in world history. Human history in its many different manifestations offers students new insights into themselves and their society. It shows them most clearly what it means to be human, how difficult the course of human history has often been. On graduation from high school, therefore, students should be acquainted with the histories of Europe, the Middle East, Africa, Asia, and the Americas. Graduates must have enough knowledge, moreover, to see these peoples as the products of their own unique historical development rather than simply as foils to reflect or contrast developments in the United States. They should appreciate the common problems that humans have faced and the variety of solutions that have been tried. They should, moreover, see that cross-cultural influences have also shaped human life from early history down to our own time. Only by understanding that the world has had many histories, each unique in its own way, yet never autonomous, can American students place themselves in the kind of global historical framework that they will need to function in the contemporary world.

The sheer scope of the world's history, its great turning points, dramatic moments, and their consequences can easily overwhelm teachers and students unless organized to create order out of the mass of historical data at their disposal. The myriad local histories degenerate into cacophony unless they are related to common experiences that have shaped human life. The comparative approach, anchored in chronology,

On graduation from high school, students should be acquainted with the histories of Europe, the Middle East, Africa, Asia, and the Americas.

Above: Guiseppe Rosaccio's World Map

187

The comparative approach, anchored in chronology, helps to bring order to world history while simultaneously deepening students' understanding of each particular place and time.

helps to bring order to world history while simultaneously deepening students' understanding of each particular place and time. Words commonly used, such as "revolution" and "war," already imply comparison among similar but distinctive events. Comparisons and contrasts reveal what is unique to each culture and why each assigns different meanings to common terms and memories.

This chapter, therefore, proceeds both chronologically and comparatively through successive eras of world history. From the origins of human life in Africa, the beginnings of civilization in the neolithic and urban revolutions of the ancient world, and the rise of the classical civilizations of Greece and Rome, India and China (1000 B.C. - 600 A.D.), this chapter continues with the expansion of agrarian civilizations (ca. 600 - 1400 A.D.), the early modern world (1400 - 1800 A.D.), the 19th century, and the contemporary era.[1] This is a dramatic story, still unfolding and filled with people and events that grip students' imaginations and bring them face to face with the great issues, aspirations, achievements, and failures in the human journey. Each of these eras has its own character, and must therefore be studied with focus upon its own time and circumstances and upon its comparative developments across societies.

MAJOR THEMES

Unifying all these eras, and building continuity for students across the centuries, are the great narrative themes introduced in Chapter II of this volume. Central among them is the **development of the many diverse societies** that have comprised humankind, their origins, changing character, and interactions throughout history. Implicit in this theme are understandings of continuity and change, of commonalities and cultural variabilities in gender roles and relationships, in family and kinship relationships, and in the social roles and organization of societies over time. What different forms has family life taken in different times and places, and how have

---

[1] In this volume the traditional (Latin) system of counting years, B.C. (*before Christ*) and A.D. (*Anno Domini, in the year of the Lord*) is followed. Students, however, should know of the alternative system, increasingly used in the contemporary world, B.C.E. (*before the common era*) and C.E. (*in the common era*).

these forms affected the daily lives of men, women, children, and adolescents and their relationships to each other? How have different kinds of social organization affected political institutions and how has social life been influenced, in turn, by developments in all other spheres—political, economic, religious, and philosophical—of human activity? What have been the consequences of social, economic, and political inequalities between groups, and the impact of those inequalities on individuals and nations? And how have differing social structures affected the place of the individual and the regard or lack of regard for individual dignity, equity of opportunity, freedom, and initiative?

Economic forces have been of such fundamental importance in determining the quality of people's lives, in structuring societies, and in directing the course of human events that they, too, must form an essential part of students' understandings of world history. Following this theme of **economic and technological development** will introduce students to the major stages in human use of the environment, to the changing ways various societies have provided for food, clothing, shelter, and comforts, from hunting and gathering to current technologies. This theme introduces students also to basic economic concepts and processes, to the different kinds of economic systems that have been tried, their basic assumptions, and their consequences in the lives of individual men and women and in the fate of nations. This theme introduces students also to the evolving connections in trade and cultural exchange among societies from earliest times, and the ever-greater scope and speed of global interactions today. Examining in that context changing patterns of regional and global economic dominance will disclose how local populations reacted at various times in history to Muslim, Mongol, Chinese, Japanese, Western, or Soviet expansionism and the effects of these developments on colonizers and on the colonized, in turn. The complementary processes of decolonization and the rise of nationalism in the modern world need to be explored. They lead to an understanding of the emergence of a truly international economy in the 20th century, challenging students to consider their own position in the world.

Technological innovations lie at the heart of some of the most profound transformations in world history, the most obvious being the emergence of agriculture, cities, writing,

> *Economic forces have been of such fundamental importance in determining the quality of people's lives, in structuring societies, and in directing the course of human events that they, too, must form an essential part of students' understandings of world history.*

In the modern era, in societies throughout the globe, technological transformations have unsettled or swept away, for better or worse, earlier patterns of behavior and expectations in social, cultural, and political life.

printing, and industrialization. Topics like these challenge students to evaluate the impact of technological change on all aspects of human life and to assess the balance between technological inventiveness and borrowing. Following this theme will also disclose how cultural or socio-economic factors have encouraged or inhibited technological innovation and how, in turn, societies have been changed by such innovations. In the modern era, in societies throughout the globe, technological transformations have unsettled or swept away, for better or worse, earlier patterns of behavior and expectations in social, cultural, and political life. To what extent is economic "modernization," as it is so often called, necessary, or inevitable, or beneficial? To what extent have different people and cultures been able to control the forces of modernization, or choose from among its products and consequences? Each major civilization and region of the world may be studied for its own special way of making the transition, or resisting the transition, from an earlier, familiar, or traditional life to so-called modern life. What have people been happy to gain, or afraid to lose, from scientific, technological, and economic change?

Such a question applies to everyone on earth, and it cannot be answered without following also the great themes of the **development of systems of political theory and organization, and of religious and philosophical beliefs and thought.** Ideas, beliefs, and values have been profoundly influential throughout history. Their impact can be explored through a variety of questions: how have different religious, philosophic, or scientific beliefs developed and spread, why have they been so popular, what conflicts have they produced, how have those holding to these beliefs viewed government and the role of individuals, how have different peoples understood themselves, and how has human understanding of the world and the cosmos changed?

It is likewise important to stress the power of religious conviction. Topics like the spread of the great monotheistic (or "salvationist") religions, the Crusades or the Reformation in the West, the conflict between Confucian humanism, Buddhism and Taoism in China, Aztec and Mayan religious practices, or the Iranian revolution deserve a prominent place in the curriculum because they are dramatic stories which illustrate how religious conviction can become the prime determinant of historical change. Religious conflict—Buddhist/Confucian, Hindu/Muslim, Christian/Muslim, Christian/Jewish, orthodox/heterodox—has likewise been a mainspring of historical change from the very earliest times to the present. Without an exploration of these issues, history becomes lifeless and explanations of change meaningless.

Just as social customs, philosophical thought, and religious beliefs have affected people's responses to geographical, technological, and economic forces, they have worked also to shape political life within and among nations. Struggles to impose law and order within societies and in the world, efforts to construct governments and institutions, the drive to seize and hold power over others, and the long human struggle for individual freedom, dignity, and democratic self government are captivating stories which form the skeletal framework of history. "Eventmental" history is important. Students need a strong chronological framework grounded in political history in order to think historically, to debate cause and effect, and to analyze the interactions of all other forces—social, cultural, technological/economic, and philosophical/religious—influencing the course of history. Attention must be given to the great variety of political systems that have developed over time, including the origins and spread of democratic ideas and practices, the forces that have encouraged and strengthened free government and those that have opposed, undermined, or destroyed it. No other story better places the American experience in world perspective. Important also to understanding the development of political theory and organization are the systems of political thought underlying alternative governmental structures; the rise in the 20th century of mass societies and their consequences for political systems, law, and international relations; the consequences of developments in military technology for the nature and growth of governments and for individual freedom; and international efforts in the control of aggression and the development of an international order in the wake of World War II.

Courses in world history should also help students to find drama and significance in the lives of individuals, in the flow of ideas and values, in human creativity wherever it is found. To these ends, studying the arts and literature of major

Students need a strong chronological framework grounded in political history in order to think historically, to debate cause and effect, and to analyze the interactions of all other forces—social, cultural, technological/economic, and philosophical/religious—influencing the course of history.

world civilizations in their historical setting is invaluable. Engaging questions are not hard to find. Of any culture, how much was truly indigenous and how much derived from neighbors or other civilizations? How did cultural change occur? How was it related to political, economic, social, or religious change? Are those works we now call great and representative of a past people's culture the works they themselves would have wanted or expected to be remembered for? What might future historians decide is representative of us, or of other modern societies? These need not be trivial questions. Confronting them in historical perspective, armed with insights gained by studying the culture of others, students will bring world history alive for themselves.

WORLD HISTORY AND THE PROBLEM OF TIME

There are many ways in which world history may be presented, but it is clear from our efforts that there is too much of critical importance for world history to be covered in a single course.

There are many ways in which world history may be presented, but it is clear from our efforts that there is too much of critical importance for world history to be covered in a single course. In Chapters I and II of this volume we strongly argued the case for a significant increase in time for history in the curriculum, with no less than two full years of world history recommended as essential for all students between grades 7 and 12, and with history recommended as a significant part of the curriculum at all grades of the elementary school, when developed in ways appropriate to the capabilities and interests of children.

Teachers fortunate enough to teach in schools providing this amount of world history instruction will find no difficulty in incorporating the following recommendations of essential understandings and perspectives. For teachers not so fortunate, selections must be made. In these cases not all of the major topics recommended in the following pages can be included, and those that are selected cannot all be given equal weight. The choices, though difficult, will be aided by considering the justifications we have presented for the importance of each era, its major themes, and the content included. Our forthcoming volume recommending various curriculum designs and appropriate standards of achievement in history for elementary, middle and high schools should be of added assistance.

UNIT I
THE BEGINNINGS
OF CIVILIZATION

SIGNIFICANCE AND TEACHING GOALS

■ MAJOR THEMES

The study of world history should begin with the origins of humanity and the first steps toward organized society and civilization. This study of early cultures and civilizations is important for several reasons. First, it launches students' exploration into the meanings of the words "humanity," "culture," and "civilization." Second, it introduces them to a variety of historical sources and evidence, and shows them that historical understanding depends upon written and non-written sources alike. Exposure to art and artifacts as well as to written documents will introduce them to the techniques of historical analysis. Third, a comparative approach to early human history allows students to grasp the common problems faced by people around the globe and the wide range of solutions that they have found. Finally, a study of the earliest societies offers teachers and students opportunities to explore basic historical issues such as race, scarcity, technology, language, law, power, and religion.

In studying the beginnings of civilization, students should be introduced to all four major themes of world history. Among these is the **economic and technological development of early human societies**, most notably their invention of farming in the Neolithic era, including plant and animal domestication—developments with vast repercussions in the ancient world. Students should learn about the technological base of agriculture and associated developments such as the invention of the plow, the wheel, pottery, and the technologies

A comparative approach to early human history allows students to grasp the common problems faced by people around the globe and the wide range of solutions that they have found.

Above: New Kingdom Ruler

of cooking, brewing, and irrigation. They should also learn the basic stages in the agricultural revolution, from hunter/gatherer societies to small farming communities to full-scale agriculture.

The formation of cities in the ancient world marked a second ecological-social development with momentous consequences.

Scribes writing in alphabetic script and cuneiform, from a wall painting at Tell Ahmar.

The formation of cities in the ancient world marked a second ecological-social development with momentous consequences. Studying the urban revolution, how it developed, and its consequences will develop students' insights into a second major theme, **the development and changing character of human societies.** Ever since their creation, cities have powerfully influenced social, cultural, intellectual, and political history. Students should understand the evolution of small farming communities into larger urban concentrations, particularly in Sumeria and Babylonia. They should understand how social classes and status groups developed along with the growth of cities, developments which can be compared with those in Egypt, India, China, and the Americas. Special attention should be given to the invention of writing in this era, and the consequences of literacy in the early civilizations of Sumeria, China, and Egypt.

The beginnings of organized political life, bringing with it both security and new forms of danger, both peace and war, illustrate a third major theme in world history, **the development of political organization.** Knowledge about the origins of states and the variety of ways in which they were ruled is crucial to building understanding of the role of states and politics in history. Though states arose at different times, the patterns of their development were roughly comparable. The histories of Mesopotamia, Egypt, Crete, and Mycenae as well as the early histories of China, India, and the Americas illustrate the use of law, the development of bureaucracies and armies, the role of religious authority, the growth of different social structures, and the development of taxation and tribute. In this early setting students can see different societies groping for principles of order and appreciate the many problems of organizing and maintaining government. These are matters that students tend to take for granted in their own society. Deeper historical knowledge can open up new perspectives on their own lives.

Finally, the beginnings of civilization provide opportunity for students to examine a fourth major historical theme, **people's development and representation of their understandings of themselves and of their place in the universe.** Introduction to the religious beliefs of the Mesopotamians, ancient Hebrews, Egyptians, and the early civilizations of India and China will provide students insights into the different ideas held by these early peoples about creation, deity, the nature of the universe, death, and the place of the individual in the world and the cosmos.

Religious beliefs of early civilizations provide insights into their different ideas about creation, deity, the universe, death, and the place of the individual in the cosmos.

■ ESSENTIAL UNDERSTANDINGS

1. **The effects of geography and the environment** in human migration, settlement, economic activity, and technology.

2. **The agricultural revolution**, its major stages and consequences.

3. **The importance of trade and the diffusion of successful technologies and ideas,** often over great distances, from the very earliest times.

4. **The urban revolution**, its relationship to agriculture, its major stages, and its consequences.

5. **The origins of political life**, administration, and law.

6. **The origins of literacy**, its various forms in ancient societies, and its consequences.

7. **Early religions**, their importance, variety, and consequences.

■ HABITS OF THE MIND

The study of the beginnings of civilization is especially valuable in developing students' **appreciation of the tentative nature of historians' descriptions of the past,** and the changes they expect, and hope, to make as new evidence comes to light. One of the intriguing aspects of this era for students is, in fact, the study of how historians and archaeologists seek to establish reliable knowledge about an age for which evidence is often so fragmentary.

The recovery of Egyptian history, for example, can be studied as one of the most remarkable achievements of modern historical scholarship. Students can be shown how historians have combined archaeological and documentary evidence to reconstruct the history and culture of a civilization for which almost all knowledge had disappeared almost fifteen hundred years ago.

The study of Egypt also allows a unique opportunity for the development of **critical thinking skills.** Until the ancient hieroglyphic script was deciphered in the early 19th century A.D., making possible the scholarly study of Egypt's ancient literature and other written texts, Egypt was the subject of an elaborate pseudo-history in which it was portrayed as a land of mystical religious ideas expressed in mysterious symbols and the ultimate source of all civilization worldwide. The fad for "pyramid power" in the 1960s and 1970s was only an extreme expression of this set of ideas. Teachers should use the opportunity provided by this contrast between the scholarly and pseudo-histories of Egypt to help students understand the nature of historical evidence and how historians use that evidence to formulate hypotheses about the past.

Study of this unit fosters, also, **comparative analyses,** as students observe the great revolutions in agriculture and urban living developing in Mesopotamia, the Nile Valley, the Indus Valley, China, and later in other parts of the world as well. The comparative approach, anchored in chronology, deepens students' understanding of human commonalities, while fostering appreciation of the importance of geographic place and cultural variability.

Egytian tomb hieroglyphics

Teachers should help students understand the nature of historical evidence and how historians use that evidence to formulate hypotheses about the past.

MAJOR TOPICS IN THE STUDY OF THE BEGINNINGS OF CIVILIZATION

1. The Origins of Human Life

2. The Neolithic Revolution

3. The Urban Revolution: Sumer, Babylon, and the Ancient Hebrews

4.   Ancient Civilization in Africa: Egypt and Kush

5.   Ancient Civilizations of India, China, and the Americas

MAJOR TOPICS AND THEIR DEVELOPMENT: ESSENTIAL UNDERSTANDINGS AND RELATED BACKGROUND FOR TEACHERS

■ *THE ORIGINS OF HUMAN LIFE*

The study of history should begin with the very origins of human life in Africa and its spread through the world. Students should be familiar with the major stages in the evolutionary development of human beings, while also understanding that new scientific discoveries are constantly changing our knowledge of that development. What was "known" only a few years ago is now less certain.

The weight of paleontological evidence today tells us that our earliest ancestors emerged in East Africa between three and four million years ago. Hominids of the type *Homo erectus* began moving out of Africa to other parts of the earth one million years ago or more. Students should know the major phases of human physical and cultural development from the early Neolithic to the revolutions of agriculture and iron, including the development of tools from the simple stone implements used by *Homo habilis* to the specialized tools of *Homo sapiens*; the development of language; the use of fire by *Homo erectus*; and developing forms of social organization, community life and culture, from the time of *Homo erectus* to that of the Cro Magnons.

■ *THE NEOLITHIC REVOLUTION*

The means of gaining food was and is of primary importance to human life. One of the earliest technological developments, with vast repercussions, was the invention of farming, including plant and animal domestication. Students should understand that this revolution occurred all around the world: first in the Middle East in the region extending from present-day Turkey to Iraq and Israel perhaps as early as 10,000 B.C., and then in North Africa, Europe, Southeast Asia, and Central and South America. Thus, any discussion

Rendering of a cave painting depicting early herding.

One of the earliest technological developments, with vast repercussions, was the invention of farming, including plant and animal domestication.

of the Neolithic period in the Middle East must be seen as a regional manifestation of a phenomenon occurring, though at different times, elsewhere in the world. Similar factors in East Asia led to the domestication of millet, rice, and yams, and in Central and South America to the domestication of beans, squash, gourds, potatoes, and corn.

To understand the significance of the Neolithic Revolution, students should begin with the nature of Stone Age hunter/gatherer economies, including the role of gender in society and work. They can then move on to the domestication of plants and animals. They should study the technological base of agriculture and associated developments such as plowing, cooking, brewing, and irrigation. Students should also understand the slow pace of technological development, for this revolution was not a sudden transformation, but one that took thousands of years.

It is essential that students understand that the Neolithic Revolution was the necessary foundation for the great civilizations that followed.

It is essential that students understand that the Neolithic Revolution was the necessary foundation for the great civilizations that followed. Through agriculture humans now controlled and regulated their food supply rather than depending on the caprice of nature. It is crucial, also, that students understand that one of the primary effects of agriculture was that it dramatically boosted the population, though in many cases it resulted in a deterioration of the standard of living enjoyed by certain hunter/gatherers, in some cases for thousands of years.

With an assured food supply it was no longer necessary for every member of the community to gather or produce food and it was possible for people to specialize in other areas of work, such as building houses or producing crafts. Housing became permanent, villages sprang up, and the arts in the form of religious wall paintings, pottery, basketry, and weaving developed. Students can develop understanding of these developments of the Neolithic period by studying the archaeological discoveries in villages such as Jericho in present-day Palestine, Jarmo in present-day Iran, Beidha in present-day Jordan, and the settlement of Çatal Hüyük in present-day Turkey, one of the largest settlements of the Neolithic period.

Finally, students should understand that these societies

were not isolated and self-sufficient. From all around the globe there is evidence that the emerging agricultural societies relied heavily on trade, sometimes over considerable distances. Students need to learn how economic organization and trade have been of fundamental importance everywhere in the world since the very earliest times; how they have not only helped to shape social relations, but have influenced the development of law and government.

■ THE URBAN REVOLUTION: SUMER, BABYLON, AND THE ANCIENT HEBREWS

The history of Mesopotamia provides students rich insights into a second of the great turning points in human history: the evolution of the small farming communities of the Neolithic era into the large urban concentrations that marked the dawn of civilization. Between 3900 B.C. and 3500 B.C. the practice of irrigated agriculture had spread to the southern, more arid valleys of the Tigris and Euphrates Rivers. Increasing concentrations of population in this region (known as Sumer), the growth of long-distance trade made necessary by the lack of stone, metals, and timber in these alluvial valleys, and the development of communication to facilitate trade may all have been factors contributing to the urban revolution occurring in the region between 3500 B.C. and 3000 B.C.

Sumer

Students should understand how the Sumerian landscape was transformed with the development of large cities with their spectacular temples and palaces. Mesopotamian society also changed with the development of ruling classes, priests, administrative bureaucracies, specialized craftsmen, and the thousands of laborers serving the temple estates. To understand the stratified social system that emerged, students must understand something of Sumerian theology and its motivation of the populace to serve the gods through labor on the temple estates in order that the temple granaries might be filled and that natural disasters, disease, starvation, and enemy attack—all believed to be punishments from the gods—might be averted.

One feature of this era deserves special attention: the

Sumerian Ziggurat

The history of Mesopotamia provides students rich insights into the evolution of the large urban concentrations that marked the dawn of civilization.

Sumerian invention of the cuneiform system of writing (ca. 3200 B.C.), developed so that temple priests could record goods entering and leaving the temple storehouses. Students will be fascinated with early forms of writing, including pictograms or logograms, cuneiform, hieroglyphics, syllabaries, and the alphabet. They should consider the status of scribes in Sumerian civilization, the administrative purposes their documents served, and the importance of writing in preserving the epic poems, myths, and legends of Sumerian civilization, notably *The Epic of Gilgamesh, The Epic of Creation,* and *The Righteous Sufferer,* comparable in theme to *The Book of Job.*

Ancient Mesopotamia also provides students important insights into early state formation, the development of inter-state alliances between kings, and the consolidation of empires.

The study of ancient Mesopotamia also provides students important insights into early state formation. They should be familiar with the broad outlines of this history, roughly comparable throughout the developing empires of the ancient world: the accession to power around 3000 B.C. of the first kings of the independent city states—military leaders to whom the priests and populace looked for protection from warring neighbors; the development of shifting inter-state alliances between kings; and the consolidation of empires, first under the rule of the kings of Ur and later under the rival kingships of Assyria in the north and Babylon in the south.

Asurbanipal hunting on horseback. Alabaster relief from Kujundschuk-Nineve. London, British Museum.

Babylon

The Babylonian Empire deserves special attention for the rule of Hammurabi, who unified all of Mesopotamia and whose capable reign illustrates the use of law, the development of a centralized bureaucracy and professional army, and the refinement of the administrative organization and written communication required to administer a far-flung empire. Hammurabi's reign exemplifies, also, the growth of foreign trade through the development of a professional merchant class; systems of taxation and tribute; and the evolution of a more complex society in which hundreds of specialized artisans provided products for trade which local merchants, in turn, dispensed to a growing class of private consumers.

The Ancient Hebrews

Students should not complete their studies of the ancient

Middle East without knowledge of the ancient Hebrews, a Semitic people whose distant origins are judged by most serious scholars to be found among the linguistically-related nomadic peoples from east of the Euphrates River who sometime after 1200 B.C. settled in that part of the Middle East today known as Syria, Jordan, and Israel.

Like the other groups who established themselves in western Asia Minor between 1200 and 1100 B.C.—the Philistines, Phrygians, Dorians, Chaldaeans, and Medes, for example—the Hebrews evolved politically from their loosely joined tribal origins into a kingdom united under the strong leadership of Saul, David, and Solomon (1020-925 B.C.). The singular importance of the ancient Hebrews does not lie, however, in their political achievements which were modest, but in their development of a unified belief system whose sacred writings, ethics, and moral teachings have, from ancient days, been a dominant shaping force in the history of Western civilization. The moral and ethical principles, the ideas of right and wrong, of justice, and of individual social responsibility embodied in the Judaic tradition—and in Christianity whose founders were all Jews and whose origins lie in Judaism—make up the core of Western religious thought and have deeply marked most subsequent Western ideologies, however secular or even anti-religious.

This model shows what the temple Solomon built in Jerusalem might have looked like.

To understand this tradition, students should be introduced to the central, compelling stories in the Hebrew Bible, recognized by scholars as a major historical source and essential for comprehending the countless references to Biblical history in Western literature and art, down to the present. Students should understand the basic tenets of the Mosaic law, the Ten Commandments. They should understand the central belief in ethical monotheism—a radical departure from other religions of the ancient world—which saw God as a moral judge, demanding right behavior and social responsibility from each individual, and holding the individual responsible for moral choice. Students should also understand the role of the prophets in calling upon their people to make themselves worthy of their destiny as the covenant people, chosen of God.

The moral and ethical principles, the ideas of right and wrong, of justice and of individual social responsibility embodied in the Judaic tradition make up the core of Western religious thought and most subsequent Western ideologies.

These understandings, together with some knowledge of the continuing development over more than two thousand years of Rabbinic Judaism, are important for comprehending the power of Jews to survive centuries of scattering and brutal oppression. They are also important if students are to understand the covenant theology of the founding Protestant sects of early America and the covenant strain resounding down through 19th-century United States history. They are important, too, if students are to understand the Biblical basis of contemporary Israeli claims to their historic lands, an important explanatory perspective on the tensions between Muslims and Jews in the Middle East today.

■ ANCIENT CIVILIZATION IN AFRICA: EGYPT AND KUSH

> *No other ancient civilization enjoyed as long a continuous history as Egypt, and the achievements made by the ancient Egyptians during the more than three and a half millennia of their history were numerous and varied.*

The history of ancient Egypt is an essential and fascinating part of world history. No other ancient civilization enjoyed as long a continuous history as Egypt, and the achievements made by the ancient Egyptians during the more than three and a half millennia of their history were numerous and varied. These included the development of a distinctive religious view of the universe and humanity's place in it, the creation of a remarkable art that contains the earliest examples of large monumental sculpture and architecture in stone, important advances in mathematics and medicine, and the invention of one of the two oldest writing systems of the ancient world. Just as important as the accomplishments of Egyptian civilization, however, was the influence it exerted on its neighbors. It inspired the ancient inhabitants of the modern Sudan to create the civilization of Kush, the earliest civilization of inner Africa. It also functioned together with the civilization of ancient Mesopotamia as a catalyst for the development of classical Greek civilization.

Much recent controversy concerns whether Egypt was part of black Africa and whether Egypt provided the foundations of Greek civilization. Although scholarly debate will no doubt continue, the best current scholarship can be summed up in four points. First, European and American classical scholars have traditionally ignored or underplayed the important influences of the Semitic Near East and of Egypt on Greek civilization. Second, ancient Egypt cannot be understood if it is pictured simply as a part of black Africa. Egypt was a crossroad of the Old World where people of diverse colors and cultural backgrounds mingled for centuries. Racially complex, ancient Egypt included a continuum of complexions from lighter-skinned Mediterranean peoples resembling the inhabitants of coastal North Africa in northern Egypt to those resembling the dark-skinned people of the Sudan in the south. Third, none of the peoples of the ancient Mediterranean world placed the significance on race given to this concept in the modern world. Hence, Egyptians thought of themselves in cultural and political terms as part of an **Egyptian** society and an **Egyptian** culture that amalgamated people, ideas, and cultural influences from throughout the region. Lastly, the contributions of Egyptian and Near Eastern civilizations to Greek civilization were many, but the ancient history of the regions connected by the Mediterranean is best understood when teachers emphasize cultural interchange, mutual influences, and—in many cases—parallel developments within these various societies.

Egyptian souls working in the fields of heaven. Painting.

A key theme in Egyptian history is the fundamental role played by the unique geography of the Nile Valley. The ancient Greek historian Herodotus called Egypt the gift of the Nile and all modern scholars agree. Egypt is essentially an enormous oasis created by the Nile in the vast North African desert. It was by meeting the challenge of this environment and exploiting its opportunities that prehistoric inhabitants of the Nile Valley created Egyptian civilization.

A second major theme in Egyptian history is the central place of religion in Egyptian culture. Students should understand that there is more to Egyptian religion than a plethora of deities represented in strange human and non-human images. All areas of Egyptian culture derived their meaning from a religious world view. Central to that world view was the idea that the gods created Egypt as an island of order surrounded by forces of chaos that constantly threatened to overwhelm it. As part of that original creation, Egypt and all of its traditions—ethical, legal, and artistic—were, therefore, inherently good. Justice, morality, beauty, all of which the Egyptians called *Ma'at,* consisted of behavior in accordance with that tradition. An important consequence of this world view was that Egyptian culture was xenophobic in its relations with foreign ethnic groups but accepting of foreign individuals provided that they assimilated to Egyptian tradition. The

All Egyptian culture derived from a religious world view whose central idea was that the gods created Egypt as an island of order surrounded by forces of chaos.

203

order embodied in Egypt, however, was precarious, and the gods had to struggle constantly to maintain it with the assistance of human prayers and rituals.

A third major theme in Egyptian history is the role of the monarchy as the primary integrating factor in Egyptian civilization. The centrality of the king has two aspects. First, in religious terms Egyptian history began with the final act of the process of creation, the vindication as ruler of Egypt of the god Horus who was henceforth incarnate in every true king of Egypt and after death became Osiris, the king of the dead. Second, the historical beginning of Egyptian history was the forcible conquest of northern Egypt by a king from southern Egypt ca. 3,000 B.C.

Being both god and man, the king was the indispensable link between the divine and human spheres, maintaining the divine order in Egypt and providing critical assistance to his fellow gods in their endless struggle against the forces of chaos.

Politically, therefore, the king represented the unity of Egypt. Being both god and man, the king was the indispensable link between the divine and human spheres, maintaining the divine order in Egypt and providing critical assistance to his fellow gods in their endless struggle against the forces of chaos. Traditional Egyptian art and architecture originated at the royal court to provide a visual representation of the king's essential role in Egyptian life and a safe repository of his body. Not surprisingly, identification with the king was the highest aspiration of an Egyptian, an aspiration made possible after death by magic which allowed persons of lesser status in the social hierarchy potentially to become Osiris just like the king.

While students need not understand the specific reigns of the Pharoahs, it will be helpful for them to be introduced to the essential features of modern historians' periodization of Egyptian history, reflecting both the more than three thousand year continuity of Egyptian cultural traditions and the constant development and modification of those traditions. Central to this approach is the division of Egyptian history into (1) periods of political unification marked by strong central government, foreign expansion, and important cultural achievements (Old Kingdom, Middle Kingdom, and New Kingdom) and (2) periods of political disunity characterized by multiple centers of power, vulnerability to foreign attack and even conquest, and cultural uncertainty (First Intermediate Period, Second Intermediate Period, and Third Intermediate Period).

Popular perceptions of ancient Egypt are largely formed

by the surviving monuments, temples, and the tombs of her royalty and nobility. Virtually unnoticed is the rest of the society that supported the priestly and governmental elite. Students should be made aware of the fact that Egyptian society was more complex and that the elites, whose monuments are so prominent, constituted only the peak of a social pyramid whose base was formed by a vast peasantry living in villages situated along the Nile.

In Egyptian society the elites constituted only the peak of a social pyramid whose base was formed by a vast peasantry living in villages along the Nile.

A variety of literary and artistic sources can be used to illuminate the life of the Egyptian peasantry as well as that of the craftsmen, scribes, soldiers, and lesser priests who constituted the remainder of Egyptian society. Teachers can also use these same sources to highlight two other unique features of Egyptian society, the minor importance of slaves in Egyptian life and the relatively privileged status of Egyptian women who performed numerous economic and religious functions and were recognized by Egyptian law as independent persons with the same legal and property rights as their male social equals.

The hieroglyphic writing system is one of the hallmarks of Egyptian culture, appearing in what is virtually its fully developed form almost simultaneously with the appearance of a unified Egyptian state, about 3000 B.C. Its complexity ensured that literacy would be the possession of a privileged minority, the scribes, who were both Egypt's administrators and the authors of its literature. Although reference to Egyptian literature most readily brings to mind the *Book of the Dead*, a 2nd millennium B.C. compilation of magic spells intended to aid the dead in achieving immortality, the range of Egyptian literature extends far beyond such funerary literature and includes short stories, ethical treatises, and a wide variety of poetic genres. Students should also be made aware of the value system transmitted by this literature, a value system marked by an emphasis on practical ethics, the rational conduct of life, and religious universalism.

An example of Egyptian hieroglyphic writing

In concluding their study of Egypt, students should be introduced to its considerable contributions to its neighbors, north and south. Much of Greek culture, particularly its art and architecture, was strongly influenced by Egyptian civilization. Egypt's role in fostering the growth of civilization in the south in the modern Sudan was even more profound.

Kush

The relationship between Egypt and her southern neighbors was strongly conditioned by geographical factors. The Nile River, north of the first cataract provided Egypt with great opportunities for irrigation, agriculture, and efficient riverine communication. These advantages, compared with the situation in the Nile Valley south of the present-day Aswan High Dam guaranteed that Egypt would enjoy significant advantages over her southern neighbors with regard to the development of civilization. Third millennium B.C. sources already reveal a combination of Egyptian military and colonial expansion in the northern Sudan and trade with the peoples of the central Sudan for luxury products originating in the southern Sudan and elsewhere in northeast Africa.

Further Egyptian imperial expansion in the 2nd millennium B.C. resulted in the establishment of outposts of Egyptian civilization almost as far south as modern Khartoum and the Egyptianization of the Kushite elite, so that after the Egyptian withdrawal from the Sudan a little before 1000 B.C. a powerful kingdom emerged in the area.

With its capital first at Napata near the 4th cataract of the Nile, and then at Meroë just south of the junction of the Nile and Atbara Rivers, Kush preserved its independence and Egyptian heritage until the 4th century A.D. Kush also provided Egypt with one of its greatest dynasties, the twenty-fifth, which reunified a divided and weakened Egypt in the late 8th and early 7th centuries B.C. and sponsored an important revival of Egyptian art and thought.

Teachers should emphasize to students that Kush was not merely a clone of Egypt. Like many cultures throughout world history, the Kushites created a distinct civilization, borrowing Egyptian artistic and architectural conventions to express their own distinctive culture. A good example of the creativity of Kush is the fact that the Kushites invented the only ancient alphabet independent of the Phoenician alphabet in order to write their still undeciphered language. Its capital of Meroe became an important center of iron-making, and a center of trade between East Asia, the Middle East, and parts of Africa. The study of Kush thus provides an opportunity for students

Kush also provided Egypt with one of its greatest dynasties, the twenty-fifth, which reunified a divided and weakened Egypt and sponsored an important revival of Egyptian art and thought.

Bronze figure of a kneeling Kushite king.

to assess the effects of cultural interchange and creativity.

■ ANCIENT CIVILIZATIONS OF INDIA, CHINA, AND THE AMERICAS

In the study of the ancient world, it is helpful to compare the early river civilizations of Mesopotamia and Egypt with those rising in the Indus Valley of India around 2500 B.C., and in the Huang Ho (Yellow), Chang Jiang (Yangtze), and Wei river valleys of China, where an advanced technology and intellectual life had developed by about 2000 B.C. Finally, students should compare these early civilizations with those of the Olmecs in Central America (ca. 800 B.C) and the Tiwanakans of Peru and Bolivia who formed the foundation of the later civilization of the Incas.

Indus Valley Civilization

Indus Head

Thanks to archaeological excavations beginning in the early 1920s, India's first urban civilization has emerged from the sands of time in the Indus Valley. Students should understand how advanced this earliest stage of Indian civilization was, with its neatly laid town planning, observable in the more than 70 sites discovered thus far, including the cities of Mohenjo-Daro and Harappa; its intricate drains and uniform weights and measures; and the ideographic writing appearing on its beautifully artistic seals. Indeed, the Indus Valley peoples were more advanced than the Aryan tribals who invaded from the northwest and appear to have conquered them around 1500 B.C. Led by their kings *(Rajas)* and priests *(Brahmins)*, the Aryans brought herds of cattle and horses to India and stout bows, arrows, and shafted axes, stronger weapons than the more civilized pre-Aryans possessed.

Aryan destruction of the Indus Valley civilization was so nearly complete that only its surviving material features provide clues to the accomplishments of this culture. The similarity in organization of its two large cities—their imposing structures rising on artificial mounds on the western boundaries of each city, their large storehouses for grain, and their symmetrically arranged urban layouts—suggest to scholars that this civilization, like Sumer, had developed a high

Students should understand the advanced state of Indus Valley civilization, its town planning, drains, uniform weights and measures, and its ideographic writing.

level of political organization, perhaps under priestly leadership, with large numbers of workers cultivating fields to provide the grains that filled the communal granaries. Evidence of trade between Mesopotamia and the Indus Valley suggests the influence of Sumerian civilization in the development of these sites. The fragmentary nature of Indus artistic remains and the still undeciphered Indus script severely limits scholars' understandings, however, of the nature of social life, beliefs, or the historical development and decline of Indus civilization.

Ancient Chinese Civilization

Historically as important as the Indus Valley civilization was the ancient civilization of China, one of the earliest and most enduring of the world's ancient cultures. Its accomplishments should be compared with those of other early civilizations to deepen students' understanding of how ancient states rose, spread, and fell, under different circumstances.

To begin, students should be introduced to the geography of East Asia that they might learn about the material factors that have influenced human societies in this region throughout Chinese history. They should know the territory in which Chinese civilization first developed, and the rivers that have provided irrigation for agriculture and supported communication across broad regions. The huge Chinese land mass—bounded by towering mountains, vast deserts, and the sea—has limited contact with other civilizations and has long been an invitation to coherence and continuity in Chinese history.

A crucial starting point for the study of Chinese history is knowledge of the Neolithic cultures of prehistoric China which, like those of Mesopotamia, Egypt, and India, first emerged in an alluvial valley in north-central China along the Yellow River and later spread to northeast China. In these regions the Chinese developed farming of wheat and millet; domesticated cattle, sheep, pigs and dogs; harvested silk; and developed techniques of weaving, irrigation projects, and flood control.

The neolithic cultures of prehistoric China developed farming, domesticated animals, harvested silk, and developed weaving, irrigation projects, and flood control.

The foundations of the Chinese state were developed during the early Xia (ca. 2000 B.C.) and Shang (ca. 1766-1122

B.C.) dynasties. Students can compare the ways in which these dynasties asserted their supremacy over large territories through armed force and religious authority with the ways other early states of the ancient world established their authority. The Shang dynasty is also important for the discovery of bronze metallurgy, which produced a metal stronger than either the tin or copper combined in its manufacture. Bronze was used in the production of beautifully decorated utensils, ceremonical vessels, spears, and chariots.

Ancient Civilizations of the Americas

Students' understanding of the origins of civilization should include the achievements of the Olmecs in Central America and the Tiwanakans, precursors of the Incan civilization in Peru and Bolivia. Though appearing many centuries after the Sumerians, Egyptians, and Chinese, these early civilizations of the Americas emerged from the foundations laid by centuries of agricultural development which began around 5000 B.C. and bred such food crops as corn, yams, squash, and avocadoes, as well as beans, gourds, and grains.

Head of an Olmec ruler fashioned from a basalt boulder.

A good place to start is the Olmec civilization (ca. 800-400 B.C.) and its impressive achievements in taming its tropical environment, creating an accurate calendar for recording the growing seasons, and developing a society characterized by a ruling class of priests and a working class of specialized laborers. Attention should be given to the religious and artistic aspects of Olmec civilization, its trade in jade and other resources, and its development of hieroglyphics to represent both objects and more abstract concepts. Though the Olmec civilization disappeared around 400 B.C., its cultural legacy was to influence later civilizations in Central America, first that of Teotihuacan and, following its decline, the even greater civilization of the Mayans, from about 400 A.D. on.

Though the Olmec civilization disappeared around 400 B.C., its cultural legacy was to influence later civilizations of Teotihuacan and the even greater civilization of the Mayans.

Students should also be introduced to the early Tiwanakan civilization of the Andes (ca. 300 B.C.) which developed a differentiated social structure of ruling elites, artisans of fine jewelry, pottery, and woven textiles, tradesmen, and agricultural laborers. Miles of roads were built to support trade—a precursor of the Incan road system—and llama trade caravans linked settlements in present day Bolivia, Chile, and Peru with the religious center of Tiwanaku.

Although these early civilizations of the Americas never developed such basic technologies as the wheel or the use of iron, they nonetheless developed their considerable achievements in complete isolation from the other centers of world civilization and without benefit, therefore, of the cultural exchange and trade that spurred the rise of civilizations in the Middle East, North Africa, and India.

UNIT II
THE CLASSICAL CIVILIZATIONS
OF THE MEDITERRANEAN WORLD,
INDIA, AND CHINA
(CA. 1000 B.C.-600 A.D.)

SIGNIFICANCE AND TEACHING GOALS

■ MAJOR THEMES

The classical civilizations of China, India, Greece, and Rome are essential topics in the study of world history. Each of these civilizations rose from the legacy of the ancient societies that preceded it, but each, also, was much more than the elaboration of its predecessors' achievements. The infusion of new peoples into these regions with the invasions of the Bronze Age not only marked the decline of the earlier riverine states; it also contributed to the cultural ferment associated with the rise of the classical age. Through these years of dynamic tension, each of these regions saw the development of new ideas, new political and social institutions, and new systems of thought that would characterize these societies and those influenced by them for centuries to come.

The classical civilizations of China, India, Greece, and Rome saw the development of new systems of thought that would characterize these societies and those influenced by them for centuries to come.

Important also in this era was the increasing interaction among the societies of the ancient world. Students will see these processes dramatically at work in the diffusion of Hellenic culture throughout the Middle East and Mediterranean world and the spread of Roman civilization throughout the Empire. Students can compare these processes of cultural diffusion and exchange with the successive periods of absorption and assimilation into traditional Chinese culture of the nomads on China's borders. They should also examine the importance of the great trade routes connecting all these regions: overland by caravan from China to Rome and from the Middle East to India; and by water from the Indian Ocean

Above: The Parthenon, Athens, Greece.

to the South China Sea.

The great nomadic invasions that overwhelmed these civilizations mark a third point of comparison between them. Symptoms of decline had emerged as early as 100 A.D. in China's Han Dynasty, and 180 A.D. in the Roman Empire, leaving both societies weakened, plagued by social unrest, and incapable of turning back the waves of invaders descending upon them. Nomadic invasions from the north had by the end of the 6th century completed the destruction of the Gupta Empire as well.

Merchants in China and India expanded their activities, linking their lands, the Middle East, and Rome through sea trade and through the great Silk Road, overland from China into the Middle East.

Studying the history of these four civilizations picks up and continues all four of the major narrative themes introduced in Unit I, the Beginnings of Civilization. Basic to understanding this age is knowledge of **the development and changing character of these societies.** Students will observe dramatic illustrations of social change, for example, in the years that followed the Aryan invasions of India's Punjab and Delhi plain. Cultural exchange between the more civilized pre-Aryans and the Indo-European invaders from the northwest created Hindu civilization, its caste system and, from the Vedic beliefs introduced by the Aryans, the religion of Hinduism, still the major faith in India today. Students should compare these developments with the social and cultural changes occurring in China and the Mediterranean states of Greece and Rome. In all cases they should give special consideration to the lives of men and women, free and enslaved; the role of the family; and the importance of literacy and education.

Black-figure vase, ca. 500 B.C.

Following the theme of **economic and technological development** will highlight for students important advances in agricultural technology and the resulting increase in yields (and hence population) in what were still agricultural societies. Manufacturing thrived, particularly in India where iron-making and steel were the most advanced in the world. Most important, however, were the advances in trade, for merchants in China and India expanded their activities, linking their lands, the Middle East, and Rome through sea trade and through the great Silk Road, overland from China into the Middle East. Students should closely examine the consequences of this growing network of cultural exchange and trade in the ancient world.

The classical age is important, also, for its **developments in political theory and organization.** The dynasties of classical China are important for establishing the highly centralized political structures that made possible centuries of effective rule over a vast territory of periodically warring states. Students should consider how the development during this time of a large trained administrative bureaucracy, the integration of units of local control under a single national code of law, and the Confucian philosophy permeating every level of society created an imperial system strong enough to survive into the 20th century.

Students should compare this example of classic imperialism with the foundations of the theory and institutions of political democracy established in ancient Greece and Rome. The study of Greece is essential, for the rationalist philosophy and intellectual tradition, the democratic ideals of liberty and equality of citizens before the law which developed in Athens lie at the heart of Western tradition and are indispensable to any understanding of how that tradition and its inner tensions subsequently evolved. Studying the Roman Republic, the poetry of Horace, and the lives of Brutus, Cassius, and Cato the Younger (who defied tyranny and warned against the abuses of arbitrary power) will reveal to students the foundations of the civic humanist tradition, central to late 17th- and 18th-century republican thought and the founding of their own nation.

Finally, this era provides students unusual opportunity to examine the **development and diffusion of the central ideas and influences of the major ethical systems and religions of the classical age:** Hinduism, Buddhism, Confucianism, Judaism, and Christianity. All evolved in important ways during this age and must be understood, for their influences have survived for centuries, into our own day, and reveal most forcibly the power of ideas and religious beliefs in history.

The study of Greece is essential, for its rationalist philosophy and intellectual tradition, its democratic ideals of liberty and equality of citizens before the law lie at the heart of Western tradition.

■ *ESSENTIAL UNDERSTANDINGS*

1. **The nature and influences of cultural synthesis and diffusion in the classical age:** Greek indebtedness to

View of the Great Wall of China

Students should understand the major characteristics and enduring qualities of imperial rule in China: the centralization of dynastic power, large trained bureaucracies, a single national code of law , a national system of taxation and tribute, and the political ideals of Confucianism.

Crete, Mesopotamia, Phoenicia, and Egypt, and the spread of Hellenic culture through the Middle East and Mediterranean world; Roman civilization and its diffusion throughout the empire; the formation of Hindu civilization in the exchanges between Aryan invaders and the Indus Valley civilization; the successive periods of absorption and assimilation into traditional Chinese culture of the barbaric nomads on China's borders; and the effects of cultural and economic exchange among all these regions through the great sea and land trade routes connecting China and Rome, the Middle East and India.

2. **The historical evolution of the theory, ideals, and institutions of political democracy** in Athens and republican Rome; the conditions supporting the development of democratic institutions and those contributing to their decline and fall.

3. **The major characteristics and enduring qualities of imperial rule in China:** the centralization of dynastic power, large trained bureaucracies, a single national code of law, a national system of taxation and tribute, and the political ideals of Confucianism.

4. **The origins, central beliefs, influences, and diffusion of the major religious and ethical systems** arising during the classical age: Hinduism, Buddhism, Confucianism, and Christianity.

5. **The major causes of the decline and fall of the great civilizations of the classic age:** Greece, Rome, Gupta India, and Han China.

■ *HABITS OF THE MIND*

The study of this unit is particularly rich in opportunities for students **to examine the complexity of historical causation.** In the stories of Chinese dynasties, of the Ashoka and Gupta empires of India, of Athens and Sparta, the Peloponnesian War, the Macedonian Conquest, the Alexandrian Empire, and Rome, students will observe the rise and decline of successive centers of power, prosperity, and cultural influence. The fall of Rome, for example, has always fascinated historians, who have offered an enormous range of explanations: technological, economic, social, religious, philosophical, and political. Few historical episodes can so well develop the habit of suspecting the single, simple answer, of considering all possible forces at work—not least the role of individuals and their character—and of not neglecting the possible intrusion of accident, unreason, or simple ignorance in the making of historic turning points. Paralleling the fall of Rome was the decline and fall of the Han Dynasty in China, an epic event that can profitably be used **to develop students' skill in comparative analysis.**

The study of Greece and Rome provides students opportunity **to exercise their own powers of critical thought and debate,** for the great issues of democracy and dictatorship, freedom and slavery, piety and impiety, personal honor and expediency, justice and oppression were subjects debated and fought over, and their records allow students to examine the great tragedies, orations, and other documents of this age.

Paralleling the fall of Rome was the decline and fall of the Han Dynasty in China, an epic event that can profitably be used to develop students' skill in comparative analysis.

Death Mask attributed to Agamemnon, King of Mycenae, immortalized in Homer's Iliad.

MAJOR TOPICS IN THE STUDY OF THE CLASSICAL CIVILIZATIONS OF THE MEDITERRANEAN WORLD, INDIA, AND CHINA

1. The Rise of Greek Civilization

2. The Rise and Fall of Rome

3. The Rise and Establishment of Christianity

4. The Rise of the Classical Civilizations of India and China

MAJOR TOPICS AND THEIR DEVELOPMENT: ESSENTIAL UNDERSTANDINGS AND RELATED BACKGROUND FOR TEACHERS

■ *THE RISE OF GREEK CIVILIZATION*

In studying Greek history, students should be made aware during the outset that the Greek achievements of its classical age were indebted to earlier advances on the part of the Minoan and Mycenaean civilizations which flourished between 2000 B.C. and 1100 B.C. During the "Dark Ages" and "Archaic Period" of early Greek history (ca. 1100-700 B.C.), contacts increased across the eastern Mediterranean, allowing the Greeks to absorb ideas and cultural innovations from the more advanced civilizations in the Near East and Egypt. These contacts allowed a shift from an oral to a written culture which marked a profound change in Greek civilization.

Building on the Phoenician alphabet, the Greeks developed an alphabet which made the learning of reading and writing much easier and hence more accessible to a wider portion of the population than it had been in the older civilizations of the eastern Mediterranean. This was a vital step in the emergence of Greek culture and provided the foundations for Greek philosophy and history. This early use of literacy can be studied by using Greek mythology, the Homeric poems, and (later) Herodotus, who is called the father of history.

The Persian Wars reveal much about the strength of Greek society and culture and the powerful desire of the Greeks to fight for their freedom against the overwhelming might of Persia.

A second topic should be the creation of the polis and the invention of citizenship (ca. 800 B.C.). The political life of Greece moved in a decisive direction with the creation of small, independent cities. The development of the polis represents the beginnings of the Western political tradition and is essential to understanding the emergence of democracy in Athens, as well as the ideals of equality and liberty, and the conditions necessary for these aspirations to be realized in a functioning system of government.

Xerxes Bridge at the Hellespont

Finally, students should know the story of the Persian Wars. They not only provide examples of stirring history, but also reveal much about the strength of Greek society and culture and the powerful desire of the Greeks to fight for their freedom against the overwhelming might of Persia. In assessing the importance of this era, students might consider whether Western history might have been different, had Persia conquered Greece.

The period of classical Greece can be studied through the histories of its two greatest poleis, Athens and Sparta. Fifth-century Athens, because of its great figures and institutions, has long been a model of democratic origins. Students therefore should know about Athenian history, organization, and achievements. They should trace its development from Solon and Cleisthenes down to Pericles. It is important that they be exposed to the art and architecture of the period, as well as to some of the great literary and philosophic works, so that they can see for themselves the questions that preoccupied the Athenians. They should be introduced to some of the mechanisms of Athenian democracy—the assemblies, popular juries, and selection of office-holders by lot—so that they can compare the direct democracy of Athens with their own representative system. This will help them recognize the strengths and weaknesses of each system and deepen their understanding of democratic institutions.

At the same time students should be given a full picture of Athenian society. It is essential that they understand the differing rights of citizens, foreigners, women, and slaves and the strains placed on political democracy by the growth of the Athenian empire and the subsequent Peloponnesian War. Many of these issues can be highlighted in the trial and death of Socrates. Plato's *Apology* offers an opportunity to discuss the nature of citizenship and justice, as well as to learn about some of the problems that Athenian democracy faced. Aristotle's *Politics* presents students with his classical, and still very helpful, six categories of government. Three were exercised for the common good: kingship, aristocracy, and polity (to which we give the name democracy); but each could be perverted, exercised only for the selfish interests of those who ruled: tyranny, oligarchy, and mob rule (for which he used the word democracy).

Central to the character of Athenian culture was Greek classicism, an ideal of moderation, of the golden mean, in the arts, architecture, and letters as well as in human behavior. It stressed balance, symmetry, order, harmony, clarity, reflection, restraint, and discipline—probably because the ancient Greeks were likely to be immoderate, impulsive, and undisciplined in their behavior. The ideal of the well-rounded man—athlete, poet, soldier, philosopher, and citizen—strongly influenced later Western views on education for free societies. The moderate, self-respecting, civic-minded citizen needed for democracy was most likely to be found in the "middle classes," Aristotle taught. Hence his insistence upon a society where the extremes of wealth and poverty had to be avoided

Euripides and Sophocles were among Athens' leading venerated dramatists.

It is essential that students understand the differing rights of citizens, foreigners, women, and slaves and the strains placed on political democracy by the growth of the Athenian empire and the subsequent Peloponnesian War.

217

if democracy was to survive.

As a complement to the study of Athens, students should also learn about the contrasting development of Sparta: how it extended its power over the surrounding territory, subjugated the local population, and created a tightly regimented social and political order admired by many of the political thinkers of antiquity as well as some in modern times. The consequences of this development can be studied through the Peloponnesian War and its effects, chronicled by the historian Thucydides. The contrast between Athens and Sparta can fuel discussion about how different political systems develop and their differing outcomes for societies and individuals, as well as about the fragility of democracy in wartime.

The contrast between Athens and Sparta can fuel discussion about how different political systems develop and their differing outcomes for societies and individuals.

Why did the classical era in Greece come to an end? How and why did the ideal of the independent city state die? This fundamental transformation in Greek society is crucial in understanding to what extent Greek ideals and values survived and were eventually disseminated throughout the Mediterranean world. Having been grounded in the classical era, students will be able to appreciate some of the changes that occurred in art and philosophy, as well as how the arrival of Greek culture affected or transformed local cultures and religions, such as Judaism or Egyptian religion, and how these in turn influenced developments around the Mediterranean.

Students should learn how Macedonia differed from the rest of classical Greece, and how the kings, Philip and Alexander, took over the Greek poleis and then extended Greek culture throughout the Near East. Knowing about the subsequent wars is less important than recognizing the divisions in the Hellenistic world that led eventually to Roman domination. Characters such as Diogenes and Cleopatra can help to introduce these topics.

■ THE RISE AND FALL OF ROME

The beginnings of the Roman Republic, as constructed by Roman historians writing centuries later, display a rhetoric of liberty and an ideal republican constitution that have influenced politicians and political philosophers in the West ever since. They also make a stirring story of heroism and adventure that students enjoy. Students should learn something about the Etruscan background and the subsequent overthrow of the Tarquins which prepared the Roman hatred of kings, an important force in their politics. At the same time, students should see the complicated nature of the Republic, and the early strains within it that led to the social Conflict of the Orders and the compilation of the XII Tables.

The process of Roman expansion, first within Italy and then throughout the Mediterranean, is an equally compelling story. It shows how people and institutions propelled expansion and then were forced to adjust to the internal changes brought about by empire. Though drawn out, Roman expansion brought about a fundamental transformation in Roman life and marked a crucial turning point in Roman history, one that has been studied and debated ever since. Students can be introduced to this debate by studying the effects of expansion on society and politics.

Students should know something about the course of expansion, especially the Punic Wars and Hannibal's near-conquest of Rome. They should learn about the spread of slavery which gradually transformed the Roman economy. It is also useful to contrast Athenian and Roman slavery, as well as other examples of dependency such as those in Sparta, Mesopotamia, and China. This kind of comparative study will reveal that throughout history men and women have exploited their fellow humans in varying forms of dependency. Roman slavery was only one kind, but it had profound consequences for every aspect of Roman life.

The most important outcome of Roman imperialism was the fall of the Republic. It is a story replete with dramatic figures such as Cicero and Caesar and a saga that students will find absorbing in its sweep and tragedy. Teachers should emphasize the strains imposed on the Republic by expansion and economic change and its subsequent social and constitutional failure to meet those strains. It is helpful for students to learn about the Roman army, not only its military aspects but also its social and political impact. The fall of the Republic involved a profound political crisis which opens up to students the interaction of the army, its officers, civilian officials, and the active public in political upheaval.

Interlinking systems of a Roman Aqueduct in ancient Rome. Painting by Zeus Diemer.

The outcome of Roman imperialism was the fall of the Republic, a story replete with dramatic figures such as Cicero and Caesar and a saga absorbing in its sweep and tragedy.

The Augustan settlement and the beginnings of the Roman Empire marked the end of the crisis and signaled a sharp turn in the nature of the Roman state, all under the guise of Augustus' claim of restoring the Republic. These events should be studied as an instance of political and institutional change, aided by traditional propaganda. The emperors themselves are fascinating subjects, illustrating the uses and abuses of power. Similarly, the growth of the city of Rome, its architecture and monuments, will deepen students' understanding of the internal dynamics of empire.

To understand the fall of the Roman Empire, students must see how truly complex its problems were including technological stagnation, economic decline social change, political instability, and outside pressures.

What makes an empire? The study of Rome shows how laws, language, army, bureaucracy, and economy each helped to knit disparate peoples into a vast empire. Studying the extent of the Roman Empire—through present-day Italy, Spain, France, Southern Germany, England, southeastern Europe, the Middle East, Egypt, and North Africa—and the Romanization of the ancient Western world offers an excellent opportunity to learn about European and Mediterranean geography. It also offers insight into the dynamics of expansion and its effects on subject peoples, such as the Jews and Britons. European historiography has tended to coopt the Roman Empire entirely into the history of Europe. In fact, Rome was a Mediterranean empire whose cultural style reflected the influence of different peoples all around the sea's rim. North Africa also played an important economic, cultural, and political role in the history of the empire, contributing, for example, several emperors, the most important being Septimius Severus, and giving the world St. Augustine, the early Christian father. Students should understand, once again, that race was not given the significance in the ancient Mediterranean world that it has been given today.

It is important to examine the Roman family amid the broader problems of Roman society and economy. Complex social developments including the inability to rise above an agrarian economy based on dependent labor, the gradual debasement of freemen, coupled with the use of bread and games to pacify the masses, and the inflation of honors at the top of society, were only some of the driving forces behind problems in the empire. To appreciate the rise and fall of the Roman Empire, students must see how truly complex its problems were, and how the empire changed internally as well as externally.

Students should consider the varying explanations historians have given for the fall of Rome. From primary sources they should explore what Romans themselves believed to be going wrong. In evaluating the causes of Rome's collapse, students should consider the role of different forces such as technological stagnation, economic decline, social change, plague, political instability, religious conversion, and outside pressure from invading Germans and nomads from the central Asian steppes.

The Roman Empire split into East and West, first as an administrative decision and then as a consequence of military collapse in the West. It would be useful for students to learn something about the major Germanic kingdoms that replaced Roman power in the West, such as the Vandals, Visigoths, and Franks. The survival of the empire in the East and the development of the Byzantine Empire is also a necessary part of the story, one requiring understanding of the origins and growth of Christianity.

Detail from an early portrayal of Jesus with his disciples at the "Last Supper."

■ THE RISE AND ESTABLISHMENT OF CHRISTIANITY

The historical development of Christianity is of profound importance, not only because it teaches students about the roots of important American religious and ethical traditions, but also because it reveals the historical power of belief and religious institutions. The birth of Christianity in the 1st century A.D. is widely judged to be one of the great dramas of history. Students need to understand how directly the early Christians drew from their Jewish roots, how the Hebrew Bible was to be combined with the teachings of Jesus to form the Christian Bible. Students should understand that the teachings of Jesus stressed traditional Jewish beliefs of love and compassion for others and the importance of entering into a right relationship with God. Students need also to reflect upon the Sermon on the Mount as expressing the "New Law" on Christian love and the doctrine of equal human worth and dignity made explicit in Christian teachings.

It is important to see the impact of St. Paul, of Greek learning, and of the early church fathers on the promulgation

The historical development of Christianity is of profound importance, not only because it teaches students about the roots of important American religious and ethical traditions, but also because it reveals the historical power of belief and religious institutions.

of Christian doctrines, particularly the Christian belief that Jesus of Nazareth fulfilled Old Testament expectations of the messiah and that in his death and resurrection he had reconciled the world to God, making possible the forgiveness of sin and the flow of the eternal life of God into the lives of human beings.

Finally, students should see the way in which Christian doctrines were disseminated throughout the Roman world. They should see how these doctrines treated women, slaves, and the family and know something about the organization of the church. They should explore Roman ambivalence to the new religion and the response of the state. How did the early church manage to survive and flourish? How did it change Roman society? Finally, students should learn about Constantine's conversion and its consequences, both for the empire and the church—one of the best examples in history of the importance of a single man's decisions.

■ THE RISE OF THE CLASSICAL CIVILIZATIONS OF INDIA AND CHINA

In making the transition from the classical Mediterranean world to that of India and China, students should be oriented to the contemporary development of all three regions during the centuries following the invasions of the Indo-European Aryans into India (ca. 1500-1000 B.C.), the Dorian invasions into mainland Greece (ca. 1200-1000 B.C.), and the overthrow of the Shang Dynasty in China by martial forces from the Wei Valley, and their establishment of the Zhou Dynasty (ca. 1100 B.C.).

As their study progresses, students should be alert to the economic linkages that developed between the classical civilizations of China, India, and the Graeco-Roman world in the Great Silk Road (ca. 100 B.C.) and the sea trade connecting all three (ca. 100 A.D.). Students should also compare the events leading to the decline and fall of Gupta India, Han China, and Rome in the early half of the 1st millennium A.D.—events that included invasions into all three regions by nomadic warriors of the central Asian steppes. Students should consider why, in their already weakened state, none of these civilizations withstood the onslaught.

Students should be alert to the economic linkages that developed between the classical civilizations of China, India, and the Graeco-Roman world in the Great Silk Road (ca. 100 B.C.) and the sea trade connecting all three (ca. 100 A.D.).

The Rise of Classical Civilization in India

By about 1000 B.C., the dawn of India's Epic Age, the conquering Aryan tribes had crossed the Punjab and settled down in kingdoms around Delhi's broad plain, which was to become the strategic site of no less than ten capitals over the next three thousand years of India's history. Students should learn that in the course of more than a thousand years following the Aryan invasions, exchanges between Aryans and pre-Aryans led to the synthesis of Hindu civilization. In many ways the conquering Aryans were culturally conquered by their captives, who had been more civilized when they first met. During the Epic Age, the caste system took shape under Aryan rulers concerned with preserving the social superiority of their own warrior and priestly classes over the indigenous peoples. The longer of India's two great epic poems, *Mahabharata*, is a tale of the prolonged struggle for power over Delhi's plain among competing Aryan cousins. The shorter epic, *Ramayana*, reflects what was probably a somewhat later stage of Aryan history. Just as students of Western civilization should read something of the *Iliad* and *Odyssey*, our students of India should read portions of both epics.

Buddhism, which was to become one of the world's major religions, emerged in the 6th century B.C. as a new form of Hinduism, which itself had developed gradually out of Aryan religious beginnings. Ancient Hinduism was many-sided, embracing both ritual (under Brahmin priests) and mysticism (as practiced by holy teachers called *gurus*). The Upanishads stressed the latter, finding a divine spirit in all the universe and its creatures. Students should be introduced to this Hindu belief in monism, the oneness of all gods and living things in the Divine One, Brahma, and they should understand something of the Hindu belief in pure and unchanging spirit transcending an impermanent material world.

Students should know of Buddhism's origins in the meditations of Siddhartha Gautama who became known as Buddha (the enlightened one). He minimized the importance of ritual and of the caste system, which had grown out of Hindu belief, and proclaimed that the devoted individual could live a holy life and ultimately achieve union with the divine (*nirvana*), escaping the inevitable suffering of earthly

Students should know of Buddhism's origins in the meditations of Siddhartha Gautama who became known as Buddha (the enlightened one).

Figure of a preaching Buddha from Hoti-Mardan.

The Gupta era provides an aesthetic tradition and architectural works of art that rival anything created in other civilizations of the world.

A view of an Indian temple

existence. Students should also know of his ethical mandate to inflict no suffering.

Buddhism's spread was aided, like Christianity's later, by its emphasis upon the spiritual equality of people, regardless of caste or occupation, by its preaching of love and charity, and, on the practical side, by its organization of monasteries. The emperor Ashoka (269-232 B.C.) was converted and supported Buddhist missionary efforts, but Hinduism under its Brahmins remained dominant in India. Buddhism's larger conversions were to take place in Southeast Asia, China, and Japan where Buddhism was "nativized"— that is, translated into existing indigenous terms, symbols, and concepts of these cultures.

By the Buddha's era there were many competing kingdoms all across India, but in the immediate wake of Alexander the Great's brief invasion in 327 B.C., India's first imperial unification was achieved by Chandragupta Maurya. The Mauryan Empire lasted from about 324 B.C. to 184 B.C., roughly as long as British imperial rule over India would last almost two millennia later. But it disappeared with the return of civil war and invasion.

The era of Gupta imperial unification (ca. 320-550 A.D.) is generally viewed as India's "Golden Age." Thanks to the beautiful Sanskrit poetry and plays of Kalidasa, India's Shakespeare, we know much about it. Hinduism dominated during the Gupta Empire, and the Hindu temple emerged as a "home" for the gods in every major center of Hindu settlement. Early Buddhist caves had Hindu temples added to them as well, the most famous being in Ajanta, Ellora, and on the Island of Elephanta, off Bombay. Gupta trade in luxury exports reached to Rome, Africa, China, and Southeast Asia. Scholars, influenced by Greek mathematical astronomy, made sophisticated contributions in both fields. Studying the Gupta era also provides the opportunity for students to understand an aesthetic tradition quite different from that of the West, and to see statues, frescoes, and architectural works of art that rival anything created in the other civilizations of the world. The invasions of nomadic tribesmen from the steppes of Asia that began in 500 A.D. continued over the next century to complete the destruction of the Gupta Empire.

The Rise of Classical Civilization in China

Understanding classical China is important, for among contemporary societies, China exhibits the strongest continuity with its ancient past. Its foundations were laid during the Zhou, Ch'in, and Han dynasties, between the years 1029 B.C. and 100 A.D., the onset of the decline and eventual fall of the Han civilization.

The Zhou Dynasty is important for uniting existing agricultural communities in a mode of feudalism. Under Zhou rule the territory of China was extended to include the Yangtze River valley, and the claim that the emperor ruled by mandate from heaven was introduced as a tenet of imperial authority.

Confucius (551-479 B.C.)

It is vital that students learn about Confucianism, one of the most enduring ethical systems in history. Living during the last years of the Zhou Dynasty (ca. 551-479 B.C.), when its rule weakened and China fell into chaos, Confucius sought to make sense of a troubled world. The basic tenets of Confucianism should be taught: its humanistic (rather than religious) emphasis; its concern with social good and with right relationships between people—husband and wife, father and son, older and younger brother, friend and friend, and ruler and subject; and its paternalistic, hierarchical political ideals. It would also be useful for older students to know that Confucius was challenged by others, such as Lao Tzu. Taoism placed more emphasis on the amoral natural universe and denied the usefulness of ethical action.

It is vital that students learn about Confucianism, its humanistic emphasis, its concern with social good, and with right relationships between people.

Students should examine the importance of the military revolution in weaponry and tactics of war that finally brought an end to the half-millenium of warfare that prevailed between 722 and 221 B.C. Mobilizing an army of over one million men and using new mass-produced iron weaponry and the centralized authority of the administrative state, the Chi'n Dynasty was able to create a unified empire of over 50 million inhabitants. Harsh and ruthless in his rule, Shih Huang-ti, or First Emperor, did away with the feudal basis of Zhou rule and established a bureaucratic administration far in advance of other civilizations, and based on well-defined offices staffed by salaried, removable officials. Students should understand how this innovation allowed a tremendous centralization of

Chinese history has been replete with crises and change and not a dull march of one dynasty after another.

the Chinese state and laid the foundations of the imperial Chinese empire that would last to 1911.

The Han Dynasty (206 B.C.-220 A.D.) capitalized on these achievements and took them further, especially by reviving Confucianism and making it part of the state apparatus. By necessity, imperial Confucianism was legalistic and rigid, but it nonetheless exerted a powerful ethical influence on government policy and sparked generations of debate about the proper role of government. Students should also appreciate the achievements of the Early Empire: the use of silk, gunpowder, and paper; the high level of artistic and literary achievement; and contacts with the world outside China through trade and conquest. Daily life, agricultural work, and ancestor worship should also be studied to give students a sense of the full dimensions of Chinese society.

Students need to examine the success and influence of Buddhism in China. One approach is to understand the turmoil of the "Dark Ages" in China during which Buddhism was introduced. The break-up of the Han Empire in the 3rd century A.D. and the political difficulties that ensued mark another important turning point about which students should be informed. This period helps underscore the point that Chinese history has been replete with crises and change and not a dull march of one dynasty after another. American students need to replace older notions of a "static" Asia with a more lively and truer picture of ever-changing East Asian civilizations. The early empire and its vicissitudes is one point at which that can be accomplished.

UNIT III
THE EXPANSION OF
AGRARIAN CIVILIZATIONS
(CA. 600-1450 A.D.)

SIGNIFICANCE AND TEACHING GOALS

■ *MAJOR THEMES*

This third unit in world history considers the 850-year period between the decline of the great classical civilizations of the ancient world and the first 15th-century stirrings of the modern world. In the Mediterranean, Christian Byzantium rose on Rome's eastern foundations and civilization spread, albeit slowly, northward through medieval Western Europe. More continuous was the recovery in China, whose influence was to spread to Japan in this same period. The Americas saw the rise of the Mayan, Incan, and Aztec empires, and Africa became home to the empires of Ghana, Mali, and Songhay in the west and Zimbabwe in the south. More dynamic than all these developments, however, was the historic rise and spread of Islam, a new faith that united the Middle East under Arab leadership, and then was rapidly disseminated with profound effects to Africa, India, southern Europe, and Southeast Asia.

Yet just as the great civilizations of the ancient Eurasian world were vulnerable to nomadic invaders looking for wealth, so too were their successors plagued by invasion and revolt. In this era, however, the invaders themselves created vast empires, uniting for a time disparate peoples and regions under the leadership of warrior bands. Thus, between 970 and 1500 A.D. nomadic invaders once again poured out of the Eurasian steppes into the settled regions of China, Eastern Europe, the Islamic Middle East, and India. Once again it was the wealth of the settled communities that attracted nomadic peoples

This age saw the historic rise and spread of Islam, a new faith that united the Middle East and was rapidly disseminated to Africa, southern Europe, and Asia.

Above: Arabian astronomers at work. Miniature from a manuscript in the University of Istanbul.

227

The wealth of the settled communities attracted nomadic peoples of the steppes whose superior mobility, horsemanship, and warlike elan awaited only the organizing leadership of a Genghis Khan or Mahmud of Ghazni to bring vast territories under Seljuk Turk, Mongol, Moghul, or Ottoman control.

whose superior mobility, horsemanship, and warlike *elan* awaited only the organizing leadership of a Genghis Khan or Mahmud of Ghazni to bring vast territories under Seljuk Turk, Mongol, Moghul, or Ottoman control.

Among the earliest and most dramatic of the waves of conquest in this era was the initial expansion of Islam, which, under Arab leadership, destroyed much of the ancient balance of power between Rome and Persia in the Mediterranean region. It was followed in the 11th century by the invasion of the Seljuk Turks who adopted Islam as a simplistic warrior faith, rapidly established control over the entire Middle East, and launched a global expansion that posed a critical challenge to Orthodox Christendom, and increased tensions all along the borderlands.

Even more momentous in world terms was the arrival of the Mongols, uniting virtually all of the Eurasian land mass under a single rule in the 13th century. This period of Mongol peace encouraged the exchange of products, ideas, and techniques across vast distances, as personified in the travels of Marco Polo. Finally, between 1300 and 1500 came the expulsion of the Mongols from China, the resumption of Turkish domination of the Middle East, and the renewed expansion of Islam into India and Europe.

Bringing order to the sheer scope of events in these centuries requires focus upon four major narrative themes. Primary among them is **the development and spread of the great world religions** whose temporal as well as spiritual influence and power stamped the character of whole civilizations in this age: Islam, Christendom, and the enduring influences of the already established faiths of the East— Hinduism and Buddhism. Following this theme will help students make sense not only of developments within these societies, but also of the conflicts that erupted between them: the continuing tensions between Islam and Hinduism in South Asia, following the Seljuk conquests, for example; and such confrontations between Christendom and Islam as the historic battles that set the northern limits of Islamic expansion into Europe, the Crusades, and the Christian reconquest of Muslim Spain. No age illustrates more dramatically for students the importance of religion in human history, and the need to understand the driving force of the beliefs and values, the ethical commitments, the hopes and fears of individuals and groups in the unfolding human story.

A second major theme follows naturally from the first: **the development and changing character of the societies influenced by these faiths.** Most dramatic were the social changes in the Muslim world, for Islam defined not only the faith of its followers, but all levels of social and political life. The Middle Ages witnessed also the first clear statement of European culture through the institution of the Church of Rome, the dominant—though not the sole—force in setting standards of right and wrong in all spheres of human activity, including attitudes toward learning, knowledge, and views of self and others.

Students will also be fascinated by the varying responses of settled societies to the nomadic challenge throughout this period: Islam's absorption of the Seljuk Turks, converting them and then drawing new strength from them; China's tolerance but final expulsion of the Mongols; India's failure to free itself from its invaders and gradual adjustment to Turkish Muslim rule; and Europe's slow-developing but deeply belligerent response to Islam.

Following the theme of **economic and technological development** will disclose the growing interdependence of different peoples of the world as conquest knit regions into empires and long distance trade intensified cultural exchanges between East Asia, the Islamic Middle East, Africa, and Europe. Historically, trade was long recognized in the Middle East as a source of both power and culture, and the merchant profession was honored. Domestication of the camel allowed the conquest of the deserts and brought the Middle East together while the expansion of Islam carried its advanced accomplishments in science, medicine, and philosophy to neighboring territories, Europe, Africa, and the Far East. In China the conversion of the Yangtze Valley into a productive rice-producing region through the development of sophisticated irrigation channels and canals created the foundations for the thriving economy of the Tang and Sung Dynasties— accomplishments followed by the flourishing overseas mercantile successes of the Mongol Ascendancy. Particularly

Vaulted Gothic arches, Lincoln cathedral, England.

No age illustrates more dramatically the importance of religion in human history, the driving force of the beliefs and values, the ethical commitments, the hopes and fears of individuals and groups.

important among the economic perspectives students should acquire concerning this era was the development of the great land bridge across Eurasia, established by the Mongols and uniting in trade and cultural exchange China, the Islamic Middle East, Africa, and Europe.

Following the theme of **the development of political organization,** students will profit from examining the variety of governmental systems developing in this same era, including the feudal kingdoms of northern Europe, feudal Japan, the Muslim caliphates, the Muslim city-states of East Africa, the West African empires of Ghana, Mali, and Songhay, and the pre-Columbian empires of the Americas. Students should understand the development in the 13th century of a period of unity across much of Eurasia through a vast military confederacy under Mongol control, and compare this period of Mongol peace with the resumption of political disorder and warfare with its collapse and the renewed invasions by the Turks of the Muslim heartlands. Within Western Europe, students will see developing in this same era the power of the Western idea of law behind documents such as Magna Carta (1215) and the Golden Bull (1356) and the foundations being laid for European states and institutions that have lasted until the present day: nations, monarchies, parliaments, common law, and European versions of Roman law and administrative structures.

The granite walls at Great Zimbabwe

■ **ESSENTIAL UNDERSTANDINGS**

1. **The rise and spread of Islam, ca. 600-1000 A.D.:** the origins and principles of Islam; the unification of the Muslim Middle East under Arab rule; its intellectual and cultural accomplishments in science, astronomy, mathematics, medicine, and geography; the spread of Islamic civilization to Africa, Portugal, Sicily, Spain, and India.

2. **The nomadic invasions from the Eurasian steppes, ca. 1000-1450 A.D.:** the invasions of the Seljuk Turks, their conversion to Islam, their conquest of the Middle East, and their expansion of Islam into Europe and India; the Mongol invasions, their unification of much of the Eurasian world, and the increased exchange between East and West; the resumption of Turkish invasions resulting

Particularly important among the economic perspectives students should acquire concerning this era was the development of the great land bridge across Eurasia, established by the Mongols and uniting in trade and cultural exchange China, the Islamic Middle East, Africa, and Europe.

in the establishment of Ottoman rule in Byzantium and the Islamic Middle East, and of Turkish Muslim conquests in India.

3. **The origins and consequences of religious conflict:** between Islam and Hinduism in South Asia and between Christendom and Islam in the Crusades and the Christian reconquest of Muslim Spain.

4. **The Medieval West:** the Byzantine Empire as heir to the Roman Empire and center of Orthodox Christendom; its conquest by the Ottoman Turks; the ascendancy of the Church of Rome in Western Europe and its religious, intellectual, and economic influence.

5. **Feudalism in Europe and Japan:** similarities and contrasts in feudal society, economy, and government.

6. **Development of the monarchies** of England, France, and Spain; struggles over authority between Church and State; origins of the English legal system and rule of law in Magna Carta and the medieval parliament of lords and commons.

7. **The flowering of Chinese civilization** during the Tang and Sung Dynasties: its commercial revolution; revival of classical learning, overseas colonization, and development of meritocracy through its examination system; its conquest by the Mongols under Genghis Khan and achievements of the Mongolian Ascendancy under Kublai Khan.

Students should understand the flowering of Chinese civilization during the Tang and Sung Dynasties, including its commercial revolution, revival of classical learning, and development of meritocracy through its examination system.

8. **The rise and spread of African civilizations:** the great migrations of the Bantu-speaking peoples; the "camel revolution" and development of intercontinental trade linking West Africa with a trans-Eurasian trading system; spread of Islam to Africa; rise of wealthy city states and empires of West Africa, their systems of government, trade, and centers of learning; the rise of the Swahili city states of the East Coast, and the kingdoms of Zimbabwe and the Kongo.

9. **The rise and accomplishments of the major sedentary**

civilizations of the Americas: the Mayan, Aztec, and Incan civilizations, their origins, elaborate agricultural systems, hierarchic societies, trade and communication systems, law codes, religions, and impressive architecture; their vulnerability to later conquest, however, in their technological developments which lagged behind those of the Eurasian world, and their isolation from the great systems of trade and cultural exchange unifying the continents of Asia, Africa, and Europe.

■ *HABITS OF THE MIND*

Study of this era offers students a rich field in which to **compare the achievements of agrarian civilizations throughout the world** and to appreciate the great diversity as well as commonalities among societies in their responses to common human needs. This era also affords students opportunity to **assess the constant tension between change and continuity.** During this era population grew, technology improved, and commercial and agricultural improvements created new wealth and opportunities. Yet for most ordinary people, in all societies, daily life remained an unchanging struggle simply to survive on their land or labor. Here students can perceive the common, unchanging needs and anxieties of people, however far away in time or space, however unfamiliar their ways of coping with life. By looking at different modes of family life in these years, students can **develop their power of historical empathy,** and free themselves from the intellectually limiting confines of present-mindedness.

Examining ways in which historians have reconstructed the African past will **develop students' respect for historical method.** The best research and writing in African history is an achievement of the past forty years. Students can appreciate something of the innovative methods in archeology, anthropology, linguistics, and oral tradition analysis that both Western and African scholars have developed to puzzle out the deep history of pre-literate peoples. Students should also be aware, however, that written documents on African history are more abundant than is often assumed, not only in modern European languages but also in Arabic, Amharic, Egyptian, Swahili, and other tongues. Examining some of these records, such as English translations of Arabic accounts of Mansa

Study of this era offers students a rich field in which to compare the achievements of agrarian civilizations throughout the world and to appreciate the great diversity as well as commonalities among societies in their responses to common human needs.

Musa, provides students engrossing opportunities to learn from primary documents.

MAJOR TOPICS IN THE STUDY OF THE EXPANSION OF AGRARIAN CIVILIZATIONS (600-1450 A.D.)

1. The Rise of Islam in the Middle East

2. Nomadic Invasions from the Eurasian Steppes, ca. 1000-1450

3. The Impact of Islam on India

4. Europe in the Middle Ages: Byzantium and Western Europe

5. The Middle Empire in China

6. Japan

7. African Civilizations

8. The Americas

MAJOR TOPICS AND THEIR DEVELOPMENT: ESSENTIAL UNDERSTANDINGS AND RELATED BACKGROUND FOR TEACHERS

■ *THE RISE OF ISLAM IN THE MIDDLE EAST*

The recovery of civilization in the Middle East in the 7th century A.D. can be traced to the rise of a vibrant new faith, Islam, among the Arab people and their rapid unification of the region. To understand these events, students should develop some insight into Islam as one of the three great monotheistic religions originating in the Middle East. Students could well begin by following the major events in Mohammed's life, his revelation, his transfer from Mecca to Medina, and his death in 632. They should come to appreciate the force of Mohammed's view that he came not to destroy but to complete the works of God's earlier servants, from Adam to Jesus. They should understand the basic moral principles Islam shares with Judaism and Christianity, and be introduced

Students should understand the basic moral principles Islam shares with Judaism and Christianity, and be introduced to the Five Pillars of Islam, duties incumbent on all believers.

233

to the Five Pillars of Islam, duties incumbent on all believers:

1. To profess that there is no god but Allah and Mohammed is his prophet; that is, a strict monotheism with Mohammed as the final prophet.

2. To pray five times daily, reciting from the Koran passages in praise of the Lord.

3. To give alms to the poor, and for the support of religion and good causes.

4. To fast from sunrise to sunset during the month of Ramadan.

5. To make the Hajj, the pilgrimage to Mecca, required of all believers at least once in their lifetime.

Following Mohammed's death, the rapid spread of Islam westward and eastward became one of the most powerful forces in the world of that time. Students should be aware that the rise of the Arabs and of Islam was made possible partly because of internal disunity and conflicts already present. The peoples of the Middle East had been only superficially united under the late Roman Empire and subsequent conflicts, whether between Romans and Vandals, between the Byzantines and Persians, or between religious groups, had weakened governmental rule and made it easier for the Arabs to establish their authority. More importantly, Islam gave the region a unity of belief and language (Arabic) that it had not had before. This does not mean that the local people simply dropped their own customs and language. Instead, they were gradually assimilated into the new; most conquered peoples embraced Islam. Students should see that early Islam, like early Christianity, won support among the poor and oppressed—they, of course, were legion—by its principle of the equality of all believers, and by the doctrine of life after death.

Students should be acquainted with the major characteristics of the Koran, which not only served as the doctrinal basis of Islam but also lay down rules for governing all society, including criminal and constitutional matters, family, and inheritance; there was no separate, civil government, no

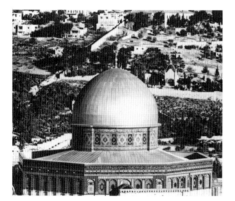

Jerusalem's Temple Mount—the traditional site of Mount Moriah—is graced by one of the most beautiful buildings in the Middle East, the Dome of the Rock.

Following Mohammed's death, the rapid spread of Islam became one of the most powerful forces in the world of that time.

secular law. It is important to know about the social and political aspects of Islam as well: the role of the four Righteous Caliphs who succeeded Mohammed, the birth of the Umayyad dynasty out of the conflicts between the caliphs, and the development of the Shi'ite sect, which held that only descendants of Mohammed should head the community, combining in one office supreme religious and political authority. The Arab empire suffered, however, as the Roman had, from the lack of means for orderly succession, conditions contributing to political instability and assassinations.

Students should understand the importance of trade and commerce in Middle Eastern society and the prestige given the merchant class as a result. They should also understand the status of other groups in the society, including religious and military leaders, scholars, the bureaucracy, powerful landlords, artisans, and the free peasantry. Although Islam did not develop a slave-based economy as Rome had done, it did import substantial numbers of slaves who at times were employed for economic purposes, but more frequently for domestic service or for military service as soldiers and sailors, and in the case of elite slaves, for positions of authority and prestige as chief bureaucrats in the administrative affairs of the society. Slavery existed in the Middle East until modern times. Slave revolts, as well as peasant uprisings, while not frequent, were invariably suppressed. Attention should also be given to the position of women in Islamic society, and to that of Christians and Jews, tolerated within Islamic society as "people of the Book."

Students should understand the importance of trade and commerce in Middle Eastern society and the prestige given the merchant classes as a result.

The Abbasid dynasty, which came to power in 750 A.D. as the result of a revolution, established Baghdad as its capital. Although they reigned until the 13th century, by the 11th century Abbasid rule had weakened, making the dynasty vulnerable to the Seljuk invasions. The centuries after 750 A.D. saw a remarkable flourishing of economy, philosophy, literature, the arts, and law. Students should know about the intellectual and cultural achievements of the Muslim world along with their political presence on the world stage during the era called the "Dark Ages" in Europe.

The wealth of the early Abbasid Caliphs rested on rich agricultural production, the development of textile, metal, and

Consultation scene of the year 1151 before the death of Mesuf B. Mehmet-Melik-Shah. Bibliotheque Hazne, Kapu Sarayi.

Scientific works written in Arabic extended and systematized knowledge of medicine, astronomy, geography, and mathematics; Islamic science led the world by the end of the 12th century.

ceramic manufacturing; and on a vigorous world trade, extending to India and China through the Baghdad crossroads. This was also a period of great creativity, primarily expressed in written Arabic although many of its intellectuals were of Iranian or other non-Arab origin. This vitality lasted well into the 13th century, when the mystical movement of the Sufi tended to subordinate secular interests to religious piety and missionary zeal. Under the Abbasids, scholars translated Greek philosophy and science into Arabic and developed an Islamic rationalism, best known in the work of Averroes, who influenced many European scholars. Scientific works written in Arabic extended and systematized knowledge of medicine, astronomy, geography; mathematics; Islamic science led the world by the end of the 12th century.

■ NOMADIC INVASIONS FROM THE EURASIAN STEPPES, CA. 1000-1450

The Middle East was subject to a series of major nomadic invasions from the steppes beginning in the 11th century and lasting through the 14th. The first of the invaders were the Seljuk Turks, who took advantage of the weakened Abbasid rule to impose their power on the Middle East. Adopting Islam as a simplistic warrior faith, these Turkish nomads conquered Baghdad in 1056, defeated the Byzantines at Manzikert in 1071, and rapidly extended their control over Asia Minor. A consequence of the massive infiltration of Turkish society into Islam was a renewed vigor to Islamic expansionism which, under Turkish military leadership, established control over Palestine, disrupted Christian pilgrimages to the Holy Lands, and launched new incursions into Christendom and Hindustan.

The Christian response to the *jihad* was the launching of the Crusades to free the Holy Lands from Seljuk control. Students can understand these clashes between Islam and Christendom by examining certain similarities between them: two world religions, committed to bringing their messages to all humankind, and the clashes that resulted between the militant followers of each faith, all around the Mediterranean. Students will also see in the Crusades, along with the start of the Christian reconquest of Muslim Spain, the Norman conquests of Sicily and southern Italy, and the rising power of the

Italian mercantile republics of Pisa, Genoa, and Venice, challenging Islamic supremacy in the eastern Mediterranean, the beginnings of European expansionism—beginnings whose full development in succeeding centuries could not have been foreseen in these early stirrings of a European civilization just emerging in the High Middle Ages from its barbaric past.

Students should try to see these events from the standpoint of the Muslim world, as well as through the lens of Europe. They should understand something of the Muslim response in Saladin's consolidation of Egypt and Syria and his successful defeat of the Third Crusade (1189-92). At the same time students should learn about the rise of the Turkish slave soldiery—the Mameluks who rose to governing power in Egypt following the end of Saladin's dynasty.

The second of the great invasions from the steppes—that of the Mongols—should occupy an important place in students' study of world history. These superb horsemen, organized in family clans as highly trained cavalry units, and ably led by Genghis Khan and his successors, swept over the settled societies of China, the Middle East, and Eastern Europe in a series of shattering conquests of tremendous destructiveness and loss of life that rapidly knit the Eurasian land mass into one vast military confederacy. Their presence was felt for several generations, especially through the vigorous leadership of Genghis Khan, Hulagu, and, in China, Kublai Khan. Only the crisis of leadership following Genghis Khan's death in 1227 spared Western Europe from Mongol conquest. As important as the Mongol conquests were their consequences. The period of Mongol peace stimulated a vast trade across Eurasia and introduced to Europe, at a particularly fortunate period in its development, such products of Chinese technology as printing, gunpowder, and the compass, all of which were to contribute to Europe's rapid rise in the later 15th century.

Mongol horseman, organized in family clans as highly trained cavalry units, swept over the settled societies of China, the Middle East, and Eastern Europe in a series of shattering conquests that rapidly knit the Eurasian land mass into one vast military confederacy.

With the recovery of Turkish ascendancy in the 14th century, under the leadership of the Ottoman sultans, Islamic expansionism once again became a dominant force in Eurasia. Beginning as a warrior state in West Asia Minor, the Ottoman Turks extended their conquests into the Balkans, and across Asia Minor to the east. They brought an end to the Byzantine Empire in 1453, set up a well-organized empire in the Middle

East, and posed a threat to Europe for the next two centuries.

■ THE IMPACT OF ISLAM ON INDIA

The strict monotheism, social ethic, and proselytizing zeal of Muslim invaders brought centuries of violent conflict to Hindu India, whose very temples were considered abominations to Allah by devout Muslims.

Followers of Islam first invaded India in 711 A.D. Then, in the 10th century, and again in the 12th, India once more came under attack, the latter time by armies of Muslim Turks entering through the northwest in what is today Pakistan, capturing the city of Delhi, and extending their control over much of northern India and into central and southern parts of the sub-continent.

Their impact was destined to be as great as that of the Aryan invasions two millennia earlier. Muslim conquerors and Mullahs brought many changes to South Asia. Students should understand how Islam differs from Hinduism, Buddhism, and all other indigenous Indian religions. The strict monotheism, social ethic, and proselytizing zeal of Muslim invaders brought centuries of violent conflict to Hindu India, whose very temples were considered abominations to Allah by devout Muslims. But millions of lower caste and "untouchable" Hindus readily converted to Islam, drawn to a faith which proclaimed the equality of all believers.

Students will find the resulting changes an illuminating lesson on the tensions between cultural continuity and change: the clashes between Hindu and Muslim social customs and religious beliefs; the introduction of new architectural styles and the development of a new language (Urdu); the increase of Hindu piety in reaction to the imposition of Muslim minority rule; and the eventual reestablishment of regional Hindu kingdoms in the south, leaving India in 1400 politically divided with a dominant Hindu majority and a Muslim minority that would continue to be an important force in India throughout the modern era.

■ EUROPE IN THE MIDDLE AGES

In the West the ancient world fell with Rome. Waves of invasion and the collapse of empire forced Europeans to create new social, political, and economic institutions, though ancient ideals lived on in the Church, art, law, literature, education, and philosophy. In this unit, students should compare developments in the two regions, East and West, that emerged from the ruins of the Roman Empire.

The Byzantine Empire

In the East, the emperors at Constantinople saw themselves as the true heirs and successors of the Roman Empire. The rich culture that developed in the Byzantine Empire is often underplayed in courses on world history, but its powerful Orthodox Christian heritage, its rich artistic traditions, and its link to Slavic Europe and Russia make it an important and rewarding subject. During the Early Empire (to ca. 650), Constantinople carried on many of the traditions of Rome, through an urban-based society and government with trading contacts all around the Mediterranean. It was not until the 7th century, with the advent of the Muslims, Lombards, and Slavs, that the empire experienced a profound crisis comparable to what the West had undergone. The invasions severely disrupted trade and urban life, forced the Byzantines to fall back behind their fortifications, and brought much of what was characteristic of the ancient world to an end.

During the Middle Empire (to 1024), the Byzantines concentrated on their landed territories rather than the sea and in this period trade and the military gained prominence. But students should recognize that the empire was still characterized by a highly centralized government under the will of the emperor. They may compare it with the decentralized feudal monarchies in Western Europe and the centralized imperial system in China. They might also compare the main elements of Orthodoxy with the Western Church. The iconoclastic controversy and the break with Rome (1054) mark important points in the development of a distinct religious culture. The Middle Empire also saw the conversion of the Slavs to Orthodoxy by Cyril and Methodius. The eventual conversion of the Russians and the transmission to them of Byzantine religious, legal, and political ideas profoundly influenced the growth of Russian culture and society. The history of this period will therefore help students understand subsequent developments in Russian history.

The story of Byzantine troubles—from conquest by their Latin "allies" in 1204, to the reconquest of 1260, to the

The rich culture that developed in the Byzantine Empire is often underplayed in courses on world history, but its powerful Orthodox Christian heritage, its rich artistic traditions, and its link to Slavic Europe and Russia make it an important and rewarding subject.

*Empress Theodora
Byzantium*

growing pressure from hostile states all around them, to the eventual triumph of the Turks over them in 1453—is interesting in itself, but it also helps to inform students about developments in the Balkans and the Near East down to the present. Altogether, Byzantine history deserves an important place in the world history curriculum.

Western Europe

The long period in Western European history from the fall of Rome to the Renaissance can best be appreciated by focusing on a few critical issues. To begin with, it is important to stress that the period was not culturally or politically uniform, but really embraced several distinctly different cultures such as the Carolingian era, the High Middle Ages, and the crisis of the 14th century.

A political theme is the creation of states. Attention should be given to the Carolingian Empire established by Charlemagne in 800 A.D. and his short-lived effort to revive the Roman empire in the West. Students can then appreciate the weakness of the kingdoms and principalities that emerged in the wake of the Empire and the difficulties rulers faced in commanding unruly and independent monarchs. The process of state-building, from the imposition of justice to the levying of taxes, is a crucial topic and can be enlivened by seeing it through the struggles of leading personalities such as St. Louis of France, Frederick Barbarossa, or Henry II of England.

The growth of monarchies in the High Middle Ages elicited a reaction from the nobility who saw their power and privileges appropriated by the crown. In England, this reaction found expression in Magna Carta, which established the principle that the monarch had to live by the same law that he demanded be followed by the nobles. This principle of the rule of law—the foundation of the English legal system and constitutional liberties—was further developed in the establishment of the English Parliament in the 13th century. Although subject to royal authority, Parliament gained significant power over taxes and legislation, prohibiting English kings from becoming absolute monarchs.

With the crises of the 14th century, the High Middle Ages

Equestrian statue of medieval knight. Last third of 13th Century. Gothic Sculpture.

This principle of the rule of law—the foundation of the English legal system and constitutional liberties—was further developed in the establishment of the English Parliament in the 13th century.

240

went into decline. Wars, peasant rebellions, and political strife came to dominate the later Middle Ages and form a necessary backdrop to understanding the emergence of new political systems in the 16th century—the beginning of the early modern era.

Another important theme is dominance and subordination—feudalism or lordship. Students should understand the role of lordship in politics, society, and economy. They need to know about the feudal system of military organization, the methods of knightly combat, and the aristocratic ideals of prowess and honor that underlay it. Characterized by armed, mounted warriors, small armies, and stone castles, feudal warfare dominated Europe for roughly 500 years and had an enduring impact on European culture and values. It is useful to compare Western practices of lordship, knighthood, chivalry, and castles with feudalism in China and Japan in order to bring out the particular characteristics of each. At the same time, students need to learn about agrarian lordship—the system of estates, manors, and serfdom that provided wealth to the clergy, nobility, and kings. In this context, it is important for students to compare medieval serfdom with slavery in the ancient and early modern worlds to help them understand how dependency evolved in European history and how both its presence and its decline were instrumental in the rise of Europe.

Students also need to understand that the peasant family formed the basic unit of agricultural production, while urban crafts were likewise based on a family organization of work involving wives, husbands, and children alike. Indeed, the history of the family, with its variations across time and classes, the development of the Church's law of marriage, and the flowering of romantic ideals in poetry offer topics that captivate as well as inform young students.

Another theme is the beginning of European expansion: the rise in population after 900, the painstaking process of land reclamation pushing back the frontiers of Europe, and the revival of trade and towns. Economic revival coincided with the launching of aggression abroad in the Crusades beginning in 1096. Europeans pushed out against the Muslims not only in the Holy Land but in the reconquest of Muslim Spain as

Characterized by armed, mounted warriors, small armies, and stone castles, feudal warfare dominated Europe for roughly 500 years and had an enduring impact on European culture and values.

The Bayeux Tapestry recording Duke William of Normandy's conquest of Britain in 1066.

well. The gradual reshaping of the political, economic, and religious geography of Western Europe is thus a fundamental aspect of the medieval period. This dramatic process must be analyzed from the standpoint of the Muslims as well as that of the Europeans. Here it is important that students be aware of Christian attitudes toward non-Christians, and their persecution of Jewish communities during the period of the Crusades and the Black Death. At the same time they should learn how vital Islamic and Jewish thought was in this period and how much they contributed to Christian philosophy and the development of science in Europe.

The theme of religion is essential because of the pervasive influence of the Church. It dominated the intellectual and cultural life of the West, competed with princes and kings for power, and strove to regulate everyday morality. The shifting balance of authority between church and state and their periodic clashes are crucial elements of medieval history. Monasticism, church reform, and the renaissance of the 12th century are important for seeing how religion, philosophy, art, and Gothic architecture developed in Europe. Similarly, students will be interested to learn how the Church organized teaching and learning from grammar schools through the medieval university system which first appeared in the 12th century.

Women working with wool

The study of the Middle Ages also opens a door to understanding gender inequalities in European history. Legally barred from the priesthood, from public office, from courts, from the universities, and from knighthood, women had to make their marks in other ways. Understanding those obstacles will help students appreciate the myriad accomplishments of women as saints and scholars, ladies and queens, workers and warriors. The importance of women in family and work in Europe can be compared with women's roles in other cultures of this same era, enabling students to evaluate the problems of discrimination based on gender. Christian Europe's rejection of polygamy (accepted by most if not all other religions) should be understood.

Legally barred from the priesthood, from public office, from courts, from the universities, and from knighthood, women had to make their marks in other ways.

The end of the Middle Ages was marked by war, internal revolt, and religious dissent. It forms a crucial period of transformation. The monarchies in England, France, and

Spain were weakened by war. Plague slashed the European population, undermined the manorial economy, and created widespread economic hardship. Students should also appreciate the spread of religious change and revolt, as mysticism, lay piety, papal schisms, and direct challenges to the authority of Rome in England and Bohemia fundamentally altered the nature of medieval Christianity. Though tumultuous, it was a fertile period essential to an understanding of subsequent developments in Europe.

■ THE MIDDLE EMPIRE IN CHINA

The Middle Empire saw a renewed flowering of Chinese civilization. The recovery of stability under the Sui was marked by increasing governmental power and by the accomplishment of huge public-works projects such as repairing the older Wall and beginning construction of the Grand Canal. Under the Tang and Sung dynasties (617-1279), China experienced rapid economic growth and population increase. Students should understand that the commercial revolution of this era was facilitated by a sophisticated system of river and land transport that helped to unify the country. It should be pointed out to students that this was the first of China's two great commercial revolutions, the second to come in the 16th and 17th centuries and, like this one, to have far-reaching implications for the formation of businesses, urbanization, agriculture, and social mobility.

Students should understand that the commercial revolution during the Tang and Sung Dynasties was facilitated by a sophisticated system of river and land transport that helped to unify the country.

Chinese contacts with the outside world also increased and brought in new wealth. The growth of great cities in southern China and the development of the compass and technological improvements of its ocean going vessels led to a flourishing trade with Southeast Asia and India and the development of a Chinese trading empire in the region. Students should also observe how centralization of government increased. Emperors tried to reduce the power of aristocrats and Buddhists and to reinforce the bureaucracy. One dramatic step in this direction was the development of the examination system and the creation of a meritocracy. It should be explained to students how this system worked so that they may contrast it with contemporary forms of government in medieval Europe, Africa, and the Middle East, and with the advent of civil service examinations in Europe much later. The examination system encouraged a revival of interest in classical learning. Scholars delved into ancient texts, producing a rich cultural heritage comparable to the classical aspect of the European Renaissance.

Students should understand the 13th-century Mongol conquest of China and their establishment of the Yuan dynasty (1260-1368) as one more of the dynastic upheavals in the course of Chinese history. This period should also be understood in the larger context of the Mongol conquests across most of the Eurasian land mass. Genghis Khan and Kublai Khan are colorful figures who amassed the largest empire in world history. Students should be encouraged to think about how they achieved this power and to examine their impact on China. For Chinese history, their importance lay in bringing China into even closer contact with the Middle East and Europe by forming an imperial bridge of which China was but a part. Students can get a sense of this contact through the travels of Marco Polo. But students need also to understand why Chinese society itself was little changed by the Mongol ascendancy. Culturally inferior to the Chinese and far outnumbered by them, the Mongols were forced to recruit Chinese officials for much of the lower administrative tasks of ruling the empire, while reserving the highest positions and prestige for foreign merchants and governmental officials— Turks, other Muslims, and even a few Europeans. When the Chinese revolted, expelling the Mongols and returning to Chinese dynastic rule, the major legacy of three generations of Mongol rule was an increased aversion to foreigners. China swiftly returned to its traditional ways.

■ JAPAN

Although historical records of Japan do not begin until about 500 A.D., students should understand that the first settlers reached the islands centuries before, through migrations which historians believe originated in Korea, Siberia, and Polynesia as early as 8000 B.C. By 200 A.D. the Japanese had developed extensive agriculture, but it was the importation of Chinese culture, beginning around 500 A.D., which gave the Japanese the foundations of their writing system and began a long relationship of borrowing, trade, and scholarly interchange with China. Through that relationship the Japa-

A Japanese Buddhist temple complex

The importation of Chinese culture gave the Japanese the foundations of their writing system and began a long relationship of borrowing, trade, and scholarly interchange with China.

nese acquired Buddhism and the beginnings of their literature, art, philosophy, technology, and political forms. They changed from a clan system to a centralized government under an emperor who proclaimed Confucian principles.

During the Heian period (794-1185), this early classical civilization reached its apogee. At the imperial court in Kyoto, the aristocracy developed a culture based on leisure, studied etiquette, and refined aesthetic taste. Students can see these elements in Lady Murasaki's <u>Tale of Genjii</u>, the first Japanese novel. They should know that while men concentrated on writing philosophy and poetry in Chinese, Japanese women used the vernacular to write diaries, poems, and novels. It is also important to stress that this standard of living, as in most parts of the world, was made possible by aristocratic estates on which poor peasants, whom the aristocracy considered as barely human, labored to produce food and wealth. Away from Kyoto, the emperor employed local warriors to maintain order in the countryside, but the growing independence of this military class sparked rebellions, eroded civil order, and steadily reduced the emperor's power and prestige in the late Heian era.

Because of its important legacy in Japanese life, medieval Japan (1185 - ca. 1600) is a richly engaging topic for students. During this period the power of the emperor further declined and authority fell into the hands of local military rulers, giving Japan a feudal society which can be strikingly compared to that of medieval Europe. The emperor became nearly inconsequential after 1185 and, during a low point in the late medieval period, was reduced to selling his poetry in the streets and did not even perform the religious functions which were among his traditional responsibilities. The *shogun*, a general originally appointed by the emperor to defend the frontiers, became the leading authority and that position gradually became hereditary. Warriors participated in policy-making, and the *shogun* possessed his own bureaucracy, the *bakufu*. Yet the countryside was dominated by powerful lords (*daimyo*) who built up power with the assistance of their vassals and created concentrated estates on which they held direct control of peasants and their produce.

This Japanese form of a warrior society developed a

A Japanese lancer. Undated Woodcut.

The Japanese countryside was dominated by powerful lords (daimyo) who built up power and created concentrated estates on which they held direct control of peasants and their produce.

particular genre of literature, epitomized in <u>The Tale of the Heike</u>, which extolled the virtues of feudal loyalty, prowess, and valor; the warrior (*samurai*) code of honor was called *bushido*. More contemplative and artistic aspects of Japanese culture, based on the meditative practices of Zen Buddhism, also deserve attention: the *No* theater, the tea ceremony, flower arranging, and ink-brush painting. All of these topics, from government to society to literature and contemplation, make exciting points of comparison with medieval Europe that help bring out the salient features of both societies.

■ **AFRICAN CIVILIZATION**

West Africa

Africa forms an important piece in the jigsaw of human history. All too often, however, students are exposed only to the Africa of colonial domination and conquest and deprived of access to the rich and varied achievements of the African peoples in the pre-colonial era. This deficiency should be overcome by having students delve deeply into the history of the cities and kingdoms of early Africa. Three themes can aid teachers and students in comprehending the complex history of this essential topic.

The first theme is the extent to which people have adapted to the land and engaged in creative enterprises—farming, building cities and kingdoms, establishing trade networks, and inventing new technologies—despite the remarkably harsh environment. Students should thus develop an understanding of the physical geography of the African continent and the special challenges it has presented to its inhabitants. From arid deserts such as the Sahara and Kalahari to lush grasslands, tropical rain forests, and mountain ranges, the geography of Africa has offered drastically different opportunities and dangers to its human inhabitants. Rich resources have enabled the growth of wealthy kingdoms, have invited waves of greedy plunderers, and have produced agricultural wealth which sustained flourishing societies ranging from nomadic bands to bureaucratic empires.

On the other hand, poor soils, physical barriers to communication, human and animal diseases, and too much or too little

All too often students are exposed only to the Africa of colonial domination and conquest and deprived of access to the rich and varied achievements of the African peoples in the pre-colonial era.

rainfall have all tested the ingenuity of African farmers, herders, and merchants for thousands of years. Climate thus has played a fundamental role in shaping the African past. Climate, soil, and vegetation have not been static. For example, students ought to know that the Sahara was once green and lush until it dried up sometime after 4000 B.C., and that the expansion of the desert in recent years has spelled human misery and disaster. Comparisons can be made between Africa's geography and that of Europe to illuminate the differing impact that soil conditions, river transport, endemic disease, and other factors have had on social and cultural change.

A second theme can be the movements and interactions of peoples across the continent. At the end of the ancient era, the population of Africa south of the Sahara was on the whole quite sparse. During the ensuing thousand years, however, African farmers and cattle herders, wielding tools and weapons of iron, gradually settled the savannas and forests, largely replacing ancient hunting and gathering folk, and setting the conditions for rapid cultural change. The movements of the Bantu-speaking peoples, who pioneered vast areas of central and southern Africa during the past 1500 years or more, constitute one of the great migrations of world history. Students should learn how iron-age food production, population growth, and long-distance trade combined to stimulate the rise of new states in the forests and southern savannas from about 1000 A.D.

Students should also realize that Africa was not isolated from contacts with other peoples and that immigration and cultural diffusion were enormously influential in shaping local societies. The Arabian Desert is merely an extension of the African Sahara; the Red Sea and the isthmus of Suez present no serious barriers to intercontinental communication. The "camel revolution" of the early 1st millennium A.D. made regular trans-Saharan travel practical, linking West Africa progressively into the trans-Eurasian trading system. Berbers in North Africa, for example, established contacts with the peoples of the Sudan across the Sahara desert in the ancient era. Similarly, Arabs traded across the Red Sea with indigenous communities along the east coast of Africa. East Africa, in fact, was a commercial and cultural crossroads with

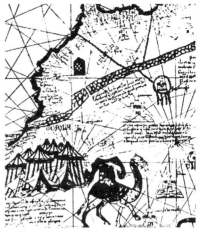
An Arab trader visits Mali.

The "camel revolution" of the early 1st millennium A.D. progressively linked West Africa into the trans-Eurasian trading system while trade across the Red Sea made East Africa a commercial crossroads with links to India, Arabia, and the Mediterranean.

links to India, Arabia, and the Mediterranean.

Students should understand the significance of this well-organized trade, chiefly in African gold, ivory, and salt, but also in African slaves, across the Sahara to the ports of North Africa, down the Nile to Egypt, eastward across the Red Sea and the Indian Ocean to Arabia, Iran, and points beyond. The resulting wealth stimulated the development of African cities and states, and furthered the spread of Islam in Africa soon after its founding. Since about half of the population of Africa today is Muslim, the importance of this world religion in the history of the continent cannot be overemphasized. As a coherent system of faith, law, and culture, Islam proved astonishingly successful in gaining the loyalty of diverse peoples in Africa. Students should learn about the conquerors, merchants, and scholar-missionaries who spread Islam from Egypt and Berber North Africa to both West and East Africa. Knowledge of this ever-spreading network of interrelations and the incorporation of Sudanic West Africa and the East Coast into the cultural realm of Islam is crucial to forming a solid understanding of African history.

A third theme is the rise of wealthy cities and states in different regions of Africa at different times. Students can begin with the Nok people in West Africa and their development of iron products, trade, and the city of Jenne-Jenno in the Niger delta. That study forms a prelude to the growth of a series of trading kingdoms in West Africa. The rich histories of Ghana, Mali, and Songhay offer students not only exciting stories but opportunities to understand the role of trade and warfare in the growth and collapse of pre-modern states. Attention should thus be paid to the rise and fall of powerful kings such as Mansa Musa (d. ca. 1337), the nature of trade within West Africa and across the Sahara desert, the diffusion of Islam and its effects on local society, and the different styles of life in cities and villages.

A good way of illustrating these developments would be to examine the city of Timbuktu, part of the great Mali Empire. From its foundation around 1100 through its rise to wealth and importance between 1200 and 1500, it became a major center of trade as well as the site of an influential Islamic school specializing in history and law, among other things. The study

Caravan to Timbuktu

From its foundation around 1100 through its rise to wealth and importance between 1200 and 1500, Timbuktu became a major center of trade as well as the site of an influential Islamic school specializing in history and law, among other things.

of African trade will help students see the crucial role Africa played in international exchange from an early time. They should realize, for example, how dependent Europe became on African gold and how it provided an incentive for European exploration and exploitation in Africa. A study of farming and village life can provide an important point of comparison with Europe and Asia, allowing students to see how differently basic functions such as agriculture can be accomplished in different environments and cultures.

Students should also be introduced to the Almoravid and Almohad empires which culturally unified large areas of North Africa and Spain between the 11th and 13th centuries. They should learn about the Swahili city-states of the East Coast and their rapid expansion of trade in African gold and ivory across the Indian Ocean after 900 A.D. It is also important for students to be familiar with the history of the gold trading kingdom of Zimbabwe with its royal aristocracy and great stone buildings. Finally, the kingdom of the Kongo deserves attention along with its rich trade based on local commodities.

Teachers should exploit the generous variety of sources for Africa to bring its history alive and to teach students how history is made. The vitality of the African past can be demonstrated through art and tales, archeology and geography. African history thus provides opportunity to demonstrate to students how the past can be reconstructed and reinterpreted out of many different kinds of sources.

■ *THE AMERICAS*

The rise of the major sedentary cultures of Central and South America deserve particular emphasis in a world history course. The Mayan, Aztec, and Incan civilizations created elaborate agricultural systems, hierarchic societies and states, tax and communications systems, law codes, and state religions. Students should understand how each developed and differed, as, for example, in their communal use of the land and in their treatment of weaker, subjugated peoples and of the lower orders in their own societies.

The Mayans, in the 10th century A.D., migrated from

The Mayan, Aztec, and Incan civilizations created elaborate agricultural systems, hierarchic societies and states, tax and communications systems, law codes, and state religions.

Peruvian sculpture, clay vessel with kneeling figure.

Students should understand the Incan civilization, its highly centralized governing system, its productive agricultural system, and its effective systems of communication and trade, knitting together a rural society spread out for nearly 3,000 miles.

Guatemala to the Yucatan Peninsula where they developed their imposing temples, an ideographic writing system, mathematics, astronomical studies, and adopted a calendar more accurate than the European calendar of that time. Students should compare these achievements with those of the Aztecs, who migrated to the central Mexican plateau in the 13th century A.D. and within the next two centuries conquered all of central Mexico. Students should understand something of Aztec religion. Their dependence on slavery and their propitiatory offerings of human sacrifice are also important to consider, not to pique student interest but as an explanatory reason for the crucial—and otherwise puzzling—support of the conquered peoples of Mexico for Cortez's rapid conquest of the Aztecs. Important also is the impressive architecture of the Aztecs, their effective governmental system, and accomplishments in developing the pictograph and calender.

Finally, students should understand the Incan civilization of the high Andes: its highly centralized governing system, all-powerful emperor, and highly structured society; its laws administered by judges; its tightly organized and productive agricultural system of terraced fields on which the wealth of the empire rested; its cities; and its effective systems of communication and trade, knitting together a rural society spread out for nearly 3000 miles from Ecuador through Chile.

Students should compare these achievements and modes of conduct with civilizations in Europe, the Middle East, India, and China. Though impressive in their architectural, artistic, and intellectual accomplishments, particularly in mathematics and astronomy, these civilizations of the Americas lagged significantly in their technological developments—they lacked the wheel and iron working technologies—and were therefore gravely disadvantaged when contact with Europe was established, and their empires engaged in conquest by Portugal and Spain.

UNIT IV
THE EARLY MODERN WORLD
(1450-1800 A.D.)

SIGNIFICANCE AND TEACHING GOALS

■ MAJOR THEMES

The 15th century marked a number of historic turning points in the human story. In the Middle East the Ottoman Turks conquered Constantinople and swiftly expanded their empire to include Byzantium, Egypt, and the Balkan lands of southeastern Europe. In South Asia Moghul conquerors established a Muslim empire in India. But after 1500, it was the Europeans who replaced the Mongols in linking different parts of the world, though on a much vaster scale than anything in the past. The consequences were the establishment of worldwide networks of trade and communication as Europeans opened the seas, expanded trade with South Asia, East and West Africa and, through conquest and colonization, ushered the Americas into the expanding global system of commerce and cultural exchange. These changes of the early modern era were far-reaching and profound, altering societies and ecological systems on both sides of the Atlantic through the exchanges of goods, plant and animal species, agriculture, precious metals, knowledge, skills, and diseases. Without understanding these events, students cannot fully comprehend many of the issues of their own day, for developments of that time set into motion consequences which continue to influence contemporary affairs in students' own lives, their nation, and the world.

Understanding this era will be aided by following all four major themes of world history. Important among them is **the development and representation of people's understand-**

After 1500 Europeans replaced the Mongols in linking different parts of the world, though on a much vaster scale than anything in the past.

Above: Typical European harbor to which trade with colonies brought influx of bullion that strengthened the mercantile state.

Renaissance Humanism, scientific rationalism, the Enlightenment, and the theological divisions unleashed by the Protestant Reformation combined to create an age notable for its intellectual, artistic, and religious ferment.

ing of themselves, their moral imperatives, and their place in the universe. From a culture dominated by a single church, Europe became in this era a pluralistic civilization, fed by many different creative sources. Renaissance Humanism, scientific rationalism, the Enlightenment, and the theological divisions unleashed by the Protestant Reformation combined to create an age notable for its intellectual, artistic, and religious ferment.

Following **the development of political theory and organization** will demonstrate to students how European monarchies, parliaments, traditions of common law, and the revival of Roman law developed in this era, eroding the power of feudal aristocrats and increasing the centralized power of nation-states. Most striking of these developments were (1) the English Revolution—a leap toward representative self-government under constitutional law, with special significance for the history of the United States; and (2) the development of French absolutism under Louis XIV, a model of centralized state building which was to have fateful consequences in the 18th century and beyond. These political developments can be compared with developments in China, India, and the Middle East.

Vital changes in this era can also be followed through the theme of **economic and technological development.** In Europe the feudal serfdom of the Middle Ages gave way to a mercantile capitalism that transformed social relations and underlay the thrust of Europeans overseas from the 16th century onward. The military revolution which occurred in Europe between 1500 and 1800 should also be understood, for it changed weaponry and fortifications, increased the size of armies tenfold, encouraged a general arms race, and provided the means for European expansion and gradual conquest of the Americas, Indonesia, and large parts of Africa and India before the end of the 18th century.

The first stages in European overseas expansion during this era and the establishment of colonial regimes in the Americas brought vast new wealth to the European economy. Comparing, by contrast, the causes and consequences of China's decision in the 16th century to suspend her vast overseas mercantile enterprises and return to traditional activities will deepen students' understanding of the relationships between economic, political, and social developments in this era.

In following the theme of **the development and changing character of human societies,** students will see the effects of all these changes—political, technological, economic, and ideational—in the daily lives of people. Expanding population, wealth, technological and commercial prowess, and the military power of competing nation-states rendered European society expansive and dynamic. The consequences of European exploration and colonization for the indigenous societies of the Americas were profound, and must be understood, for they left whole populations decimated through the ravages of diseases introduced by the Europeans, and resulted in the racial intermixing, social hierarchies, and cultural changes that have influenced the special character of Hispanic American societies to this day. The fateful rise of the Atlantic slave trade and its complex effects in African and American societies must also be understood, as well as the system that supported it—a system in which a relatively small group of people, including African kings and merchants, along with American planters and European shippers, exploited vast numbers of Africans for material gain. Students must understand these events and the deep moral issues they raise if they are to comprehend their effects in the subsequent history of Africa, and their continuing legacy in the western hemisphere, even into our own day.

The fateful rise of the Atlantic slave trade and its complex effects in African and American societies must be understood, as well as the system that supported it—a system in which a relatively small group of people exploited vast numbers of Africans for material gain.

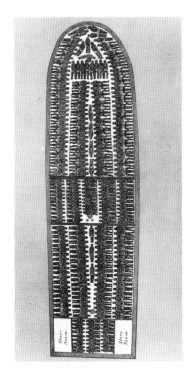

The lower deck of a slave ship plying between Africa and America during the 18th-century slave trade.

■ ESSENTIAL UNDERSTANDINGS

1. **European overseas expansion and the development of worldwide networks of trade and communication,** as Europeans established supremacy of the seas, expanded trade with South Asia and East and West Africa, and through conquest and colonization brought the Americas into the global network.

2. **The intercontinental exchanges—in goods, plant and animal species, agriculture, precious metals, knowledge, skills, and diseases**—and their social, economic, and ecological consequences for Europe, Africa, and the Americas.

3. **The rise of mercantile capitalism in Europe**, powering European expansionism and preparing the way for the "Atlantic economy" of the 17th century.

Students should understand the rise of mercantile capitalism, powering European expansionism.

4. **The importance of the changes in European thought and culture brought on by the Renaissance, the Protestant Reformation, the Scientific Revolution, and the Enlightenment:** the leading thinkers and the influences of each; the relationship of these developments to the political, economic, religious, and cultural contexts of the time; their far-reaching consequences for European societies and their American colonies, and for the course of modern history.

5. **Major political developments in absolutism and revolution in Europe:** French absolutism under Louis XIV, establishing the model for most European governments; and the Glorious Revolution in England, establishing Parliament's supremacy over the crown and expressing ideals of liberty and principles of law on which English colonists would later draw in their 18th century revolution and establishment of government.

6. **The consequences of European expansionism for the indigenous societies of the Americas:** the devastating epidemics following the introduction of Eurasian diseases that decimated native populations; Spanish and Portuguese conquests and the complex racial intermixing and fusion of cultures accompanying development of their colonial systems, first around the silver mines of Mexico and Peru and later the sugar industries of Brazil and the Caribbean.

7. **The rise of the Atlantic slave trade** as part of an international economic system in which a relatively small number of people exploited vast numbers of African workers forcibly transported to the Caribbean, Central and South America, and later to North America; consequences for the societies of Africa and the Americas.

8. **Comparative developments in the rise of the Ottoman Turk and Moghul empires:** Ottoman Turk expansion-

ism in the Middle East, North Africa, and Southeastern Europe, following the defeat of Constantinople; nature of Ottoman institutions and society; and the causes of their inability to keep up with rising European power. Conquests of India by Muslim Mongols, consequences of their unification of India, and the religious conflicts contributing to the Moghul Empire's decline.

9. **Comparative developments in China and Japan:** China's maritime superiority to Europe under the Ming Dynasty; consequences of suspending its seafaring expeditions and returning to isolationism; causes of China's dynamic economic development and consequences in the improved lives of peasants; and China's territorial expansion. Japan's unification under Tokugawa, growth of its market economy, and related changes in culture and society, including the closure of Japan to Europeans.

In studying the Renaissance, students should cultivate the habit of tolerating complexity in human affairs, for this period offers a memorable lesson in the co-existence of human progress and regression.

■ HABITS OF THE MIND

Studying the early modern era will nourish the full range of historical habits of the mind. In studying the Renaissance, for example, students should cultivate the habit of **tolerating complexity in human affairs,** for this period offers a memorable lesson in the co-existence (and often the symbiotic relationship) of human progress and regression, best taught through social history. The "new horizons" and "fresh ideas" so much glorified in survey textbooks coincided with rural penury, urban misery, and added hardships for the working poor. Likewise, economic progress under capitalism brought a final end to the protection offered by the guilds. All pretense of setting just prices, or restricting monopoly, or enforcing peasants' rights under manorial contracts was dropped. The underside of the Renaissance's creative productivity was harsh and demoralizing for many Europeans, and well-laced with cruelty and corruption.

Voltaire visited by Frederick the Great

Students may also **develop their powers of historical empathy** by placing themselves in the daily life of men, women, and children of all these societies in the early modern era. What were their experiences of change and continuity? How much were their aspirations, their joys and burdens, affected by the thunder and pageantry of great events and

255

Robert Estienne (Robertus Stephanus). Renaissance printer and founding father of a dynasty of typographers.

Students should debate to what extent they as Americans are still children of the Enlightenment, holding an essentially optimistic view of human nature, believing that a proper use of science, reform of unnatural and unreasonable institutions, and the education of all citizens will promote harmony and progress.

personages, and how much did their lives remain the same? Historical empathy should be extended, by means of memoirs and imaginative literature, to the lives of artists, religious and political reformers, explorers, conquistadors, and the Africans and indigenous Americans caught up in European expansion from the 16th century onward.

Students' **recognition of the power of ideas** may be reinforced by study of scientific discoveries in the 17th and 18th centuries, and in the popularization and application (or misapplication) of scientific beliefs to the ordering of human life and society. They should debate to what extent they as Americans are still children of the Enlightenment, holding an essentially optimistic view of human nature, believing that a proper use of science, a sensible study of human behavior, a reform of unnatural and unreasonable institutions, and the education of all citizens will promote harmony and progress in all spheres of human life.

MAJOR TOPICS IN THE STUDY OF THE EARLY MODERN WORLD

1. Early Modern Europe

2. The African Encounter with Europe

3. The Encounter of the Americas with Europe

4. China and Japan in the Early Modern Era

5. The Rise of the Ottoman and Moghul Empires

MAJOR TOPICS AND THEIR DEVELOPMENT: ESSENTIAL UNDERSTANDINGS AND RELATED BACKGROUND FOR TEACHERS

■ EARLY MODERN EUROPE

The era of early modern Europe is usually taught as comprising the years from the early 15th century to the French Revolution, beginning with the Italian Renaissance and ending with the 18th-century Enlightenment. During this era new ways of viewing the world, human nature, arts, learning, and religion altered the world views of many Europeans, deeply affecting Western thinking, down to the present. Two aspects of this age require particular attention. First were the effects of the ever-widening European contacts with other cultures around the world; and second was the swift change in thinking brought about by Humanism, the Reformation, the Scientific Revolution, and the Enlightenment.

The Renaissance

What should students know about the Renaissance? First, they should explore the question, never wholly answerable, of what brings about a great age of artistic, literary, and intellectual creativity. Time should be taken for students to enjoy great paintings, sculpture, and architecture from the era, and to sample some of its livelier writings. They may debate whether Machiavelli was mainly a rascal or reformer, whether Castiglione's *The Courtier* represents a well-rounded education, whether there is anything in Pico's *Oration on the Dignity of Man* that a serious Christian could not accept.

Students should understand the legacy of the Renaissance, its great works of arts and letters; its ideals of education, prowess, and personal character; its rescue of Greek and Roman culture; its exaltation of individualism and self-consciousness.

By such exercises, student should come to their own definition of Humanism, and see its tripartite nature: partly an extension of medieval Christian views, partly a rediscovery or rebirth ("renaissance") of pagan classical culture, partly new and innovative in its language and literary forms and in its pursuit of learning, not least of historical truth and perspective. Students should also ponder the legacy of the Renaissance, Italian and northern, to later centuries: its great works of arts and letters, still serving as models and inspiration; its ideals of education, prowess, and personal character; its rescue of Greek and Roman culture; its exaltation of individualism and self-consciousness.

Cathedral of Santa Maria Del Fiore, Florence, Italy.

The Renaissance period was, however, not simply a matter of high culture. It can also be used to show the difference between urban and rural living, between the worlds of trade and business and the worlds of agriculture and lordship. It should set forth clearly the contrasts and comparisons between the roles of men and women both of high and low estate in the culture, politics, and daily work of the times, as well as the differing opportunities and experiences of rich and poor.

The nature of towns and trade in the Middle Ages is essential to an understanding of the rise of city-states and civic culture in Italy during the 14th and 15th centuries. The role of literacy in commerce and banking as well as in religion is an important theme, and one that can be linked with students' earlier study of the ancient world. In this respect, they must learn about the impact of printing from the 15th century onward, and the ways in which it influenced literacy, writing, and education. Finally, students should learn how certain values of the Italian Renaissance were exported to the rest of Europe, and their impact on other societies and cultures. How, for example, did Northern Humanism differ from its Italian counterpart, and how did it affect the northern religious, intellectual, and political scene?

European Exploration and Conquest

The study of the Renaissance moves easily into one of the most historically consequential developments of this period: European overseas exploration and conquest. Students should follow the stages by which European ventures expanded overseas: the Portuguese in Africa and Asia, the Spanish in the Americas, the French, and English efforts that followed later. The necessary background is a consideration of changing economic, social, and military developments after 1500: the military revolution beginning in 1500, the growth of population, inflation, urbanization, and agricultural change.

Students should learn about the emergence of capitalistic forms of enterprise, whether in trade, manufacturing, or agriculture, in order to understand what powered European expansion and to appreciate later the changes introduced by industrialization.

Students should learn about the emergence of capitalistic forms of enterprise, whether in trade, manufacturing, or agriculture, in order to understand what powered European expansion and to appreciate later the changes introduced by industrialization. These changes helped to prepare for the development of an "Atlantic economy" in the 17th century, and the growth of European settlements throughout the western hemisphere. The emergence of an Atlantic economy completed a long process by which essential commodities such as sugar and cotton moved westward from their Asian homelands to the Islamic world, through North Africa to Spain and the Atlantic Islands, and finally to the New World.

The sagas of exploration, conquest, and colonization are of critical importance in understanding world history. Students should begin by seeking to explain the circumstances propelling Europe to global domination for more than three centuries, setting up forces that have helped to shape the world's politics and economy to this day. It is vital that this expansion be seen from the standpoint of other peoples as well: the impact of colonization on indigenous peoples, the near destruction of the native population of the Americas, in large part through disease introduced by the Europeans; the rise of the plantation system; and the fateful rise of the Atlantic slave trade. European expansion was a complex process involving the clash of cultures, the birth of new societies, and the destruction of some old ones—not just the saga of brave adventurers.

Reformation and New Monarchies

The Reformation and the rise of the new monarchies were two processes in the 16th century that had long-term repercussions, shaping politics and society over the following centuries. The division of Christianity into competing sects and the conflict among them was of fundamental importance in shaping politics and society over the following centuries. American students need to understand the issues leading to the Protestant Reformation and problems that belief and intolerance caused within European society, since these form the backdrop to their own history and led to virulent religious conflict between and within nations. Teachers should focus on the major theological, differences that divided Christians, countries, and classes. The compelling biographies of Reformation era figures such as Erasmus, Martin Luther, Thomas More, Theresa of Avila, Francis Xavier, or Elizabeth I provide a rewarding approach to the study of this crucial period.

Religion was an important aspect of the development of the so-called New Monarchies. Building on the precedents of the Middle Ages, monarchs tried to create more powerful and stable institutions, but were constantly dogged by the problem of religious conflict. It was hard to get political conformity when there was such diversity of belief. Students thus need to see how the problems of state-building and religion often collided and produced such great conflicts as the Dutch Revolt and the Thirty Years War. They also need to appreciate the practical problems that ambitious rulers faced: changes in

The Reformation and the rise of the new monarchies were two processes in the 16th century that had long-term repercussions, shaping politics and society over the following centuries.

Martin Luther. After a painting by Lucas Cranach (elder).

military technology that demanded larger armies; increasing budgets that demanded greater taxation; and popular resistance and revolt that demanded new forms of suppression.

Students need to examine the Protestant Reformation as the first successful revolution in European history against an established order. It offers a prime lesson in the complexity of historical cause, demonstrating how religious ideals were joined by powerful economic, social, political, and personal interests to weaken what had long been regarded as an invulnerable Roman church. Together with the tragic wars and civil wars of religion and the renewal of the Inquisition, the Reformation also brought forth new strains of spirituality and civic ideals, and the reinvigoration of the Roman church itself.

The Protestant Reformation offers a prime lesson in the complexity of historical cause, demonstrating how religious ideals were joined by powerful economic, social, political, and personal interests to weaken what had long been regarded as an invulnerable Roman church.

Finally, students should consider how the events of this period influenced the 17th-century quest for religious freedom in the colonization of the Atlantic seaboard of North America by dissenting Protestant sects. Students should consider how this quest for religious freedom carried grave personal risk for dissenters in this period but was to culminate in the religious freedom clauses of United States state and federal constitutions of the late 18th century, one of the keystones of the civil liberties students enjoy today.

Absolutism and Revolution

Two political developments in this era should be singled out for particular attention because they were of such momentous importance in shaping events beyond their day. The first was the development of absolutism in France under Louis XIV. It laid the foundations for French power in the 17th and 18th centuries and served as a model for most governments in Europe including the Prussian and Russian. The institutions and social structure of France are important for understanding the Ancien Régime and its subsequent crisis, which led to the French Revolution.

In direct contrast, royal attempts to establish absolutism in England, and to win approval for the doctrine of divine right, failed completely. By the end of the 17th century when absolutism reached its apogee in France, the English Revolution had established Parliament's supremacy over the crown.

Since England and France are only 20 miles apart, and had shared many common characteristics from Roman times onward, the question leaps forth: why this drastic divergence in the early modern period? Examining the differences between English and French geography, historical experiences, economic and social development, and political and legal traditions will reveal to students some of the conditions friendly to the appearance of free self-government and those hostile to it, conditions which still support or obstruct political freedom in parts of the modern world. For American students, knowledge about the causes and consequences of the Glorious Revolution provides an essential background to understanding the development of the American Revolution and political institutions of the 18th century. The ideals and principles of law that sprang from the English Revolution had a long history that had shaped English-speaking people's ideas about popular resistance and liberty.

The Scientific Revolution and Enlightenment

The final area of study in the early modern period of Western history should be intellectual and cultural history. It cannot be separated from political, social, or economic changes, but it forms an important body of knowledge in itself that is of the utmost importance in understanding the development of the modern world. Students should learn about two essential elements: the Scientific Revolution and the Enlightenment.

Students need to follow the gradual emergence of what is now known as scientific method. The foundations can be laid in their study of the Middle Ages, but students then need to see how modern science emerged out of the context of Renaissance and early modern culture. The exciting discoveries of this period—the heliocentric universe, the development of scientific method, the use of mathematics, advances in medicine and chemistry—need to be a part of every student's historical understanding. It is not enough that students simply learn the great steps in the development of scientific thought; they should understand how those changes emerged out of the broader culture of the period. Thus, thinkers such as Copernicus, Galileo, Bacon, Descartes, and Newton should not be taught as simple links in an inevitable chain of scientific achievement, but as struggling within the contexts of their

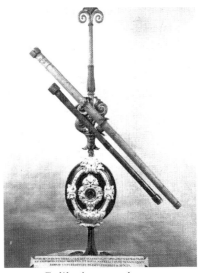

Galileo's own telescope

The exciting discoveries of this period—the heliocentric universe, the development of scientific method, the use of mathematics, advances in medicine and chemistry—need to be a part of every student's historical understanding.

261

times to understand the universe and how it worked.

Students should also learn how scientific assumptions of an orderly universe, accessible to rational understanding, spread into other realms, such as politics and economics. This study leads to a consideration of the Enlightenment. Students should understand 18th-century rationalism because it, too, has had a profound impact on their own history and is still very much part of our intellectual heritage. The study should not be limited to philosophy, but should also take in religion and the arts, to demonstrate the wide-ranging changes brought about by intellectual shifts on the part of influential Europeans—and Americans as well.

The Newtonian vision of a universe of order, harmony, and predictability stirred dreams of human progress and perfectibility.

The Enlightenment's optimistic faith in the discovery and application of natural law to human life—as in the works of Hobbes and Locke, Montesquieu and Rousseau—was to inspire reforms and revolutions in many corners of the world. The Newtonian vision of a universe of order, harmony, and predictability stirred dreams of human progress and perfectibility. The first great upheavals to be marked—though surely not "caused"—by Enlightenment thought were the American and French Revolutions, and they opened the modern era of world history.

■ THE AFRICAN ENCOUNTER WITH EUROPE

The arrival of Europeans in Africa in the 15th century marks an important turning point in African as well as European history. It is an essential part of European overseas exploration and colonization. At the same time, it set African history in a fateful new direction.

Munster's woodcut map of Africa, printed in 1540.

In the 15th and 16th centuries, European mariners, drawing partly on technology developed earlier in the Islamic lands and China, produced ships and navigational devices that opened the major oceans of the world to long-distance shipping. Thus, the regions of Africa facing the Atlantic quite suddenly joined a world network of seaborne communications. For a time after 1500 the Portuguese dominated the sea lanes around Africa. Students should compare the effects of Portuguese activity on African life with their impact (together with that of the Spanish) on Asia and the Americas. They should see that although the Portuguese took forceful control of certain ports of Morocco and the East Coast, they conquered very little African territory. Their trading stations existed at the pleasure of local African rulers who supported the slave trade; by the early 17th century Portuguese influence was in decline everywhere on the continent except Angola and Mozambique.

The export of millions of slaves from Africa to the Americas over three and a half centuries (and also eastward across the Red Sea and Indian Ocean to Arabia, Iran, and parts of Asia) is a topic of central importance in both world and American history. Students should clearly apprehend that the trans-Atlantic slave trade was one of the most harrowing episodes of organized brutality and injustice in world history. Published accounts by enslaved Africans such as Olaudah Equiano vividly describe the horrors of the trade. In a world perspective, students will see that the slave trade was part of an international economic system that united European capital and technology, American plantation production of sugar, coffee, tobacco, and cotton, and African labor to produce enormous volumes of marketable commodities and huge profits. The slave trade was also a system of forced migration: Africans became, against their will, settlers and colonists in the Americas, contributing their labor and cultures to the development of new societies.

Students should also consider the complex effects of the slave trade on African societies—on demography, economic life, family life, and the rise and fall of kingdoms. They should be led away from the romanticized view that institutions of slavery in Africa itself were largely benign, that European or Arab traders roamed the continent kidnapping innocents, and that no Africans profited from the sale of fellow humans. They should recognize, rather, that the slave trade was a system in which a relatively small group of people, including African kings and merchants along with North and South American planters and European shippers, victimized and exploited much larger numbers of both African and Amerindian workers. They should understand that the slave trade in Africa was not a scene of chaos but a highly organized commercial system in which African rulers and merchants controlled the terms of slave exports.

Bronzework from Benin. Attention to intricate detail and a combination of smooth and carefully worked surfaces distinguish this vivid image of a Beni warrior.

In a world perspective, students will see that the slave trade was part of an international economic system that united European capital and technology, American plantation production, and African labor to produce enormous volumes of marketable commodities and huge profits.

■ THE ENCOUNTER OF THE AMERICAS WITH EUROPE

Two factors gave Europeans an overwhelming military advantage: the devastating epidemics which destroyed local populations in the 16th and 17th centuries and the disparity in military technology which rendered weapons of the indigenous societies relatively ineffectual in the face of European armament.

The European exploration and conquest of the Americas from Columbus onward is an indispensable subject. Students should try to view the arrival of the Europeans and the conquests by Cortez and Pizarro from the standpoint of the indigenous peoples, as well as of the Europeans.

Students should understand how local conditions facilitated the conquest of the Americas by Europeans. Rather than banding together to oppose the Europeans, native societies often allied with the invaders to give them greater leverage against their traditional enemies at home. The Europeans usually found it easier to deal with the large settled groups than with the smaller nomadic bands. In fact, the small groups sometimes had greater military success against the Europeans and often survived much longer, especially in regions which the Europeans found inhospitable or unprofitable. Two factors, however, gave Europeans an overwhelming military advantage: the devastating epidemics spread by European diseases which destroyed local populations from the 1490s forward, and the disparity in military technology which rendered weapons of the indigenous societies relatively ineffectual in the face of European armament. Together these factors help explain the success of the European conquest and should be emphasized in teaching this period.

Students should also understand the dynamics of conquest from the side of the invaders. They should see how the Europeans found the local sedentary civilizations somewhat compatible with their own in structure and organization, enabling the Europeans to adapt local systems to their rule, to extract taxes and labor, and later to carry out conversions to Christianity. The acceptance of Catholicism, at least the outward forms of it, was remarkably wide and rapid among native Americans. Students should also understand that in many ways the Spaniards were immigrants much like the European immigrants to North America. They did not all come as an army organized and financed by the state or as crown representatives. They came looking for profit and a better way of life and once they had established their authority, they sent home for wives and families, and created a colonial society among the indigenous people.

Aztec Calendar

Students need to learn about the dynamics of the colonial society that developed in Central and South America, in part to compare it with North America's colonial history. They should understand that the newcomers were mainly looking for means of support so that they could improve their conditions. Most came looking for a commodity of high value that would reap high rewards. What they found exceeded their expectations; precious metals could be quickly exported in the small ships of the time. Silver was the most important asset and it was located primarily in central and northern Mexico and the central Andes.

These became the two areas of most intense development and experienced the heaviest Spanish immigration at first. The Spaniards used the local population for labor and built up local government and society. A colonial system—built around silver mines, a capital (Mexico City and Lima), and seaports—quickly emerged. The cities became centers of trade and artisanal crafts, much like those in Europe. Silver mining was a huge enterprise with impressive technological innovations, so that Mexico and Peru led the rest of Latin America into the 18th century. A later, third area of development was in Portuguese Brazil, based on the sugar industry, which drew it's labor force from the rapidly expanding African slave trade.

The Spaniards also had introduced slavery, bringing Africans into the western hemisphere. Because Africans had many of the same immunities as the Europeans and because they were familiar with the Europeans' technology (such as iron and the horse), they were often given positions of responsibility and acted as intermediaries between the indigenous population and the Spaniards. In the Caribbean, as in Brazil, slavery was more widespread and concentrated in sugar production. American students should learn how various regions were opened up for cash crop exploitation and the critical role that slavery played in the process.

It is also important that students understand the complex racial and cultural intermixing that went on during this colonial period. The Spanish sat atop the social pyramid but, over time, intermarriage among various groups produced a highly complex racial situation. Each group was given a different

A colonial system—built around silver mines, a capital (Mexico City and Lima), and seaports—quickly emerged, with cities the centers of trade and artisanal crafts.

It is important that students understand the complex racial intermixing of the colonial period and the fusion of cultures—Spanish, indigenous American, and African—that resulted.

name by the Spaniards (*mestizo*, for example) and assigned a stratum in the hierarchy. The Hispanic group at the top gradually expanded as mixed groups beneath them acquired Hispanic culture and sought entry into the elite. By the early 19th century, therefore, this elite was much bigger than it would have been had it been solely dependent on the biological reproduction of the Spanish.

Despite the impact of Hispanic culture on the indigenous peoples during the colonial period, they retained much of their older culture and mores. There was thus a fusion of cultures, producing, for example, a distinctive brand of Christian practice. Outside of the central areas, where it took longer for Spanish culture to penetrate, indigenous ways were preserved much longer and in purer form. In the Caribbean and northern Brazil, however, the indigenous population rapidly became a small minority in the face of European immigration and the arrival of enslaved Africans in vastly larger numbers than in North America. There, the culture was determined much more by the mix of European and African elements than by the survival of indigenous cultures. These many variations gave many of the Hispanic-American countries a special character of their own, which they retain to this day.

Finally, students should understand the changes that came about with the rise of the Atlantic trade system and the improvements in shipping during the 18th century. Whereas Mexico and Peru had been the centers of development earlier, the initiative shifted to sites along the Atlantic coast which had the resources to produce goods for the new commodity trade. Precious metals were depleted, but markets for sugar, hides, and other products expanded. Former peripheral areas such as Argentina and Venezuela then became of central economic importance and experienced the cycle of colonial development that had occurred elsewhere earlier.

■ CHINA AND JAPAN IN THE EARLY MODERN ERA

Early Modern China

The 15th century opened in East Asia with China technologically capable of surpassing European supremacy on the seas. Throwing off the resented Mongolian leadership (1368

A.D.), China expanded her land borders and her influence over the neighboring regions of present-day Korea, Vietnam, and Tibet. The flourishing sea trade between China, India, and the coast of Southeast Asia developed during Mongolian rule (1264-1368 A.D.) was eclipsed between 1405 and 1423 by the even greater maritime expeditions to India, the Middle East, and Africa undertaken by the Ming Dynasty—vast expeditions that exceeded in scale European ventures of a century later. Suddenly, however, these expeditions were suspended, the merchant class was subordinated, and China returned to its historic isolation.

Students might consider the consequences for world history had these seafaring enterprises continued, and had the permanent colonies the Chinese established in the Philippines, Malaysia, and Indonesia perhaps been expanded. Students should compare the global range of European expansion during this era with China's inward return to traditional patterns: building internal strength within the vast empire, spreading traditional ideas more widely throughout society, and returning the Chinese scholarly class to preeminence in government and in the cultivation of traditional values.

Throughout the late Ming and early Ch'ing (Manchu) dynasties of the 17th century, China underwent continued economic growth. Phenomenal population increases were made possible by more efficient farming. Agriculture and diet were changed by the introduction of new crops from the Americas which helped overcome scarcity and famine. The expanding population sparked internal migration and the colonization of new territories. It also fueled urban development, one of the hallmarks of this period. The dynamic 17th-century Chinese economy underwent another cycle of growth, producing a second commercial revolution, the so-called "sprouts of capitalism." Students can compare the Chinese experience of small commodity trade, cotton textiles based on cottage industry, and the proliferation of local markets with European economic changes during the same period. Such a comparison will help to underscore the dynamism of the Chinese economy. Economic ferment, moreover, produced improvements in the quality of life. Not only were there more products available, but there was also a greater degree of peasant freedom, as the bonds of dependency were gradually

The dynamic 17th-century Chinese economy underwent another cycle of growth, producing a second commercial revolution, the so-called "sprouts of capitalism," and improvements in the quality of life.

Silk being woven on a "waist loom." After a Japanese woodcut.

eased. Peasant rebellions—which, again, should be compared with similar uprisings in Europe from the late 14th century onward—were partly responsible for this development. Finally, commercial contacts with the rest of the world broadened and deepened, especially after the arrival of the Jesuits in the 16th century. Altogether, it was a period of startling energy. Students should be introduced to these changes to help sharpen their historical understanding and to help them understand comparable developments in other parts of the world.

Political change was also important. The borders of China expanded to their fullest extent, encompassing neighboring peoples in Tibet, Manchuria, and other areas. Students should be aware that under the Qing dynasty, founded by the Manchus, the process of centralization that had begun in the Early Empire was continued and strengthened.

Early Modern (Tokugawa) Japan

Medieval Japan ended in the civil wars that rocked the shogunate, which came to an end after the shogun Tokugawa established his power at Edo (Tokyo), in 1603. It is interesting to compare techniques used by Japanese and European rulers to gain control over their feudal vassals. The Tokugawa restricted the lords and required them to spend half of their time at the capital in Edo, where their wives and children resided as hostages of the government to ensure order.

Students should see how political changes affected the social and economic sphere as Japan became more unified and integrated. Increased rice production and small crafts led the way toward a commercialized economy, which benefitted from an improved road system. Taxation based on villages rather than on individuals encouraged the growth of communal cooperation and communal habits of frugality and diligence. Under such burdens, peasants frequently revolted to secure concessions. Commercialization spurred the growth of cities and strengthened the merchant class.

Students should see these developments against the medieval background, when the social hierarchy was rigid and the warrior (*samurai*) class had made up only about 6 to 7

Increased rice production and small crafts led the way toward a commercialized economy, which spurred the growth of cities and strengthened the merchant class.

Tokugawa Teyasu, appointed Shogun in 1603, was able to build a centralized administration that ensured the "Pax Tokugawa" for two and a half centuries.

percent of the population but occupied the highest positions of authority and status. Below them ranged the merchants, artisans, and peasants. With the spread of a market economy, many merchants became wealthy and many *samurai* fell into debt to them. Similarly, there was greater differentiation within the village community, as rich peasants outpaced their economic neighbors. Within the cities, where schools developed, merchants created a distinctive culture of their own, characterized by novels such as <u>Five Women Who Loved Love,</u> by puppet and kabuki theater, and by haiku poetry.

Students will want to know that these developments occurred against the backdrop of traditional Japanese ambivalence about outside influence. When the Portuguese introduced Christianity and European trade to Japan in 1543, they brought along firearms, tobacco, corn, and potatoes. But in 1639 Japan closed itself to the Europeans. Christianity was proscribed and the Japanese permitted only a few Dutch merchants to trade.

■ THE RISE OF THE OTTOMAN AND MOGHUL EMPIRES

The Ottoman Empire

The early modern era saw a resurgence of Muslim power in the rise of two large empires: the Ottoman Turk empire in the Middle East and the Moghul empire of the Mongol conquerors of India. Students should understand both. The Turks, earlier converted to Islam, captured Constantinople (1453) and made it the capital of their empire. Students should know something of Ottoman government: the role of the sultan, the bureaucracy, and the army, including its slave soldiers, the elite Janissary corps. They should recognize the sources of Ottoman power and, later, the sources of the empire's decline, particularly the decay of the agricultural sector. Prospering early from the conquest of other Muslim states and of southeastern Europe, the Ottomans were in the long run unable to keep up with rising European power, especially as they failed to develop their own commerce, technology, and industry. Like Peter the Great of Russia, the sultans sought to borrow military technology. Unlike Peter, they were not prepared to undertake broader structural changes in government, in law, or in economic and social life.

An Ottoman Sultan on horseback and richly garbed.

The early modern era saw a resurgence of Muslim power in the rise of two large empires: the Ottoman empire in the Middle East and the Moghul empire of the Mongol conquerors of India.

The Moghul Empire, Its Rise and Fall

The last great wave of Muslim conquerors came to India in 1526, when Moghul (Mongol) Central Asians launched the Moghul Empire, establishing India's longest lived era of unification. Students should learn something about Moghul rule, especially focusing on its two longest reigns: that of Akbar ("The Great") from 1556 to 1605 and of Aurangzeb, 1658-1707, when Moghul power reached its peak and entered its long decline. Students will find the exploits of Akbar appealing in their personal daring and heroism, but they should understand also his cultivated interests in books, painting, and architecture, and the tolerance he demonstrated for both Hinduism and Christianity, introduced by Portuguese Jesuits. Under Aurangzeb, tensions between Muslim and Hindu were renewed by the destruction of Hindu temples and attacks on the Hindu population. Rising Hindu unrest and the development of the militant Sikh religion should be examined in comparison with the religious wars of Europe during this same period. The stresses of religious conflict contributed to the rapid decline of the Moghul empire in the 18th century.

European Expansion into India

The last of the great invaders of India were the Europeans. The arrival of the Dutch, French, and British must form part of students' understanding of European expansion. But it is essential that their arrival also be viewed from the standpoint of the Indians and its impact on their culture. The Europeans triumphed largely because of the breakdown of the Moghul Empire from internal rivalries, invasions from Afghanistan, and the break-up of the imperial bureaucracy. The shrewd leader of the French East India Company, Dupleix, foresaw this disintegration and was the first European to take advantage of it and loosen India from Moghul control. He was followed by the British leader Clive. The establishment of the British East India Company's merchant warriors along the Indian coasts and its control of Indian trade should be understood as a vital part of this story. In effect, a relative handful of Europeans managed to wrest control from the Moghuls. The long-term consequences of these events—foreshadowing European imperialism of the 19th century—were to change the course of history in South Asia.

The history of this era demonstrates to students that the British triumphed largely because of the breakdown of the Moghul Empire from internal rivalries, invasions from Afghanistan, and the break-up of the imperial bureaucracy.

UNIT V
THE WORLD IN THE
19TH CENTURY

SIGNIFICANCE AND TEACHING GOALS

■ *MAJOR THEMES*

For much of the world, the contemporary era of human history begins with two great revolutions, one political and the other economic, both of them with enormous consequences in social, cultural, and ideological life. The French Revolution, together with its American predecessor, proclaimed to the world that three human aspirations were both righteous and reachable: national unity and independence; democratic self-government and civic equality; economic and social justice. The other upheaval, the Industrial Revolution, already underway in 1800, is still transforming societies, politics, cultures, and ideologies the world over. It is not possible even to begin to understand the present-day world without a thorough grasp of the paths these revolutionary movements have taken over the last two centuries, together with the forces and ideas they have spawned.

Especially important in this era were the great democratic revolutions in America and France and the ideals they proclaimed to the world. Following the major theme of the **development of political theory and organization** will help students understand how these precedents influenced the democratic revolutions of Latin America in the early 19th century, and the renewal of revolution in France in 1830 and again in 1848, when democratic revolutions swept much of Western Europe. Political democracy advanced in this era, particularly in Western Europe, as did important advances in social legislation.

For much of the world, the contemporary era of human history begins with two great revolutions, one political and the other economic, both of them with enormous consequences in social, cultural, and ideological life.

Above: American iron mill, middle of the 19th century. Steel engraving.

The 19th century witnessed two profound economic changes, affecting societies throughout the globe: the Industrial Revolution and the worldwide expansion of European imperialism.

In the Middle East, the late 19th century witnessed the rise of intellectual movements that tended to emphasize human rights, constitutions, and elections and that culminated in constitutionalist movements in Turkey in 1876 and a constitutional revolution in Iran in 1905, leading to adoption of a Western-style constitution. Students will appreciate these developments when contrasted with earlier efforts of Middle Eastern rulers to emulate Western industrialization and establish "reforms from above," but without relinquishing their centralized power.

Also important to understanding this era is the theme of **economic and technological developments and their social, cultural, and political consequences,** for the 19th century witnessed two profound changes affecting societies throughout the globe: the Industrial Revolution and the worldwide expansion of European imperialism. Neither of these developments nor their consequences in the 20th century can be understood without carefully examining them from the perspectives of both the Europeans and of those societies of Africa, Asia, and the Middle East affected by them. In following this theme, students will become aware of the national rivalries for raw materials and resource markets that propelled European imperialism. With such 19th-century military developments as the iron-clad steamboat, mobile field artillery, and heavy armaments, Europe's control of the seas was extended to East Asia, and with its 19th-century land conquests in India, Africa, and East Asia, Europe had by century's end established economic dominance over much of the globe as well.

Following this theme will allow students to explore the consequences of the spread of industrialization, of the networks of railroads, and of worldwide shipping and communication that increasingly linked societies throughout the world. It will open, also, discussion of the 19th-century rise of African, Asian, and Middle Eastern nationalism and resistance to foreign control. Japan's experience in remaining relatively free of a Western imperial presence and its success in adapting Western industrialization as it sought to "catch up" with the West provides an enlightening and contrasting perspective on these events and on Japan's 20th-century development as a major industrial power.

A third major theme in the study of this era is the impact of **philosophical and religious thought** in the lives of millions of ordinary men and women. Students need to know the basic tenets of the major 19th-century ideologies that developed in these years—Conservatism, Liberalism, republicanism, and socialism—and how each tried to deal with the effects of the democratic and industrial revolutions. Later in the century appeared those ideologies exalting force: militant nationalism, Social Darwinism, revolutionary Marxism, militarism, racism—the precursors of 20th-century totalitarianism. Students need to understand these ideologies in their European context where most arose, but also in their development in the second and third worlds, as they were adapted to the special circumstances of time and place.

Students need to know the basic tenets of the major 19th-century ideologies that developed in these years—Conservatism, Liberalism, republicanism, and socialism— and how each tried to deal with the effects of the democratic and industrial revolutions.

Karl Marx and John Stuart Mill

■ ESSENTIAL UNDERSTANDINGS

1. **The French Revolution:** its causes, conditions, and consequences; contrasts with the American Revolution; influences on 19th-century revolutions.

2. **The democratic revolutions in Latin America:** their causes, comparisons with the French and American revolutions, and their consequences at all levels of the social hierarchy.

3. **The Industrial Revolution:** the stages in its development, effects on daily lives of people, and on European 19th-century imperialism.

4. **The 19th-century "isms:"** their political ideas and effects on social, political, and economic agendas in various nations of the world; contrasts between the major 19th-century ideologies of Conservatism, Liberalism, republicanism, and socialism and those exalting force: militant nationalism, Social Darwinism, revolutionary Marxism, and racism.

5. **European imperialism:** its motivations, rivalries, character, and consequences.

6. **Effects of imperialism and reactions** in Africa, the Middle East, India, East Asia, and the Americas.

■ HABITS OF THE MIND

World history of the 19th century is rich in events and perspectives that cultivate historical habits of the mind. Novels, memoirs, and biographies will help students move into the era and **develop empathy for the lives of people** touched by the enormous changes wrought by the Industrial Revolution and the democratic revolutions of that time. Essential are the works of Charles Dickens, but also writings that capture the experiences of peoples from other nations and walks of life.

Novels, memoirs, and biographies will help students move into the era and develop empathy for the lives of people touched by the enormous changes wrought by the Industrial Revolution and the democratic revolutions of that time.

Tolstoy visits Chekhov, dramatist and short-story writer.

The complexity of interests and aspirations behind the surge of European imperialism prior to the First World War presents a great challenge to students' **historical imagination and powers of judgment**. The use of original sources is particularly valuable here, not only in analyzing cause, but in exploring the different methods of the imperial powers and the different responses of the colonized peoples, reflecting the effects of their own geographic, social, cultural, and religious resources. The stories of imperialism are full of paradox and heavy with consequences, still unrolling in the present day, terribly costly down to the third and fourth generations. In most of the former European and American colonies and client states, the hopes for national dignity, free government, and social decency are far from fulfilled. Advocates of democracy remain prey to extremists of left and right who are well-armed with force and simple answers.

MAJOR TOPICS IN THE STUDY OF THE WORLD IN THE 19TH CENTURY

1. The French Revolution

2. The Spread of Democratic Revolution to Latin America

3. The Industrial Revolution

4. Classes and "Isms" of the 19th Century

5. European Nationalism and Its Progress

6. European Imperialism and Reactions in Africa, India, East Asia, and the Middle East

MAJOR TOPICS AND THEIR DEVELOPMENT: ESSENTIAL UNDERSTANDINGS AND RELATED BACKGROUND FOR TEACHERS

■ *THE FRENCH REVOLUTION*

For historians in the Western world, the French Revolution ranks with the decline and fall of Rome and the great war of 1914-18 as one of those cataclysmic events whose causes call forth almost obsessional attention. To understand the French Revolution, it may be preferable to examine the impact of the Revolution before turning to its causes, especially if it is to be studied in contrast to the American Revolution. And it would nourish students' political sophistication to remember the English Revolution as well.

All three revolutions took nearly a century to achieve a settled, agreed-upon constitutional system. American students need to recall that it was not until 1865, after a civil war far bloodier than all the French revolutions added together, that the United States imposed agreement over its federal system. The French took 86 years, from 1789 to 1875, as did the English, from 1603 to 1689. Yet all these revolutions occurred in relatively prosperous, secure societies of substantial political and administrative experience and sophistication, with large, confident middle and lower-middle classes and widespread ownership of property. From this perspective students should better understand the political difficulties facing so many nations in the world today.

Secondly, the causes and conditions of the French Revolution may be contrasted to those of the American, as part of the explanation of the French fall into extremism, civil war, and military dictatorship between 1789 and 1815. Those who blame the disintegration only upon radical French ideologues oversimplify the contrasts. Our revolution was for the most part directed against outsiders, not compatriots. Ours was largely free of class divisions and class hatred; we had suffered no privileged aristocracy or clergy; relations between rich and poor, in town and country, were less strained. We enjoyed the advantages of great distance from Britain and of massive, probably decisive, aid from the French. Their revolution was attacked by several foreign powers across land

The causes and conditions of the French Revolution may be contrasted to those of the American, as part of the explanation of the French fall into extremism, civil war, and military dictatorship between 1789 and 1815.

Symbolic figure of Equality. Popular woodcut.

borders. Our political leaders and legislators had, for the most part, long experience in the daily workings of representative government. Theirs had substantially less. Religious issues were minor in America. In France the question of the Church tore the nation, including the political moderates of the Center, in half.

Our political leaders and legislators had, for the most part, long experience in the daily workings of representative government. French leaders had substantially less.

Economic conditions, too, were worse in France. Depression, unemployment, inflation, food shortages, and fear of famine all made the task of peaceful political settlement much harder. Regional and provincial rivalries were more divisive in France than the American colonies' well-known suspicions and hesitations. Once again, all of these factors are still alive in a world where democracy struggles to be born and to survive.

Thirdly, students need to understand the several stages of the French Revolution, from the moderate compromise over limited monarchy in 1789-91 through radicalism, reaction, dictatorship, and the return to moderate compromise in 1815. Not for nothing has France been called the West's laboratory of political experiment. Each stage and each faction represents an ideology and a set of group and class interests that were to become active in most world societies ever since. The very vocabulary of Left, Right, and Center originated in 1789.

■ *THE SPREAD OF DEMOCRATIC REVOLUTION TO LATIN AMERICA*

Students can observe the spread of revolution and movements for independence to European colonies in Latin America in the early 19th century. The drive for independence was widespread and eventually produced the political geography that we know today. Students should understand how revolt began in the areas of newer development along the eastern seaboard, in the former fringe areas, and then spread to the more settled regions of older development, the former central areas such as Peru and Mexico. Students can compare those revolts with our own War of Independence and with the French Revolution, and ask what impact the French and North American experiences and 18th-century liberal ideals of liberty, equality, and individualism had on the peoples of Latin America.

Portrait of Simon Bolivar (1785-1830). South American soldier, statesman, and revolutionary leader.

It is important to point out that the revolutions for independence in Latin America were led by local elites who wanted freedom from European power but were not eager to disturb their own positions atop the social hierarchy. Students need to see that, following these revolutions, Latin America remained under the economic dominance of Europe. Portugal had replaced Spain as the major trading partner in the 18th century, and Britain replaced Portugal in the 19th century. The great disparities in the distribution of wealth, coupled with ineffective constitutions in most Latin American countries, helps to explain the abiding contrasts in wealth and poverty, and the continued restlessness of those at the bottom of the hierarchy. At the same time, students should see the strides taken toward industrialization in the form of factories and railroads. All of these issues can be raised to get students to think about how truly "revolutionary" the Latin America revolutions were and what degree of continuity existed between the colonial period and that of independence. Such studies are much complicated and enlivened by examining the very different experiences of the Caribbean islands, including the Haitian Revolution, inspired by the French Declaration of the Rights of Man and Citizen.

The revolutions for independence in Latin America were led by local elites who wanted freedom from European power but were not eager to disturb their own positions atop the social hierarchy.

■ THE INDUSTRIAL REVOLUTION

The study of the transformation of the modern world's economy can begin with the development of fundamental industrial processes in England during the 18th century, their spread to the European continent and America during the 19th, and the changing nature and spread of industry in the 20th. Because it is one of the most powerful transformations in history, industrialization must be stressed in world history. Its origin in England should be understood as a unique historical event. Though transferred to France and the United States earlier than to Russia, Japan, or China, for example, the Industrial Revolution was uniquely an English anomaly originating independently nowhere else in the world.

Toussaint L'Ouverture meets with the French generals in Haiti to make peace after his guerrilla troops defeated them in battle.

With the Industrial Revolution came the technology for the systems of transportation and communication that rapidly linked the industrial world, its markets, and the resources of the non-industrialized world in growing systems of economic exchange. Shipping reduced transport time between continents from months to weeks; the telephone, telegraph, and wireless provided unprecedented ease and speed in communication; railroads knit the industrialized continents of Europe and North America and, introduced with 19-century European imperial expansion abroad, railroads penetrated deep into Africa and Asia.

The telephone, telegraph, and wireless provided unprecedented speed in communication; railroads knit the industrialized continents of Europe and North America and penetrated deep into Africa and Asia.

Promontory, Utah, May 10, 1869—joining of rails with golden spike.

Students need to learn not only about the technological changes introduced with industrialization, but the social and economic effects that followed the changes associated with industrialization. The impact on the family, on women and children, and on artisans should be studied. The formation of working classes and working-class political movements as well as the rising power of the middle class in Europe should be understood, as should the role of capitalism, banking, and trade in the growth of industrial economies.

Students should also appreciate the fears raised by industrialization, the revolts against it—whether by Romantic writers and artists, or by Luddites, who took direct action by destroying machinery—and the resistance by several social classes to the new economic formations. By its radical effects on economic life, the Industrial Revolution raised great and unprecedented social, cultural, moral, and political problems, many of which cut across and complicated the optimistic expectations about the future that were stirred by the Enlightenment and the American and French Revolutions, products of a simpler, pre-industrial age.

■ CLASSES AND "ISMS" OF THE 19TH CENTURY

The study of modern European and world history cannot proceed before students clearly understand the several social classes and subclasses in these societies, and how they relate to economic structure, to political factions, and to each other. Students need to know who people are, where they live, how they support themselves, what they fear or hope for, how they define fairness and the good life, all those things that draw them to this or that ideology and political party.

Difficult as it may be, students must also acquire understanding of the major 19th-century ideologies. These include Conservatism and Liberalism (capitalized, to distinguish them from today's terms), radical republicanism, and the several forms of socialism. Students need to know which groups and classes tended to support which ideology, and why. They need answers to a battery of questions about each ideology. What were its main political ideas, its economic and social programs? What were its views of human nature, human needs, human potential? Its beliefs about industrialization, class, gender, religion, and education? What was its vision of the future? To what extent did it embrace the aims of the triple revolution, and in what order? Like their current versions, these 19th-century ideologies had to wrestle with problems posed by technological and economic change. And like their current versions, they were shaped by combinations of theory and experience, of ideals and special interests, that students should recognize as they work to define their own stances on public affairs.

Students must acquire understanding of the major 19th-century ideologies: Conservatism and Liberalism, radical republicanism, and the several forms of socialism.

■ EUROPEAN NATIONALISM AND ITS PROGRESS

Whether one considers nationalism a progressive or regressive force, its power to inspire or enrage people throughout the world cannot be denied. Together with political democracy and social decency, a secure and independent nationhood remains a foremost aspiration of most world societies. Is it conducive to free self-government and social justice, or is it their enemy? World history of the 19th and 20th centuries can be mined for examples that cut in several different directions. In 19th-century Europe, the unifications of Italy and Germany may be used as cases in point, provided there is time enough to present instructive nuances and complications in each event.

More clearly retrograde was the militant nationalism of the late 19th century. Laced with Social Darwinism, racism, and militarism, it represented ideologies of force and inequality. The ugly side of mass politics should be critically examined in relation to demagoguery and the appeals to pride, fear, and anger that sought to justify the subjugation if not the annihilation of other, "lesser" peoples. The self-serving transfer of Darwin's (simplified) views on biology to human affairs produced up-to-date excuses for racism and imperialism, later to take the 20th-century form of Fascism and Nazism.

■ **EUROPEAN IMPERIALISM AND REACTIONS IN AFRICA, INDIA, EAST ASIA, AND THE MIDDLE EAST**

The growth of imperialism in the 18th and 19th centuries should be taught as a profound alteration in the lives and habits of the indigenous peoples, as well as of the colonizing societies themselves.

Imperialism has been an enduring aspect of human history and has had profound consequences in our own time. Students should study the rise of the formal and informal British Empire after the American Revolution and its relationship to industrialization and to the increasing competition for overseas markets and resources. Thus, students should learn about the race for Africa and the penetration of Europeans into the Far East, including the expansion of the Russian Empire eastward and southward across Eurasia. The growth of imperialism in the 18th and 19th centuries should be taught not simply as an aspect of the "rise of the West," but as a profound alteration in the lives and habits of the indigenous peoples, as well as of the colonizing societies themselves.

Students should be encouraged to examine the complicated motives and forces behind the imperialist urge. How important were economic hopes—new, cheaper sources of raw materials, new markets, new, safer places to invest? Were such economic expectations fulfilled? By examining the motivations behind imperialism, students may approach answers to these questions and measure the other driving forces: national pride, national rivalries, racist ideologies, the search for a balance of power, the desire for military bases, as well as for missions to Christianize, and the humanitarian impulse to carry the benefits of modern medicine, education, law, and justice to the rest of the world. Only by examining major colonies can students approach the reality of imperialist impact on the colonized, which must serve as background for the later study of decolonization and new forms of nationalism.

The Great Trek in South Africa

Africa in the 19th Century

European imperialism in Africa should be seen in the larger context of 19th-century developments in the economies of Africa. In that century the slave trade gradually gave way to a growing international commerce in African commodities and European manufactures. Thus, the lives of African peoples, along with Asians and Latin Americans, and with rural peoples in the United States and Europe, became increasingly bound up with a rapidly changing global economy. In

Africa, the reach of international trade in ivory and rubber, guns and textiles deep into the interior of the continent belies old-fashioned notions that it was 19th-century European adventurers and missionaries who "discovered" Africa. Students might discover for themselves some of the great dramas of that century—Islamic reformation and revolution in West Africa, the rise of Shaka and the Zulu empire, and the appearance of new "gunpowder kingdoms" in East Africa.

The invasion of Africa and the setting up of colonial regimes took longer, was more costly, and turned out much differently than European governments expected, for most African peoples resisted conquest tenaciously. And when they were not resisting, they were actively trying to negotiate the terms of the New Order. Bismarck, Gladstone, and Leopold II are important figures in this drama, but so are prominent resistance leaders such as Abd al-Qadir of Algeria, Samori Turé of the Western Sudan, Menelik II of Ethiopia, and Cetshwayo of the Zulu.

The setting up of colonial regimes took longer, was more costly, and turned out much differently than European governments expected, for most African peoples resisted conquest tenaciously.

Direct European rule over Africa lasted on the whole less than a century. Yet the colonial experience, set against the background of the two World Wars and the Great Depression, brought immense changes to the African scene. Students should know of the major colonial systems and their policies, comparing, for example, the British and French empires on such points as education, labor recruitment, taxation, economic investment, and civil and political rights for the governed. Students should also consider two other subjects: 1) the wrenching disruptions of African life that colonial policies produced, such as long-distance labor migration, rapid urbanization, and lowered standards of living; and 2) the creative responses of Africans to these disruptions, illustrated by the appearance of new urban ethnic associations, "Africanized" Christian churches, labor organizations, and movements of political protest.

Students may look for evidence by which to consider the balance sheet of colonialism. Did the European rulers "modernize" Africa with roads, railroads, harbors, and schools and thus better prepare its people to cope with world economic forces in the later 20th century? Or did they largely exploit Africa's agricultural and mineral riches, invest less in education, development, and technology than they might have done and lay preconditions for the "cycle of poverty" that has afflicted many newly independent nations? Or was reality a complex mixture, incorporating elements of both aspects of European rule?

Study of colonialism in Africa should pay special attention to the peculiar case of South Africa, which resembles Algeria as a colony where European settlers moved in to create and sustain an industrial state founded on doctrines of racial control and separatism.

Study of colonialism in Africa should pay special attention to the peculiar case of South Africa, which resembles Algeria as a colony where European settlers moved in to form a substantial minority. Considering the attention of the world on South Africa today, students should know the main lines of its history, especially the factors that led a fairly small European settler minority to create and sustain an industrial state founded on doctrines of racial control and separatism.

India in the 19th Century

The period of British domination in India is a crucial example of imperialism at work and needs emphasis in a world history course. Even after the East India Company emerged as the pre-eminent power in India following the defeat of the Hindu armies in 1818, hundreds of puppet Maharajas were left on local thrones throughout the subcontinent. Among the efforts by the Indians to recover control was the "Sepoy Rebellion" in 1857-58, in which Hindus and Muslims alike rallied in an effort to overthrow British rule in the Anglo-Indian War. Students should learn about the varying responses of Indian regions, as well as religious and economic groups, to the consolidation of British rule (the *Raj* as it came to be called). The educational role of British reforms and reformers—Christian, Utilitarian, and Liberal—should also be stressed. The negative side of the Industrial Revolution in transforming India's economy (as it had England's), displacing millions of Bengali, Madras, and Bombay handspinners and weavers, and depressing the local economy, is basic to understanding relations between Britain and India.

The Sepoy Rebellion. Attack on the Sealkote Mutineers by General Nicholson's Irregular Cavalry. Engraving.

The birth and development of Indian nationalism provides a counterbalance to this tale of domination. The Hindu resistance to Christian missionary efforts at mass conversion sparked an intellectual movement to recover the great works of Hindu civilization. The national political movement born in the wake of the Anglo-Indian war provided a rallying point for Indians embittered by British domination. The replacement of the East India Company by direct British rule ushered in the last phase of colonization (1858-1947) in which the British essentially tried to hold the line against rising nationalist tides. The birth of the Indian National Congress in 1885 marks an important stage in that process, but it is important to show that more radical elements and Muslim aspirations already much complicated the scene. Our students should understand that Indian pluralism and provincial, linguistic, and cultural diversities compounded the problems of nationalist leaders, who could communicate with one another, after all, only in the English language they had learned in British universities. If the English language was important politically, the railroads, telegraph wires, and penny posts were important socially and economically, helping to integrate the vast subcontinent with its enormous population. An appreciation of British legal and constitutional reforms and their effects is important. These transforming processes can be contrasted with the powerful currents of continuity and conservatism among most of the population, who had always lived out their lives far from the rulers, native or foreign, under village headmen or councils. The rules of "caste" should be re-introduced here to help students understand the lasting complexities of Indian life.

The replacement of the East India Company by direct British rule ushered in the last phase of colonization (1858-1947) in which the British essentially tried to hold the line against rising nationalist tides.

The Middle East in the 19th Century

Students should know that at least as early as the 18th century Middle Easterners made a number of serious attempts to catch up with Europe in military strength, industry, and technology, and to modernize governmental systems. Many of these attempts, especially in earlier periods, may be understood under the heading, useful also elsewhere in the world, of "modernization from above"—attempts by a ruler or ruling group to modernize and to build up new military forces without giving up (in fact with strengthening) their own power.

The perception of a need for radical change came about mainly as a result of new relations with Europe, arising both from the Industrial Revolution which spurred Europe's search for export markets and raw materials, and from the successful

Austrian and Russian counter-attacks to the Ottoman conquests that had brought Muslim armies across the Danube and as far north as Vienna, Poland, and Ukraine. Also weakening the Ottoman Empire were the wars that Europeans carried into the Middle East and North Africa, including Napoleon's invasion of Egypt in 1798, followed by Russian wars with Iran and the Ottoman Empire, by wars of colonial conquest by France in Algeria in 1830 and Britain in Egypt in 1882.

Students should understand that with its proximity to Europe, the Middle East was both early to emulate Europe and early to resent it. Emulation and resentment can both be studied in the rule of Muhammed Ali (1804-48) in Egypt. He tried to build industries, rebuild his armed forces, centralize government, and begin large-scale cotton exports. He also hoped to conquer most or all of the territory of his nominal overlords, the Ottoman rulers. Britain and other European powers stopped him and forced him to agree to a compromise with the Ottomans that limited his economic and military development. Such unequal treaties, enforcing low tariffs on goods imported from Europe, were imposed on many Third World countries after wars, and made it more difficult for them to develop industries. Students should understand how this practice caused resentment toward the West which has continued into the present day.

A combination of new ideas and discontent with old regimes led to constitutionalist movements in Turkey, temporarily in 1876 and again in 1908, and to a constitutional revolution in Iran during the period 1905-1911.

Finally, as background to understanding 20th-century developments in the Middle East, students should consider the importance of various intellectual trends that developed in this region since the mid-19th century. These tended to be less autocratic than the earlier trends seeking "reforms from above," and eventually tended to stress constitutions, elections, and human rights. Both male and female authors wrote about increased women's rights from the late 19th century on. Some intellectuals wanted essentially Western liberal systems, while others tried to reinterpret Islam in ways that stressed modern values. A combination of new ideas and discontent with old regimes led to constitutionalist movements in Turkey temporarily in 1876 and again in 1908, and to a constitutional revolution in Iran during the period 1905-1911. In both cases Western-style constitutions were adopted. Most Arab constitutions, however, came after they were detached from the Ottoman Empire following World War I.

Japan in the 19th Century

Students should compare British imperialism in India with the commercial opening of Japan to the West. As the Japanese economy became more sophisticated, and Western powers ever more expansive, pressures built up to open Japan to Western trade. American students should know about Commodore Matthew Perry's demand in 1853 that the Japanese allow trade with the Americans, but it is essential that they see this event from the Japanese standpoint, within the context of economic, social, and cultural developments within Japan. With the "opening" of Japan, Western civilization replaced Chinese civilization as the dominant outside influence in Japanese life. The pattern of borrowing and adaptation continued, though in a very different context.

The Meiji Restoration in 1868 and Japan's rapid industrialization are the central events marking the late 19th-century transition to modern Japan. Students should learn that the events by which the emperor was once again placed at the center of the state created a powerful centralized, oligarchic rule that had repercussions throughout Japanese life. Determined not to be overborne by the Western powers, the Meiji government sent scholars and observers to Europe and the United States to bring back useful methods of strengthening the economy, education, the army and navy, government, and administration. Under a German-style constitution, the emperor controlled cabinet, budget, and legislative initiative. Industrialization likewise proceeded under the reform impulses of the aristocratic, military, and business elite that dominated imperial politics. Banks, railroad, steel, and ship manufacturing quickly expanded. The course of this industrialization was marked by the close alliance between the biggest businesses and industries on the one hand and the imperial bureaucracy on the other. Japan's particular way of achieving industrialization should be compared with that taken by Russia, Europe, the United States, and presently-developing countries so that students may comprehend the many alternatives available.

As in other parts of the world, industrialization had profound consequences for social and cultural life in Japan. Borrowing form the West, the Japanese changed their style of

Determined not to be overborne by the Western powers, the Meiji government sent scholars and observers to Europe and the United States to bring back useful methods of strengthening the economy, education, the army and navy, government, and administration.

dress and haircut, but they did not alter some of their traditional attitudes toward family, women, religion, or courtesy. An industrial proletariat appeared in the cities. Many of these were young farm girls who went to work in the cities, and for the first time used their independence to agitate for better working conditions. They were part of a newly-emerging mass culture with newspapers, magazines, dance halls, coffee shops, and the *moga* or modern girl. This apparent capitulation to European culture appalled many in upper-class and rural society, who in response deepened their attachment to the emperor, to self-discipline, and to a belief in the superiority of traditional Japanese culture.

In strong contrast to Japan, 19th-century Chinese leadership resisted Western industrialization, seeing no benefits in undertaking fundamental changes that were in conflict with traditional Confucian values.

China in the 19th Century

In strong contrast to Japan, 19th-century Chinese leadership resisted Western industrialization, seeing no benefits in undertaking fundamental technological and expansionist economic changes that were in conflict with Chinese tradition and Confucian values. But while resisting change, the imperial dynasty had grown too weak to control unrest and uprisings in its own population, or to force out growing Western influence through trade in China's open port cities. Thus, China in the 19th century presents students an important case study of the effects of a waning empire, local unrest, and a succession of imperialist clashes with small military contingents pressed into service in defense of European commercial interests. The Opium War of 1839-42 with the British, the success of Anglo-French forces in entering Peking in 1857, and the humiliating defeat of China in the Sino-Japanese War of 1894-95 together led to China's capitulation to demands by England, France, Germany, Russia, and Japan for long-term leases on key ports and adjacent territories. The consequences of the forcible opening of China to Western imperialism, combined with the accumulated tensions within Chinese society itself, did much to shape the course of 20th-century history in East Asia. China collapsed into rebellion and civil war, then moved through a half-century of war and revolution, bringing forth the present Communist regime.

Tzu-Hsi, Chinese Empress (1835-1908). Photograph.

UNIT VI
THE WORLD IN THE
CONTEMPORARY ERA

SIGNIFICANCE AND TEACHING GOALS

■ *MAJOR THEMES*

Studying the history of the 20th century is of special importance if students are to understand the world in which they live and the major developments of the closing decade of the century. The great forces moving in the contemporary world cannot be understood without also understanding the momentous events and turning points of this century. The historical perspectives they offer are simply indispensable for unraveling the causes and likely consequences of unfolding developments in the world today. Without these understandings, students face the events of their times incapable of judging their relative significance or their power to affect human lives in profound and lasting ways. The bewilderment of so many American students who greeted the fall of the Berlin Wall with the puzzled query, "What's the big deal?" is stark testimony to the costs that follow when students fail to develop the historical perspectives essential for comprehending their world.

The major narrative themes **of political and social organization** are central to understanding the developments of this century. To Europeans who entered the 1900s confident in their economic and political leadership of much of the world, the 20th century appeared to promise unbroken progress. The war of 1914-18 tore across and ruined such hopes. Out of it arose conditions that would ease the way for Bolshevik, Fascist, and Nazi revolutions, for worldwide economic depression, and for a second world war more destructive than the

The great forces moving in the contemporary world cannot be understood without also understanding the momentous events and turning points of this century and the historical perspectives they offer.

Above: Thousands of Muskavites gather on August 21, 1991, after the attempted coup of Soviet hardliners failed.

Student activists work on what they call the "Goddess of Democracy" at a campus near Tienanmen Square.

The worldwide quest for democratic institutions, political freedom, and human rights as the century draws to a close must be understood.

first. Through most of the latter half of the 20th century, East and West have been divided by the Cold War. Also caught up in the East-West conflict have been the multitude of newly independent and struggling nations, born in the Middle East from the break-up of the Ottoman Empire following World War I, in Africa and Southeast Asia with the dissolution of European empires following World War II, and in Asia and the Pacific with the postwar dissolution of Japan's imperial expansion of the prewar years. As the century entered its final decades, the Soviet Union, the last of the world's great empires, was confronted with these same powerful forces of 20th-century nationalism and independence, sweeping through its linguistically and ethnically diverse republics and captive states. Understanding these events and the turbulence associated with the economic, political, and social struggles within all these regions provides students essential background for assessing the significance of the closing decades of the 20th century.

The worldwide quest for democratic institutions, political freedom, and human rights as the century draws to a close must also be understood, not only in terms of the immediate drama of such historic events as the fall of the Berlin Wall, the tragedy of Tienanmen Square, the struggles to end South African apartheid, Gorbachev's revolutionary opening of the Soviet Union, or the aborted 1991 coup of the Soviet Union's "Committee of Eight"—an event widely judged by analysts at the time as the most significant in 20th-century Russian history. Students must be able to review these developments in the context of a century that has also witnessed the rise of totalitarian states of the Left and the Right whose human rights violations have been of unprecedented violence in their programs of state-sponsored genocide, terror, and forced collectivization at the cost of millions of lives. Against these developments students should observe the dramatic extension of democratic ideals and institutions in the 20th century, suggesting to many analysts that the struggle for democracy has emerged as the dominant political force in the world today. Only the long view of human history can inform students' judgments on this question and on the historical significance of the years in which they live.

A second major theme is equally important for understanding the 20th century and its upheavals throughout the world: the theme of **technological, industrial, and economic development.** The Industrial Revolution of the 19th century was to lead to full industrialization of Japan and the West in the 20th, and to its spread in this century to Russia, China, South Asia, and to parts of Latin America. The consequences have been profound, setting into motion worldwide population movements; expanding the number of major economic powers in the world; and bringing to increasing numbers of the world's population the enormous benefits of improved health, higher standards of living, trade, and global communication; but bringing also the heavy costs that "modernization" exacts on the environment and human societies. Much of the upheavals in the developing world can be examined in terms of the tensions and resistance evoked by the deep systemic changes set into motion with the industrialization of traditional agrarian societies.

Also important have been the changes brought about by the rapid emergence of a global economy, and of the instruments and institutions of international corporations, trade, and agreements that are revolutionizing the world in which students live. How these developments have emerged in the 20th century, and how deeply they now reach into the lives of students, defining the challenges, opportunities, and stark economic realities they must be prepared to face, are all understandings to be fostered in this study.

Throughout their study of the contemporary world, students should consider the **major currents of thought** that have shaped the world. Contributions of Marx, Freud, Einstein, and Keynes, for example, should be part of their vocabularies, and understood for their influence on the social, economic, scientific, and political developments of the century.

The rapid emergence of a global economy, and of the instruments and institutions of international corporations, trade, and agreements are revolutionizing the world in which students live.

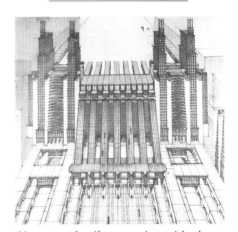

Airport and railway station with elevators and funiculars over three-levelled street drawn by Antonio Sant' Elia, 1914.

■ *ESSENTIAL UNDERSTANDINGS*

1. **The First World War:** origins and consequences.

2. **The Bolshevik Revolution:** its historical context, immediate causes, and consequences.

3. **Totalitarianism of Right and Left:** tenets of Marxist/

Leninist and Fascist/Nazi ideologies; methods in the seizure of power in Russia and in Germany; the consequences of the Stalinization of Russia and of Nazism in war and genocide.

4. **The Second World War:** its causes, participants, scope, and consequences.

5. **Postwar Developments:** the Marshall Plan, NATO, the Warsaw Pact, the rise of the Cold War, formation of the United Nations, the Universal Declaration of Human Rights, and the Helsinki accords.

6. **The worldwide quest for democratic institutions, political freedom, and human rights:** the ideals, major events, and turning points of this quest in the 20th century.

7. **East Asia in the 20th century:** Japanese imperial expansion and the consequences of World War II; the Chinese Civil War, the establishment of the People's Republic of China, Mao's Cultural Revolution, and the rise and suppression of the students' democratic movement of 1989; the postwar economic success of Hong Kong and Japan and the consequences in the world economy.

8. **The Middle East in the 20th century:** Nationalism, a force contributing to the break-up of the Ottoman Empire; the discovery of oil and its consequences in Middle Eastern internal developments and international relations; the creation of Israel; major causes and consequences of Arab-Israeli conflict; Islamic revivalism and its consequences.

9. **Decolonization in the 20th century:** the major movements in Africa and India to establish independence, the legacy of European colonialism in Africa and India, and major developments—political, economic, and social—in the newly independent states.

10. **Latin America in the 20th century:** Causes of 20th-century revolution and unrest in poverty, disparities in

The importance of such postwar developments as the Marshall Plan, NATO, the Warsaw Pact, the rise of the Cold War, formation of the United Nations, the Universal Declaration of Human Rights, and the Helsinki accords should be understood.

land distribution, economic dependency, and population pressures; economic industrialization and programs of land reform; intellectual and artistic achievements.

■ HABITS OF THE MIND

In all of their studies, students should look deeply into the specific contexts in which the events of the 20th century unfolded, and which must be taken into account if these issues and events are to be understood. It is particularly important that students be presented with differing perspectives and interpretations of these issues and events, that they might develop their **powers of critical analysis and judgment,** essential for informed citizenship.

While history is more than the story of individual men and women, it is nonetheless important for students to recognize the power of the individual in influencing the turn of historical events. Woven through the dramatic story of Indian politics since the 1920s, for example, was the unique, astonishing career of Mahatma Gandhi, whose influence in India and upon worldwide movements of civil disobedience was so great. No figure could do more to develop students' **habit of looking to the importance of individuals in history** and at the same time to help them appreciate the limits that other forces often place on the individual's highest aspirations. In Gandhi's case, it was the tragedy of violent partition at the very moment his dream of Indian independence had been won. His assassination followed soon after.

Great numbers of novels, memoirs, biographies, reportage, and films offer students many paths to **historical empathy and escapes from present-mindedness.** They make clear, too, the sometimes sharp cultural diversities that mark the world's peoples beneath the surface of their shared humanity. There is, indeed, no more powerful entry into the perspectives of those who witnessed the developments of this era than through such works as The Diary of Anne Frank and Mathabane's Kaffir Boy.

Even more clearly than the history of earlier times, world history of the 20th century should prepare students to **live with uncertainties about today and tomorrow, to realize that**

Mahatma Gandhi engaged in spinning on board the cross-channel steamer en route to Folkstone.

Students should be presented with differing perspectives and interpretations of issues and events to develop their powers of critical analysis and judgment.

not all problems have solutions, and that much business will remain unfinished, exasperating, even perilous. But this has been the human condition always, and not a reason for easy cynicism or resignation. The last two centuries have, in many ways, been the most progressive in history, with revolutionary improvements in human health and the quality of life for millions upon the planet. While there are too many failures and cruelties to encourage undue optimism, there are also too many instances of survival and amelioration, of devotion to human welfare and to the defense of basic human rights to allow us the luxury of pessimism. This, perhaps, is the most valuable of history's perspectives that students may grasp from studying the contemporary era. It is a perspective gained from a close study of both political and social history, by looking at ordinary families, men, women, and children as they struggled with the forces and conditions of their day, together with the famous, the powerful, the creative individuals whose names appear in the textbooks.

World history of the 20th century should prepare students to live with uncertainties about today and tomorrow, to realize that not all problems have solutions, and that much business will remain unfinished, even perilous.

MAJOR TOPICS IN THE STUDY OF THE CONTEMPORARY WORLD

1. Europe in the 20th Century

2. China and Japan in the 20th Century

3. The Middle East in the 20th Century

4. Decolonization in the 20th Century: African and India

5. Latin America in the 20th Century

6. Bringing Historical Perspectives to Events of the Closing Decades of the Century

MAJOR TOPICS AND THEIR DEVELOPMENT: ESSENTIAL UNDERSTANDINGS AND RELATED BACKGROUND FOR TEACHERS

■ *EUROPE IN THE 20TH CENTURY*

In approaching the study of World War I, students should

have the opportunity to review European conditions which had developed by 1914, and the reasons for the extraordinary sense of European prosperity, progress, and optimism as the new century opened. Nationalism had triumphed in Italy, Germany, Rumania, Bulgaria, Greece, and throughout Latin America; the American Union had survived intact in spite of the Civil War. Vigorous nationalist movements were active in "subject areas" of Europe. Those who believed that universal nationhood (excepting their own colonies) was one of the conditions for world peace were expecting much of the future.

Students should have the opportunity to review European conditions by 1914, and the reasons for the extraordinary European optimism over the coming century.

Political democracy, too, seemed to be making steady progress. Americans had abolished slavery and Russians, serfdom. The vote was being extended in most nations of the Western world, though not to women as yet. Elections, parties, assemblies, public debate, and freedom of speech, of the press, and of religion had emerged across the European map—or so it was claimed. The rise of effective labor unions and the passage of social legislation—led by Great Britain and Germany—promised better economic security and social justice for the industrial working classes. Most Marxist parties were revisionist, ready to rely on the peaceful workings of the parliamentary system.

Turn of the century view down the Avenue d'Opera; Paris. Street scene with carriages and people. Opera House in the distance. Photograph.

Students will be most struck, however, by looking at social history of the pre-war period, most especially at the history of the family. The eradication of many diseases, rising standards of living, the spread of public education, the growth in middle-class employment, the stable value of most European currencies, widespread confidence in national or party leadership, and a century without a major European war—all stirred people's hopes for the future of their children. Students should consider also the texture of daily life among ordinary people in order to appreciate the degree to which the great war of 1914-18 destroyed human hope, and tortured the bodies and minds of Europeans.

The First World War

The conflict that erupted in August 1914 should be examined for the underlying causes that permitted a single incident—the assassination of an archduke of the ruling

Hapsburg family by a Serbian nationalist—to embroil an entire continent in war. Students should consider the status of the interlocking European monarchies of the time; the intense national rivalries among the imperial powers; the extraordinary level of military preparedness on all sides; and the network of alliances formed to maintain the balance of power, with Great Britain, France, and Russia aligned on one side, and Germany, the Austro-Hungarian Empire, and the Ottoman Empire on the other.

By analyzing the diplomatic miscalculations and failures in communication that rapidly drew one nation after another into the conflict—from Austria's threat of retaliation, to Russia's support of its Serbian ally, to Germany's fielding of troops against Russia, to French and British entry in support of Russia—students will gain an instructive lesson in failed diplomacy and crisis mismanagement. Particular attention should be paid to the impact of military technology upon the origins of war as well as upon the war itself. The introduction of new artillery and tanks, combined with the murderous incompetence with which the war was waged, condemned the continent to four devastating years of trench warfare, with massed armies facing one another along a front extending for hundreds of miles, and with tens of thousands of lives sacrificed on each day an offensive was tried. Students should analyze the importance of the United States' entry into the war, the outbreak of revolution in Russia, the abdication of Kaiser Wilhelm II, and the sheer exhaustion on all sides which helped to bring the conflict to an end.

German shock troops ready for spring offensive, March, 1918.

In the wake of World War I there arose the Bolshevik Revolution, Italian Fascism, the Great Depression, German Nazism, and the origins of World War II.

Students should consider the conditions confronting the negotiators of the Paris Peace Conference—the unprecedented scale of economic ruin and social upheaval resulting from the war, the clashing national interests of the victors, and the personal roles of Woodrow Wilson, Georges Clemenceau, and Lloyd George. Students should assess the terms of the peace treaty, including the guilt clause; heavy German reparations; the establishment of the League of Nations; and the creation of a number of new and unstable states in Eastern Europe from territories of the collapsed monarchies of Germany, Austria, and Russia. The consequences were profound. Far from making the world safer for democracy, the war and its settlement rendered much of the world more hostile. In its wake arose the Bolshevik Revolution, Italian Fascism, German Nazism, the collapse of the world economy, Japanese expansionism, and the origins of World War II. No other event so much shaped the 20th century.

The Russian Revolution and Its Aftermath

Students should examine yet another turning point of the 20th century, the Bolshevik Revolution, and recognize its setting amid the social chaos and human suffering brought by the war. But a deeper understanding requires a review of the Russian government's failure to deal with fundamental economic, social, and political problems once assassination cut short Alexander II's attempts at reform in 1881, and the outbreak of war in 1914 cut short the feeble beginnings of the parliamentary system born of the Revolution of 1905. Students should examine the immediate causes of the Spring Revolution of 1917, consider Germany's interest in assisting Lenin's race from Switzerland to Moscow to assume leadership of the revolution, and analyze how the easy defeat of the Kerensky government by Lenin's Communist Party in the autumn illustrates the familiar plight of moderates caught between extremists of Left and Right in unstable, developing societies.

Russian Revolution, 1917: Seamen from the cruiser, Aurora, keeping order with fixed bayonettes.

The development of Soviet totalitarianism opens with Lenin's dispersal by force of the freely-elected Constituent Assembly in 1918. Its progress should be followed through the Stalinist period of forced collectivization, police state purges, mass executions and deportations, the "Stalinization" of culture, and the generalized terror and repression that, to one degree or other, marked Soviet society until recently. The international repercussions of expansionist messianic Communism should not be neglected, nor should the power of ideas, in this case revolutionary Marxist-Leninist dogma, to justify and to propel human actions. Selections from writers such as Orwell, Koestler, Solzhenitsyn, Djilas, Pasternak, and Valladares will present students with vivid portraits of totalitarianism in this century.

Soviet totalitarism should be followed through the Stalinist period of forced collectivization, police state purges, mass executions, and generalized terror and repression.

Europe Between the Wars

The two decades that followed 1918 saw the full sprouting on the European continent of the seeds of disaster sewn by the war. Students need to examine how moderates in the Weimar Republic were unable to satisfy a defeated people's demand for a restoration of national power and prestige, maintain a workable democracy, or overcome the economic, social, and psychological ravages of inflation and depression. Economic analyses should reveal the depth of the problems that brought on the crash of '29, including the agricultural overproduction of farmers in Europe and America, the low purchasing power of large sectors of the population, protectionist policies that hiked tariffs and stifled international trade, and the reckoning that followed the speculative excesses in the stock market.

Rise of Nazi Germany: Thousands of German troops listen as Hitler speaks at the Nuremberg Rally of 1936.

Attention should be given to Hitler's use of anti-Semitism to mobilize support for the Nazi party and his policy of Aryan superiority that led to the horrors of the Holocaust.

Students should examine the sources and power of Nazi ideology and the appeal of Hitler to a variety of groups who, embittered by Germany's defeat, found in his policies the promise of a rebuilt, fully employed, re-militarized Germany firmly opposed to communism and to the demands of the socialist Left. Students should examine the steps taken by Hitler, once in power, to establish a totalitarian state—the control of the press, the creation of the Gestapo, the purge of opponents, the abolition of political parties and free trade unions, and the effective use of mass propaganda. Particular attention should be given to Hitler's use of anti-Semitism to mobilize support for the Nazi party and, once in power, his policy of Aryan superiority and racial purification that led, first, to the systematic denial of rights and freedoms of its victims and then to the "Final Solution" and the unprecedented horrors of the Holocaust. This policy should be understood not just for the scale of its atrocities, but for what it demonstrated of the power of the totalitarian state to systematically select and eradicate its victims—primarily Jews, whose losses exceeded six million, but also Poles, gypsies, homosexuals, the handicapped, and Christians who protested or worked actively to save Jews.

Students should realize that fascism was not restricted to Germany alone, but found strong public following in Franco's Spain, in Italy under Mussolini, and in Hungary and Rumania. To study what the totalitarians of Left and Right had in common and how they were different—both in theory and in practice—is also critical to the political education of students.

The Second World War

In approaching study of World War II, students need to analyze the reasons for the passivity of the democracies, British, French, and American, in the face of aggression. Steps had been taken through the Washington Naval Conference of 1921 to limit armaments, and through the Kellogg-Briand Pact of 1928 to outlaw war. But these agreements lacked enforcement powers, as did the League of Nations whose powers were limited to debate and consideration of sanctions. In considering the inaction of the democracies in the face of aggressions by Japan, Italy, and Germany, students should consider the economic, social, and political problems that preoccupied the former Allies at home, and the prevailing orthodoxies of thought about the causes of war, current in the 1930s. They should examine the policy of appeasement, justified by Prime Minister Neville Chamberlain, following the Munich Conference of 1938, as having achieved "peace in our time"—a historical illustration of the fact that good intentions can have disastrous results when the policy itself is seriously flawed.

The course of the war, how and where it was fought, is important to students' understanding of the entire postwar world, of the memories and assumptions of their elders, not only at home and in Europe, but in the entire world. It was far more destructive than the first world war of economic and social orders, of political systems, of cities and resources, and of human life, as new weapons struck, from Rotterdam to Dresden, Leningrad to Hiroshima.

Students should examine the major phases of the war, from the period of intense danger (1939-42), when it appeared the Axis powers might win; through the second period (1943-44) when in both theaters of the war Allied fortunes seemed to turn around, the war against the Nazi submarines was being won, and the invasion of Normandy proved a success; through the final stages of the war (1944-45) when victory was achieved by the Allies in Europe and in Asia. Students should be aware of the enormous courage and sacrifice of the British as most of Europe fell and Britain stood alone. Churchill's

Churchill's leadership in mobilizing the nation to resistance should be understood, as should Charles de Gaulle's leadership of the French resistance forces and the coordinated Allied effort under the command of Dwight Eisenhower in Europe and Douglas MacArthur in the Pacific.

Winston Churchill gives his victory sign.

New York celebrates the news of Germany's surrender.

Students need to understand the effects of the war in the division of Germany, the establishment of the Soviet Union's sphere of influence in Eastern Europe and Asia, and the rise of the Cold War.

leadership in mobilizing the nation to resistance should be understood, as should Charles de Gaulle's leadership of the French resistance forces and the coordinated Allied effort under the command of Dwight Eisenhower in Europe and Douglas MacArthur in the Pacific.

Students should also understand the entry of the Soviet Union on the side of the Allies following Germany's invasion in 1941, the enormous Soviet losses in the defense of Leningrad and Stalingrad, and the successful Soviet offensive on the eastern front. Finally, students should examine the wartime meetings of Churchill, Roosevelt, and Stalin at Tehran (1943) and Yalta (1945), and their agreements concerning postwar international security, including guarantees of a Soviet sphere of influence on its western borders. Soviet invasion of Japanese-held Korea and Manchuria in the closing days of the war was to leave them in control of Mongolia, Manchuria, and North Korea at the war's end.

Europe and the Soviet Union in the Postwar Era

American students need to understand the effects of the war in the division of Germany, the establishment of the Soviet Union's sphere of influence in Eastern Europe and Asia, and the rise of the Cold War. Students should appreciate the fundamental differences between the divided, passive policies of the democracies following World War I and their active cooperation after 1945, expressed in economic, political, and military matters, including NATO's role in holding the balance of power during the Cold War in Europe. In particular students should understand the commitment of most nations since 1945 to cooperate in developing an open international trading system and stable economic and monetary conditions—a commitment expressed, for example, in the Bretton Woods Conference of 1944 which created the International Monetary Fund and the World Bank; the Marshall Plan; and the development of the General Agreement on Tariffs and Trade (GATT) by the seven leading industrial nations, the G-7.

In this context, West Germany underwent a stunning economic recovery and established what is generally considered to be among the stablest democracies in Western Europe and the freest form of government that Germany has ever had. Students might consider how, under a Basic Law that emphasized human rights, the principles of the Enlightenment, and Western liberalism, the state was demythologized and the army, for the first time in German history, ceased to be a self-governing body. Under a series of able and responsible leaders West Germany was able to meet its social and economic problems by the wise use of democratic procedures and to maintain a foreign policy firmly connected with the West, and cognizant of the need to repudiate territorial ambition and to atone for the sins of the past.

By the 1960s the Western democracies had developed a level of prosperity that contrasted sharply with the stagnation of Eastern Europe under Soviet control and that proved irresistible to the peoples of Eastern Europe. In particular students should examine developments in the European Common Market and the 1992 creation of the European Economic Community, developments which have thrust a more economically united Europe into the vanguard of the world's leading economic powers as the 20th century draws to a close.

Examining, by contrast, political, economic, and social conditions in the Soviet Union and just one of its satellite states—Poland, for example—is important if students are to understand the postwar years under Soviet-style communism isolated, in Churchill's phrase, by an "iron curtain" separating East from West. It is also important for students to examine the long-developing causes of the Soviet Union's economic collapse in the closing decade of the century. On the one hand, students should understand the massive industrialization of Soviet society under Stalin and Khrushchev, catapulting the nation into superpower status after World War II. Economic analysis of the Soviet command economy, including its failure to develop a pricing mechanism essential for guiding centrally controlled economic decision-making, is also important if students are to understand its weaknesses in a postwar global economy of a complexity unanticipated in 19th-century Marxist thinking.

Students might consider how the Cold War served to bolster the failing system by convincing the Soviet people of the need for the enormous sacrifices required for military

East Berlin policemen repair a section of the Berlin Wall damaged by Wolfgang Engels, a mechanic, who rammed an armored car through the structure to escape to West Berlin on April 17, 1963.

The Western democracies had developed a level of prosperity and dynamism that contrasted sharply with the stagnation of Eastern Europe under Soviet control and that proved irresistible to the peoples of Eastern Europe.

build-up and massive mobilization in the face of foreign threat from the West and from China on its eastern borders. The effects of widespread education, however, and of some liberalization of Soviet domestic policies were to lay the groundwork for the democratic movements that would emerge with Gorbachev's introduction of *perestroika* and *glasnost* and that would rapidly overtake both.

Cold War Tensions and the Avoidance of General War

Students should understand the Cold War tensions that escalated during these postwar years: the overwhelming presence of Soviet armor and troops in Eastern Europe, utilized to crush democratic uprisings in Hungary (1956) and Czechoslovakia (1968) and to back the Polish government's repression of Polish labor-led uprisings in the late 1970s; the crisis of the Berlin Blockade and the building of the Berlin Wall; the counter-presence of NATO's nuclear force in Europe; and the growing fear that the Cold War would escalate into a shooting war, with central Europe once again the theater of military confrontation, and this time of nuclear devastation.

U. S. Delegation signs the United Nations Charter, June 26, 1945. President Truman at left.

Particular attention should be given to the question how, in the climate of sustained Cold War confrontation, World War III was averted, one of the supreme accomplishments of the postwar era. Students should appreciate the efforts made to restrain violence and forge an international order in the wake of World War II. The Atlantic Charter, the creation of the United Nations, the Universal Declaration of Human Rights, and the Helsinki Accords have all helped to define the ideals of order and justice in the contemporary world. Students should also understand the broad outlines of foreign policy of the Western democracies and of the Soviet Union in these years—in particular the "containment of communism" policy forged in the Truman administration; the "balance of terror" sustained by a massive arms build-up on both sides; and the relaxation of the Cold War as the 1980s drew to a close.

Attention should be given to the question of how, in the climate of sustained Cold War confrontation, World War III was averted, one of the supreme accomplishments of the postwar era.

In taking stock of the extraordinary pace of change in the Soviet Union and Eastern Europe as the final decade of the century got underway, students will become aware of the national and ethnic rivalries within and between various Soviet Republics and within the various Eastern European states freed from Soviet control in the final decades of the century. Students might well ponder the difficulties ahead in establishing democratic institutions and maintaining peaceful relationships in what historically has been a volatile region. Slovenia, Croatia, and Serbia, for example, provide instructive insights for students to consider.

Western Thought and Culture

To enrich their study of the modern world, students should be introduced to major currents of scientific thought and to developments in the spheres of culture, philosophy, and religion. Of these, scientific research has been a dominant force in Western civilization in this century, transforming our understandings of the conscious, the unconscious, and the irrational; of space and time; of general relativity and quantum mechanics; of elementary particles (quarks) and the forces of nature; of molecular biology, genetic structure, and DNA replication. The work of Sigmund Freud, Madame Curie, Albert Einstein, Werner Heisenberg, and such pioneers of DNA research as Oswald Avery, W. Cochran, Francis Crick, and James Watson should be generally understood by students and appreciated for their enormous impact upon 20th-century thought and for their applications in atomic weaponry, space explorations, technological advances, medical discoveries, and health care.

Students should be introduced to major artists and architectural trends of this century, their innovations, and the social context in which they were conceived. Included, for example, should be the cubist movement led by Pablo Picasso, the atonal and dissonant innovations in music led by such major composers as Arnold Schoenberg and Igor Stravinsky; the innovative architectural forms that changed the skylines and urban space of modern cities; and selected works from writers such as Thomas Mann, T. S. Eliot, W.B. Yeats, James Joyce, and Virginia Woolf.

Finally, it is important to consider how religion has responded to the intellectual challenges and political stresses of the modern world. Issues of evolution, scientific indeterminacy, social injustice, the Holocaust, and mass warfare have tested the entire range of Christian and Jewish

Model of a DNA molecule, after a pattern by Dr. Van R. Potter.

Students should be introduced to major artists and architectural trends of this century, their innovations, and the social context in which they were conceived.

301

doctrines. How have religious leaders and thinkers such as Martin Buber, Reinhold Niebuhr, Pope John XXIII, and Vatican II responded to these challenges and how have these faiths remained a vital force in the Western world?

■ *JAPAN AND CHINA IN THE 20TH CENTURY*

No comprehension of the contemporary world is possible unless students also develop understanding of important 20th-century developments in China and Japan as they repeatedly cut across and interacted with foreign policy, military, and postwar economic developments in the Soviet Union and the West.

Japan in the 20th Century

Japan entered the 20th century already well-advanced as an industrial nation and soon embarked on an aggressive expansionment policy in Asia and the Pacific that would help to embroil much of the planet in World War II. Victorious in wars against China and Russia in 1895 and 1905, Japan annexed Korea in 1910, making it an imperial power as well. Students should understand something of the course of events in East Asia from Japan's imposition of its "21 Demands" on China during World War I to its invasion of Manchuria and Northern China in 1937. American students will benefit from examining these developments from the standpoint of the Japanese, who saw their population exploding against very limited resources and land area, their trade with the United States choked by high tariffs imposed after World War I, and their dignity insulted by the failure of the Allies to give Japan's delegates status at the Paris Peace Conference. Flushed by their military victories, and in the context of worldwide depression and unchallenged aggressions by Hitler and Mussolini, it proved easy for military leaders such as General Hideki Tojo to establish increasing control over Japan's political system and to launch the nation on a policy of armed expansion.

The Japanese saw their population exploding against very limited resources and land area, their trade with the United States choked by high tariffs imposed after World War I, and their dignity insulted by the failure of the Allies to give Japan's delegates status at the Paris Peace Conference.

Japan's seizure of French Indochina, its alliance with Nazi Germany and Fascist Italy, and its military expansion into Malaya and Burma put Japan on a collision course with Great Britain and the United States. The success of the

Japanese attack on Pearl Harbor, the course of World War II in the Pacific, the first, frightful use of atomic bombs, and the American occupation of Japan under the exceptional leadership of General Douglas MacArthur had a profound effect on Japanese life and attitudes, and must be part of every student's study of world history.

Americans need to grasp the significance of their rewriting of the Japanese constitution renouncing war, restoring universal suffrage, and providing safeguards for freedom of speech and the press. In examining Japan's economic and technological boom of the 1960s, students should consider how Western influences were adapted within a culture that remained specifically Japanese; and how the prominence of Japan in trade and world affairs continues to have a profound impact upon both the Japanese and American ways of life and students' own future prospects.

Sun Yat-sen (1866-1925), Chinese revolutionary leader.

China in the 20th Century

The 20th century in China has been marked by a half-century of violent political change, affecting a huge proportion of the world's population, with profound repercussions beyond China's borders. Students should understand how the cumulative impact of population growth, the increasingly adverse population-to-resource ratio, industrialization, and the import of Western ideas transformed Chinese society in the early 20th century, giving rise to an urban proletariat and professional elites with unsettling consequences for a historically traditional society.

Students should understand something of the republican reform movement led by Dr. Sun Yat-Sen and the consequences of the 1911 Revolution which abolished the weakened imperial system and established a short-lived republic, lacking in the institutions and leadership skills required for stable democratic government. The Japanese invasion in 1931, its seizure of Manchuria, and its 15-year occupation, controlling vast parts of China, should be recognized. Most important, students need to understand the Chinese civil war between the Kuomintang and the Communists and the establishment of the People's Republic of China in 1949 under the leadership of Mao Tse-Tung as one of the events that have

Students should understand something of the republican reform movement led by Dr. Sun Yat-Sen and the consequences of the 1911 Revolution which abolished the weakened imperial system and established a short-lived republic, lacking in the institutions and leadership skills required for stable democratic government.

Peasants at Xiaotian, a village at Shandong Province in eastern China, constructed a new school with the extra money they were able to earn under the family responsibility system.

An assessment of the costs and contributions of Maoist Communism in China should take into consideration the record in public health and agricultural output; examine the question whether collectivization improved the lives of peasants; and consider the effects of the introduction of the family responsibility system.

shaped modern world politics.

Students should understand the major outlines of communist policy in China, including its destruction of nearly a million of its political opponents among China's educated, land-holding, and ruling classes; its collectivization of agriculture and launching of a series of five-year plans to industrialize the nation; and its institution of centralized control over education as an agency of Maoist doctrine, its control of information, and its attack on all forms of religion. Mao's Cultural Revolution attacked whatever remained of traditional Chinese hierarchical values or vestiges of Western influence in the society. The liberalizing influences introduced after Mao's death supported the opening of China to trade and cultural relations with the West, but the brutal suppression of the 1989 student demonstrations calling for a more democratic system revealed the strong hold and fear of instability of the aging communists still in power.

An assessment of the costs and contributions of Maoist Communism in China, though very difficult to do at this time, should take into consideration the record in public health and agricultural output; examine the question whether collectivization improved the lives of peasants; and consider the effects of (and reasons for) the introduction of the family responsibility system. It is important also for students to consider the special situation of Hong Kong, its dynamic capitalism, and its 1997 reunification with mainland China on the expiration of Britain's 99 year lease.

■ THE MIDDLE EAST IN THE 20TH CENTURY

No understanding of the contemporary world is possible without comprehension of the Middle East, a region in which the West has been involved for most of this century, and in which strong forces of local and pan-Arabic nationalism, Islamic fundamentalism, and Arab-Israeli conflict intersect with powerful international interests in Middle Eastern oil and strategic access.

Nationalism

Students can understand much of what has happened in

the Middle East through most of the 20th century as part of the age of nationalism—a period when religion seemed of little importance to the elites and division developed between those who identified with the borders of the many new states that had been set up mainly by the British and French after the dissolution of the Ottoman Empire following World War I, and those who identified instead with a larger pan-Arab nationalism. Among the former were Turkey's radical reforming president Ataturk, who ruled in the interwar period, and Reza Shah Pahlavi, the founder of a new Iranian dynasty. While both brought to their countries a new wave of Western style modernization from above, the consequences were different. Attaturk paved the way for a democratic republic. Reza Shah established a dynasty which was overthrown by a religiously-inspired revolution under his successor.

Elated countrymen welcome Nasser, Egypt's President, after his decision to nationalize the Suez Canal, July 28, 1956.

Oil

Since the discovery of oil by the British in Iran in 1908, access to Middle Eastern oil has become of increasing importance in relations between this region and the world. The biggest oil yields have been in the least populous countries, whose rulers could generally buy off their people with high incomes and benefits; the more populous countries—notably Iran, Iraq, and Algeria—have, by contrast, undergone numerous internal and external struggles partly tied to oil. With the importance of oil to the industrialized world, the Middle East has been more subject to outside interference than perhaps any other region of the world.

Arab-Israeli Relations

To understand the continuing Arab-Israeli tensions in this region, students need to understand the long-held (pre-World War I) Zionist dream of a Jewish state as a haven for the millions of poor and persecuted Jews living mainly in Poland and Russia, a dream encouraged by the Balfour Declaration of 1917 proposing a Jewish homeland in Palestine. The rise of Hitler and the plight of the survivors of the Holocaust provided enormous force to Zionist demands for an independent state in Palestine.

Major events following World War II included the United

Since the discovery of oil by the British in Iran in 1908, access to Middle Eastern oil has become of increasing importance in relations between this region and the world.

Nation's 1947 Partition Resolution following the British government's declaration of its intention to surrender the Palestine Mandate; and the creation in 1948 of the new state of Israel which functioned under democratically-elected leaders such as Abba Eban and Golda Meir. The succession of Arab-Israeli conflicts that followed should be examined from both sides of the cultural divide: the continued refusal of most Arab states to recognize the legitimacy of Israel; the importance of the peace accord with Egypt; the problems raised by Israeli military occupation of a region of over one million Palestinians, after 1967; and the mounting pressures from the United States and the Soviet Union following the 1991 Gulf War to resolve these issues in a comprehensive Middle East peace settlement.

A major postwar trend in the Middle East and the Muslim world has been Islamic revivalism, which came to the world's attention with the Iranian revolution of 1978-79.

Islamic Revivalism

In addition to nationalism and patriotism, a major postwar trend in the Middle East and the Muslim world has been Islamic revivalism which, although a much older phenomenon, came to the world's attention with the Iranian revolution of 1978-79, led by Iran's Shi'i religious leaders. In other countries where religious leaders are less united and political, student and professional Islamists lead mass discontents that create a dilemma for governments with democratic tendencies—Jordan, Egypt, Algeria, and Tunisia—because the electoral strength of the Islamists raises the question whether they would safeguard democracy and minority rights were they to come to power.

Golda Meir addresses the 15th general assembly of the United Nations in New York, October 10, 1960.

In all this, students should develop the following major understandings: 1) Islam can be and has been interpreted differently in different times and places, and so could encourage rationalist thought in the Abbasid period and parts of the modern period, while primarily stressing conformity in other periods. In modern times Islam has even been given leftist and socialist interpretations. 2) Much of what has happened in the Middle East is not to be explained by Islam, but by factors like ecological decline (salination and desertification of the soil), the partly resulting growth of nomadic populations, and the decline of agriculture; the outstripping of economic growth by population growth, leading to crisis conditions in many countries; the disruption and dislocation of traditional societies by sudden and often violent modernization; and the strong backlash against some aspects of modernization, notably the emancipation of women. Students should also learn that it is best to be sparing in the use of the words "Islamic," "Muslim," and "Arab" unless they are sure that is really what they mean; often what is meant is "Middle Eastern," or the more specific geographic terms, Southwest Asia and North Africa.

■ DECOLONIZATION IN THE 20TH CENTURY: AFRICA AND INDIA

One of the important developments following World War II was the dismantling of the European colonial system, a process that proceeded peacefully, through revolutionary means, in most African nations, but that broke into violence between Hindu and Muslim populations in the events leading to Indian independence. One of the important goals of world history education is to put these developments into historical perspective, to examine how the radical new ideas of constitutionalism, republicanism, civil liberty, and nationalism propagated in Western Europe and North America in the 18th century proved enormously alluring to peoples all over the world in the ensuing two hundred years. Western colonialism could not escape its fundamental contradiction: European countries professing democratic ideals ruled alien peoples with authoritarian methods.

Africa in the 20th Century

In Africa, articulate leaders such as Jomo Kenyatta, Kwame Nkrumah, Julius Nyerere, and King Muhammad V successfully organized large-scale movements to terminate the colonial order. Tumultuous changes on the world scene after World War II much hastened the decolonization process.

Before relinquishing their colonies, the French and British fitted them out with European-style governing and legal institutions which many new nationalist leaders cast aside in favor of one-party states. In approaching this post-independence phenomenon, students should critically assess the assumption that Africans had not been "ready for democracy." Study of world history since the 17th century should prepare

Tumultuous changes on the world scene after World War II much hastened the decolonization process.

Kenya's Premier Jomo Kenyatta is pictured at the Nairobi Airport, in Kenya, June 5, 1964.

students to consider the great difficulties and very long process of instituting bills of rights and genuinely representative governments even in relatively secure and advanced societies, not to speak of new countries where the first priority is the overthrow of colonial power, where the population lacks experience with democratic processes, where ethnic and kinship bonds may be much stronger than patriotic feeling, and where economic problems are profuse and intractable. The special case of South Africa and the protracted struggle over its policies and institutions of racial apartheid also should be analyzed.

In the early years of independence some African countries did reasonably well economically, but many later experienced negative growth rates. Students should ponder the many complex factors affecting economic development, including high birth rates, extended droughts, low world market prices for export goods, "neo-colonial" intervention by Western governments or corporations, failed national policies of socialist collectivization, political instability, and civil conflict.

The demand by the India National Congress that all power be transferred to itself, and the parallel demand by the Muslim League for Muslim independence set the stage for the struggle that followed.

Study of obdurate economic and political problems, however, should not detract students from an appreciation of the popular movements of political reform in a number of African states and the lively social and cultural life of contemporary Africa—the creative experiments with new farming technologies, the vibrant life of Christian churches and Islamic communities, the achievements of novelists and playwrights such as Chinua Achebe, Wole Soyinka, and Cyprian Ekiwenzi, and the great influence African artists are having on world art and music.

India in the 20th Century

Events in the 20th century profoundly altered the course of Indian history. Although the British government sought to introduce constitutional reforms sufficient to retain the loyalty of Indian princes, Muslims, landlords, and liberal Hindus, the efforts were unsuccessful. The demand by the India National Congress that all power be transferred to itself, and the parallel demand by the Muslim League for Muslim independence set the stage for the struggle that followed. Students will want to know about the dramatic roles of great Indian leaders such as Mahatma Gandhi (1869-1948) Jawaharlal Nehru (1889-1964), and M. A. Jinnah (1876-1948) in the struggle for independence.

Since the independence of India and the establishment of Pakistan as a separate Muslim state in 1947, the history of South Asia has followed contrasting paths: continuing modernization and reversion to traditional ways. Three wars between India and Pakistan over Kashmir and the 1971 Bangladesh War, as well as the growing Hindu-Sikh conflict over the Punjab, all reflect an unhappy tradition. Indian developments—as a modern military power with its own satellite-launching capability and the growth of sophisticated indigenous industry—reflect modernization, as does fast-growing Indian urbanization. Students should never forget, however, that most of India's population remains peasant, and half live close to the knife edge of starvation. The struggle of political democracy to survive and prosper under such conditions is one of the most significant stories of our time. Readings from leading authors of the day, including Nirad Chaudhuri, Bajo Rao, and Bibbutibbushan Banerji, will help to provide important perspectives on Indian life and accomplishments.

Muslim founder of Pakistan, Mohammed Ali Jinnah

■ LATIN AMERICA IN THE 20TH CENTURY

Finally, it is vital that American students know the historical trends in Latin America during the 20th century. The countries of Latin America are some of the United States' closest neighbors, with deeply shared economic and military concerns. The study of modern Latin America is thus essential for understanding the alignment of power in the hemisphere today, the quality of life of the citizens of Latin American countries, and the role of Latin America in world politics and economics.

Students should understand how the United States gradually replaced Europe as Latin America's major trading partner, and how the dynamics of trade channelled Latin American economic growth in particular directions.

Students should understand how the United States gradually replaced Europe as Latin America's major trading partner, and how the dynamics of trade channelled Latin American economic growth in particular directions. This topic can help students ponder global issues, such as what does "development" mean? How do nations grow or develop? How do advanced nations affect them? What is "dependency" and is it an adequate description of the complex political/economic relations that entwine Latin America and the United States?

At the same time, students need to be sensitive to internal developments in Latin American countries. They should appreciate that each has its own history and traditions which help to determine its present-day policies. Thus, the factors of urbanization, growth of a middle class, and the problems and rise of trade unions and professions occurred all over Latin America but at different times and in varying combinations. The problem of poverty is enormous and demands attention. American students should understand that in terms of land and resources Latin America has been one of the wealthiest regions in the world. Nevertheless, it has experienced an exceptionally high rate of poverty. How did this come about and what consequences has it had for political and social change? Why have less well-endowed regions, such as Japan, created such wealth?

It is vital that students understand the roots of rebellion in poverty and in the great disparities in the distribution of wealth and power which stretch back into the 19th century.

These issues form the backdrop to understanding Latin American revolution in the 20th century: Mexico (1910-1940); Guatemala (1944-1954); Bolivia (1952-1964); Cuba (1959-present); Chile (1973-present); and Nicaragua (1979-1990). It is vital that students understand the roots of rebellion in poverty and in the great disparities in the distribution of wealth and power which stretch back into the 19th century. They also need to understand the exceptions to the common picture, as in Costa Rica, and the importance of recent democratic elections—for example, in El Salvador and Nicaragua—which returned democratically elected governments to power. Only this kind of historical perspective can overcome preconceived or popular notions about Latin American politics and help them intelligently evaluate their own government's policies.

Library at National University, Mexico. All four walls of the library are covered with famed murals.

Finally, a study of Latin America must include a consideration of intellectual and artistic achievements. It will help students comprehend the search for self-identity which has fueled politics and revolution, as well as art and literature, in the 20th century. They should be introduced to Latin American writers such as Borges, Paz, Llosa, Márques, Mistral, and

Neruda. They should study paintings and murals that have made Latin America such a lively force in modern art. As in every other region of the world, a well-rounded appreciation of the achievements and attractions of life in Latin America as well as its problems will make its history more interesting for students and will go a long way toward breaking down preconceptions, stereotypes, and misinformation.

■ BRINGING HISTORICAL PERSPECTIVES TO EVENTS OF THE CLOSING DECADES OF THE 20TH CENTURY

As students consider the closing decades of the 20th century and the great issues and events of their own time, their understandings and insights into these events will depend upon the depth of the historical perspectives and habits of mind already nurtured in their preceding years of historical study. None of these events arises full-blown in the headlines of today. All have developed from decisions and events already long underway. The special power of historical study is its ability to cast contemporary events in their unfolding historical context and thereby to foster more penetrating causal analyses and greater wisdom in responding to them. Only in understanding how these developments came about will students be able to judge the debates about them and confront intelligently the choices to be made in days to come.

If their history courses have regularly brought such issues alive, probed their historical antecedents, and engaged students in thinking deeply about them, then students will have been well prepared for the citizenship responsibilities confronting them. For these purposes, no curriculum field is more important or of more enduring worth.

Children play on the rubble of wall pieces in front of the Reichstag building in Berlin the day after East Germany started to dismantle the wall.

The special power of historical study is its ability to cast events in their unfolding historical context and thereby to foster more penetrating causal analyses and greater wisdom in responding to them.

Picture Credits

U.S. History

1 NCHS. **23** NCHS. **45** Bettmann Archives. **51** Bettmann Archives. **52** Reproduced as published in *America 1585: The Complete Drawings of John White*, edited by Paul Hulton, copyright 1984, by The University of North Carolina Press, drawings, copyrighted by the Trustees of the British Museum, with the kind permission of the copyright owner. **53** Bettmann Archives. **55** Bettmann Archives. **57** National Archives. **59** Metropolitan Museum of Art. **62** Pennsylvania Academy of Fine Arts. **63** Trustees, British Museum. **64** Bettmann Archives. **66** Fine Arts Museum, San Franciso. **69** Library of Congress. **70** Library of Congress. **71** Library of Congress. **72** Bettmann Archives. **73** Bettmann Archives. **74** NYHS. **75** Dover Publications. **77** Library of Congress. **80** Dover Publications. **83** Dover Publications. **84** Dover Publications. **85** NYPL. **88** Bettmann Archives. **89** Library of Congress. **90** Museum of American Textile History, North Andover, MA. **91** Bettman Archives. **93** Library of Congress. **94** Library of Congress. **96** NYHS. **97** NYPL. **99** Seaver Center for Western History. **101** Dover Publications. **102** Bettmann Archives. **103** Dover Publications. **105** Frederick Meserve Collection. **107** National Archives/Henry E. Huntington History Institute, Library and National Gallery. **109** Library of Congress. **110** NYHS. **112** NYPL. **113** U. S. Military History Institute, Carlyle Barracks, PA. **114** Bettmann Archives. **117** NYPL. **119** Bettman Archives. **121** Bettmann Archives. **122** Library of Congress. **123** NYPL. **124** Brown Bros., NY. **126** Bettmann Archives. **127** Evanston Historical Society, Illinois. **130** Dover Publications. **131** Bettmann Archives. **132** Bettmann Archives. **133** Dover Publications. **135** Bettmann Archives. **136** Dover Publications. **139** Library of Congress. **140** Library of Congress. **141** Bettmann Archives. **142** Bettmann Archives. **143** Louis Lozowick, *Chicago*, 1923, oil on canvas, Lee Lozowick, Prescott Arizona. **147** Dover Publications. **148** Bettmann Archives. **149** Whitney Museum of American Art. **151** Bettmann Archives. **153** Bettmann Archives. **156** Library of Congress. **158** AP/Wide World Photos. **159** Culver Pictures. **161** Bettmann Archives. **165** Bettmann Archives. **166** Bettmann Archives. **167** Bettmann Archives. **169** Bettman Archives. **170** AP/Wide World Photos. **171** Bettmann Archives. **173** AP/Wide World Photos. **175** Bettmann Archives. **177** AP/Wide World Photos. **178** Bettmann Archives. **179** Magnum Photos. **182** Bettmann Archives. **184** Bettmann Archives. **185** Bettmann Archives. **186** AP/Wide World Photos.

World History

187 *"Columbus and the Discovery of America,"* Jackdaw Publications, Ltd. **193** Bettmann Archives. **194** Carole Collier Frick, UCLA. **196** Art Resource, NY. **197** This illustration was reproduced as published in *The Neolithic Revolution*, by D. M. Knox, copyright 1980, with the kind permission of the copyright owner, Greenhaven Press, St. Paul, MN. **199** Carole Collier Frick, UCLA. **200** Bettmann Archives. **201** Jewish Theological Seminary, NY. **203** Bettmann Archives. **205** Art Resource, NY. **206** Staazliche Museen, Berlin. **207** Art Resource, NY. **211**From _The Greek World_ by Roger Ling, copyright 1988, Equinox (Oxford) Ltd **212** Carole Collier Frick, UCLA. **214** Bettmann Archives. **215** Carole Collier Frick, UCLA. **216** Carole Collier Frick, UCLA. **217** Bettmann Archives. **219** Bettmann Archives. **221** Art Resource, NY. **223** Bettmann Archives. **224** Art Resource, NY. **225** Art Resource, NY. **227** Bettmann Archives. **229** Bettmann Archives. **234** Bettmann Archives. **236** Bettmann Archives. **240** Art Resource, NY. **241** Art Resource, NY. **242** Bettmann Archives. **245** Bettmann Archives. **247** British Museum, London. **248** Longmans and Green & Co., copyright 1857. **249** Bettmann Archives. **251** Bettmann Archives. **253** Bettmann Archives. **255** Biblioteque Nationale, Paris. **256** Bettmann Archives. **257** Reproduced as published in _Art & Architecture in Italy 1250-1400_ by John White. **259** Bettmann Archives. **261** Scala/Art Resource, NY. **263** NYPL. **264** Bettmann Archives. **267** Carole Collier Frick, UCLA. **269** NYPL. **271** Bettmann Archives. **273** Bettmann Archives. **274** Bettmann Archives. **275** Bettmann Archives. **276** Bettmann Archives. **277** Bettmann Archives. **278** Bettmann Archives. **280** Bettmann Archives. **282** Bettmann Archives. **286** Bettmann Archives. **287** Bettmann Archives. **288** Bettmann Archives. **291** Bettmann Archives. **293** Bettmann Archives. **294** Bettmann Archives. **295** Bettmann Archives. **296** Bettmann Archives. **297** Bettmann Archives. **298** Bettmann Archives. **299** Bettmann Archives. **300** Bettmann Archives. **301** Bettmann Archives. **303** Bettmann Archives. **304** _Beijing Review_. **305** AP/ Wide World Photos. **306** Bettmann Archives. **307** Bettmann Archives. **309** Bettmann Archives. **310** Bettmann Archives. **311** Bettmann Archives.

NYHS - New York Historical Society
NYPL - New York Public Library